death + dishonor ∴ the unwanted facts (knowledge) of Strategic bombing

D0220142

ABOUT THIS BOOK

Terrorism and the United States' self-declared war on terrorism are the defining leitmotifs of the times we live in. They are being used throughout the Western world to justify widespread derogations of civil liberties and the overwhelming use of force, increasingly via strategic bombing.

These aerial bombardments are aimed either explicitly at civilian populations as a matter of strategy or deployed in circumstances where extensive civilian deaths are guaranteed but are euphemistically written off as collateral damage or accidental. In this important book, Professor Beau Grosscup recounts the engrossing history of aerial bombardment of civilian populations throughout the 20th century right up to the present day in Afghanistan and Iraq.

He shows how certain European colonial powers, notably Britain, initiated its use between the two World Wars; how wholesale bombardment of civilians was an instrument of choice used by all the major contestants of the Second World War. And how, since then, it has been refined conceptually and practised extensively by the United States in Korea, Vietnam and more recently in the Balkans, Afghanistan and Iraq. Beau Grosscup exposes the labyrinth of rationalizations put forward, in particular by the United States, that attempt to exclude strategic bombing from being labelled state terrorism, and he further exposes the race, gender and class biases that lie behind these justifications of aerial bombing of 'other' people.

This unique modern history of strategic bombing exposes the dirty secret about the so-called 'clean' use of air power and aims to rally public support against the politically motivated manipulations of the terrorism issue by the Western bombing nations. The author asserts that if terrorism is to be diminished in the future, the role United States aerial bombing plays in sustaining the global cycle of violence must be recognized and confronted.

ABOUT THE AUTHOR

Beau Grosscup is Professor of International Relations, California State University, Chico. He has made a special study of terrorism for many years, and is the author of *Newest Explosions of Terrorism*, now in its 4th edition.

BEAU GROSSCUP

STRATEGIC TERROR

THE POLITICS AND ETHICS
OF AERIAL BOMBARDMENT

SIRD
KUALA LUMPUR

Zed Books
LONDON AND NEW YORK

Strategic Terror was first published in 2006 by
In Malaysia: Strategic Information Research Development (SIRD),
No. 11/4E, Petaling Jaya, 46200 Selangor
In the rest of the world: Zed Books Ltd,
7 Cynthia Street, London N1 9JF, UK and
Room 400, 175 Fifth Avenue, New York, NY 10010, USA.

www.zedbooks.co.uk

Cover designed by Andrew Corbett
Set in 9/13 pt Georgia by Long House, Cumbria, UK
Printed and bound in Malta by Gutenberg Ltd

Distributed in the USA exclusively by Palgrave Macmillan, a division of
St Martin's Press, LLC, 175 Fifth Avenue, New York, NY 10010.

A catalogue record for this book
is available from the British Library

US Cataloging-in-Publication Data
is available from the Library of Congress

ISBN 1 84277 542 1 hb
ISBN 1 84277 543 X pb
ISBN 978 1 84277 542 4 hb
ISBN 978 1 84277 543 1 pb
ISBN 983 2535 832 (Malaysia)

Contents

For Cooper Grant

My treasure, my heart, my peace ...
were that I could follow in your footsteps

Acknowledgements

This book belongs to many people, especially those who have expressed contempt for terrorism wherever it occurs, whoever the perpetrator is and for whatever reason. Unknown to most of you, individually and collectively you have been my mentors. May these pages give you more reason to persevere?

My thanks go to all the students in my Politics of Terrorism classes at California State University, Chico, with a special salute to those who, in the post-11 September 2001 jingoistic climate, listened patiently to, thought deeply about, and argued constructively with the ideas of this dissident student of terrorism. The support from the CSU Chico Summer Scholars Program, the insistence of my Department of Political Science and California Faculty Association colleagues that sabbaticals are essential to democratic intellectualism in an increasingly corporate academic culture, and the many venues that invited me to test my ideas were all instrumental to this project. Grateful appreciation goes to the editorial staff of Zed Books, especially Robert Molteno and Anne Rodford for their patience, hard work and encouragement, all of which made for a most constructive professional experience. Professors Beverly Crawford, Mimi Riley, John Martin, Miriam Monges, Joseph Russo and Scott Sibary, I am indebted to your soul-filled friendship, first-rate intellect and considerable expertise. I am particularly appreciative of your insistence that we sort through my various confusions. Finally, I am deeply beholden to Richard 'Ricky' Nadeau for his incessant interest in and invaluable help with this project. Besides epitomizing in theory and practice the true meaning of intellectual, you are a magnificent person and public treasure.

George Charles 'Beau' Grosscup III
Cohasset, California

Abbreviations and Acronyms

ACTS	Air Corps Tactical School
BBC	British Broadcasting Corporation
CEP	Circular Error Probable
CSIS	Center for Strategic and International Security
DU	Depleted Uranium
FBI	Federal Bureau of Investigation
IRC	International Red Cross
IRA	Irish Republican Army
JCS	Joint Chiefs of Staff
NATO	North Atlantic Treaty Organization
NLF	National Liberation Front
OPEC	Oil Producing Exporting Countries
PGM	(Precision-Guided Missile)
PLO	Palestinian Liberation Front
Psyops	Psychological Operations
RAF	Royal Air Force
SAC	Strategic Air Command
SHAEF	Supreme Headquarters Allied Expeditionary Force
UNICEF	United Nations International Children's Education Fund
UNITA	National Union for Total Independence of Angola
USAID	United States Agency for International Development
USSBS	United States Strategic Bombing Survey
9/11	September 11 2001

This book is about strategic bombing and the issues that surround it. Several of them, in particular the two questions of whether it is effective military strategy and whether air power alone can win wars have been well chronicled and thus need not be dealt with here. It is important to note that many observers, mostly from the ranks of or otherwise connected to the Western military profession, have examined them in excruciating detail. By most of these observers, both questions have been answered in the negative. A few, mostly ardent proponents of air power, argue that the record is mixed and thus the jury is still out. Regardless, strategic bombing continues, not just as a weapon in the war-making arsenal of today's major powers but, for most of them, the weapon of choice.

Over the past quarter-century the rise in the popularity of strategic bombing has occurred within a Western political context in which concern with terrorism has risen to prominence. As a strategy that purposely targets civilians and their livelihoods, the question of whether or not strategic bombing constitutes terrorism could have been from its very conception, and in the contemporary political climate should now be, a most poignant and pressing concern. That it has always escaped the level of scrutiny given to the strategic military questions noted above can be ascribed to two factors. First, military professionals have always dominated the discourse on air power, its nature, use and effect. Whether a particular strategy constitutes terrorism is not their chief concern. Historically, if it brings victory in war, they could not care less about the terrorism issue. Second, the obvious political stakes involved make close scrutiny of the question 'Is strategic bombing terrorism?' particularly dangerous to the leaders of the self-anointed 'family of nations' who have a huge political stake in sustaining their argument and imagery that terrorism is a morally reprehensible deed of the foreign 'other.' Thus, they have worked diligently to avoid the question being asked, and when it has been asked, they have made sure their violence escaped the 'terrorism' label.

The genesis of this inquiry was a trip to Dresden, Germany, in June 1999 at the time of the US-led NATO bombing of Kosovo-Serbia. The incentive to investigate the question came from two sources. First, pre-trip research on the World War Two bombing of Dresden provided eyewitness accounts of the bombing and an introduction to the many controversies that surround it. Incentive also came from on-site visits, notably to the meadows of the Elbe river where the city's civilians had fled to escape the raging fires and sticky goo of Allied napalm – only, it is alleged, to have North American pilots mow them down with strafing fire.[1] Also notable was a trip to the Altmarkt (old market) where, after the bombing ended, 25,000 rotting bodies had been stacked for mass cremation. With further research, it became clear that most of the ongoing debates about the what and why of the Dresden bombing serve as a microcosm for the intellectual universe of strategic bombing. This is especially true of the question of whether or not strategic bombing is terrorism.

To this day, the obvious yet unspoken mission of the defenders of the aerial bombardment of Dresden is to debunk the accusation that it was a terrorist bombing. This is most pointedly demonstrated in the debate over whether this city, known as the 'Florence of the Elbe,' was a legitimate military target. Or did thousands of civilians suffer and die in an Allied demonstration bombing to influence post-war negotiations with the leader of the Soviet Union, Joseph Stalin? To defenders of the bombing, Dresden *was* a military target. Although they agree that 50 percent of the city's homes were destroyed, they argue that its industrial base, communications network and strategic proximity to the Soviet Red Army advance made it an obvious candidate for aerial destruction out of military necessity.[2] To critics of this view, Dresden is an illustration of how flexible the concept 'military target' is.

Likewise, terrorism is at the center of the debates over how many civilians died at Dresden and whose account of the effects of the bombing is credible and thus should matter. On the human toll, the figures range from the initial British toll of 16,000 to German estimates of 250,000. Later, some British researchers agreed on figures close to 100,000. The official US Air Force total is 25,000 to 30,000. The lower figure is intended to make the point that civilians were not purposely targeted and died as unavoidable and thus 'acceptable' casualties of war, rather than from a policy of terrorism. Conversely, the high figures are meant to suggest the bombing was indiscriminate or wanton, that is, terrorism. The figures in the middle range are open to interpretation and thus also enter the debate. Finally, defenders of the bombing assert that the longstanding belief that the attacks on Dresden caused a human catastrophe of immense proportions is a product of Nazi misinformation, is indeed virtually the last lie of Joseph Goebbels's propaganda machine. Coming as it does from 'reliable' Allied sources, this explanation carries tremendous weight, especially since it accuses an enemy well known for telling the biggest of lies of lying one more time. This 'truth' holds sway despite a Supreme Headquarters Allied Expeditionary Force (SHAEF) document of 18 February 1945 celebrating the effect of Allied 'terror bombings.' Within North American military circles the SHAEF press release is now summarily dismissed as 'ill-advised,' a dismissal that is perhaps the final but necessary episode in the long and dogged Allied effort to uncouple the bombing of Dresden from terrorism.[3] Discarding one's own words and findings if they prove to be politically inconvenient is a practice that runs throughout the history of strategic bombing.

The dramatic terrorist events of the 1972 Munich Olympics, designated in Western political lore as the start of the contemporary age of terrorism, raised the questions of what is terrorism? who are the terrorists? and what is their agenda? in new and urgent form. This effort to understand it should have focused greater scrutiny on strategic bombing as a military strategy that targets civilians, on its doctrine and more significantly on the bombing nations' application of it. Why it hasn't or, more pointedly, how the bombing nations both past and present can target civilians and civilian infrastructure yet escape the 'terrorism' label is a primary focus of this inquiry.

The task begins with the origins of strategic bombing doctrine. The primary concerns are its relation to traditional military doctrine, the racist, class-biased and gendered context in which it was conceived, and the social and political position of those who created and championed it. The point here is twofold: first to unpack the assumption that targeting civilians is the most likely way to win wars of the future. Second, to explain the obvious hypocrisy of the European and North American imperial nations which, as they rained terror from the skies on their colonial and neocolonial subjects, sent their diplomats to The Hague and the League of Nations intent on protecting their own civilians from aerial bombardment on legal and moral grounds.

Investigation into the theory and practice of strategic bombing reveals some important realities about the general context in which it takes place. First, strategic bombing has occurred and continues to occur within a context of privilege. From the beginning, the proponents of air power have been privileged to be on the cutting edge of weapons technology. Thus, they have been first to think about its application, to determine how it is to be used, and on whom. They also have the privilege of defining and enforcing the terms and concepts that guide the political discourse on strategic bombing. Together, these two privileges have resulted in the most important privilege of all, to bomb civilians with virtual impunity while monopolizing the discourse on terrorism.

Second, strategic bombing has always been done in a rigidly polarized political and moral context of 'us' and 'them,' in particular in the context of 'self' and 'other' terminology that determines who is friend and who is to be bombed and why. This has provided a nearly perfect political context for the bombers to reject any critical assessment of strategic bombing. It has also been crucial in avoiding any negative connotations being attached to their bombing, most important any 'credible' link with terrorism.

Finally, the context in which strategic bombing has occurred demonstrates how central 'seminal' events, postured as an unprovoked attack on the 'civilized world,' are to the justification for and public acquiescence in a vengeful 'anything goes' approach to bombing. This is true of World War Two in general and, for the United States in particular, the Japanese attack on Pearl Harbor. The 'threat of communism' that rationalized the Cold War also justified wholesale terror from the skies over Korea and Vietnam. The terrorism of the Munich Olympics, Iraq's 'cruel' invasion of Kuwait, and the alleged humanitarian disaster of ethnic cleansing in Kosovo all served to mobilize Western public opinion behind a 'whatever it takes' approach to bombing while silencing its critics. The events of 11 September 2001 (9/11) were dramatic and tragic, but in relation to strategic bombing they simply provided another opportunity for a bombing nation to test the theory of strategic bombing in pursuit of an answer to the question: can air power alone win war? The post 9/11 'revenge' bombings exhibited and continued patterns of behavior that had been developed over almost a century of strategic bombing. The most important of these patterns was the invocation of a rationalization system by which the bombing nations seek to avoid the charge of being terrorists.

My inquiry begins with the 2003 US-led invasion of Iraq in which it was hoped that the strategic bombing plan known as Shock and Awe would play the pivotal, indeed sole, role in 'regime change.' That it did not is consistent with the historical record of strategic bombing and puts another nail in the coffin of the efficacy claim. Still, unfortunately for millions of people, its failure also means that the experiment in 'technowar' whose principal aim is to break the civilian political will to resist by means of the 'clean' application of the technology of mass destruction is to continue. At the very least, investigation of Shock and Awe will introduce the controversies and discernible patterns that nearly a century of strategic bombing has provoked. I hope also that it will force serious reflection on whether or not the Shock and Awe bombing of Iraq deserves, as I. F. Stone said of the US Cold War bombing of Korea, the label of 'terror from the skies.'[4] If so, an important and ambitious first step in challenging the privileged position of the strategic bombers and their political allies will have been taken.

Shock and Awe!!
Shock and Awe!!

In early March 2003, the United States Defense Department formally introduced Shock and Awe, its war plan for the impending attack on Iraq.[1] The idea was to blast the so-called 'axis of evil' nation with 3,000 bombs and missiles over 48 hours for the purpose of 'shocking the Iraqi leadership into submission quickly.'[2] Almost overnight the phrase 'Shock and Awe' held a prominent place in the US lexicon. On the Internet, late-night television programs and among political pundits, the catchy slogan was evoked to make fun of or draw attention to people or events. Soon, there was virtually nothing that couldn't be 'Shocked and Awed.' According to *Tonight Show* host Jay Leno, 'John Kerry finally cleared up his position on military action in Iraq. He said he voted yes on shock, no on awe.' The website military.com unabashedly offered a new feature, 'SHOCK and AWE,' showing 'raw battle footage on video, gritty photos from the front lines, the latest on military games and simulations, and stories and intel you won't get anywhere else.' To this day, the prominent place of Shock and Awe in political and commercial imagery appears secure. 'Dick Cheney's Shock and Awe' referred to a revealing photo of the Vice President on the 2004 campaign trail 'that leaves little to the imagination.' British citizens were described as being in a collective state of 'Shock and Awe' after the London bombings of 7 July 2005. The Winx Club, a new product for children, is marketed as five girl dolls who 'kick booty' and encourage kids to get ready to 'Shock and Awe.'

The public and pundits may have chortled over the slogan, but to the war planners and their critics Shock and Awe was serious business. For Pentagon officials, the 'cleanest' and quickest way to win their 'necessary' war was 'to have such a shock on the system that the Iraqi regime would have to assume early on the end was inevitable.'[3] Pentagon officials briefed the particulars of the plan to newspaper reporters with the following statements:

> US Air Force B-2s, F-1117As, B-52s, F-15Es and RAF Tornados will be in the first wave: 'Their targets in the first hours have been chosen to lessen destruction of Iraq's infrastructure but maximize the destruction of Saddam Hussein's family, military and political machine.' 'B-52 bombers flying out of Diego Garcia and B-2 stealth bombers will attack the barracks and bases of the elite Republican Guard and government offices ... Amid the noise and horror of this initial onslaught, ...[4]

> By the time Iraqis see the dawn at the end of the first night, their country's military and political infrastructure is likely to have been shattered, say analysts. Key leaders will have disappeared, entire military units will have been obliterated, power supplies will have been shut down but the visible damage will be surprisingly small, according to the attack plan.[5]

> If by this time Saddam is still resisting, military planners have factored in a short political pause to allow his capitulation. If no white flag is seen, the assault on Baghdad will begin ... At this stage, the political imperative to keep civilian casualties to a minimum will have to be put to one side. The attack on Baghdad will use overwhelming force.[6]

In reality, said one Pentagon official to CBS News, 'There will not be a safe place in Baghdad.'[7]

Critics of the war plan included Pentagon officials and anti-war activists. Questioning the effectiveness of the plan, a senior Pentagon official referred to it as a 'bunch of bull.'[8] According to anti-war organizer Bill Hackwell, 'The Bush administration is preparing to turn the US war machine, the biggest armada in history, on a poor country and cause a bloodbath like we have never seen.'[9]

Though Pentagon officials declared, 'The sheer size of this has never been seen before, never been contemplated before,' there wasn't anything new about Shock and Awe. It was merely a restatement of the doctrine of strategic bombing; a theory articulated at the end of World War One asserting that air power alone could and should win wars. Though its basic assumptions have remained, the application of the doctrine has gone through various reformulations. In 1996, the theory of Rapid Dominance, or Shock and Awe as it was soon anointed, became the latest version.

Primarily the brainchild of retired Air Force General Charles Horner and defense expert Harlan K. Ullman of the National Defense University,

'Shock and Awe' builds on the ideas of Sun Tzu and Karl von Clausewitz. They pictured war as 'a deception' with elements of 'fog, friction and fear.'[10] Writing in classic strategic bombing (and gendered) terms, the architects of Shock and Awe present the central aim as:

> ... to destroy, defeat, and neuter the will of an adversary to resist. ... to affect the will, perception, and understanding of the adversary to fit or respond to our strategic policy ends through imposing a regime of Shock and Awe. ... Our intent, however, is to field a range of capabilities to induce sufficient Shock and Awe to render the adversary impotent. This means that physical and psychological effects must be obtained ... The target is the adversary's will, perception, and understanding.[11]

The key objective is to have the same impact on the enemy's will using conventional weapons as the atomic bombing of Hiroshima and Nagasaki had on Japanese civilians and leadership. As Horner and Ullman write: 'The Japanese simply could not comprehend the destructive power carried by a single airplane. This incomprehension produced a state of awe.'[12]

'SHOCK AND AWE' AND TERRORISM

In assessing the description of Horner and Ullman, Edward Spannaus, law editor of *Executive Intelligence Review,* argues that 'Shock and Awe' is nothing more than a sanitized version of the mass terror tactics used in World War II.'[13] Noam Chomsky also associated Shock and Awe with terrorism, asserting: 'we saw this repeated again in the attack on Iraq, spun as "Shock and Awe", which is simply a niceified phrase for Causing Terror.'[14] Though sparsely, the connection was also to be found in Internet discourse. For example, Nathan Newman urged, 'let's end the hypocrisy of labeling attacks on civilians by enemies "terrorism" and our own use of it "shock and awe."'[15]

By invoking the word 'terror' to describe past and present Western bombing policy, Spannaus, Chomsky and a few others took a rare and brave step. Rare in that since the inception of strategic bombing, government and military elites from the bombing nations have adamantly avoided and effectively excluded from 'legitimate' public discourse any connection between terrorism and their use of air power. It is a brave step as historically those who dared to make the link found their ideas derided as unpatriotic in public discourse and unwanted in the corridors of power.

In the post-9/11 context the 'war on terrorism' dominates the Western mindset. The 'global scourge of terrorism' is universally condemned and billions of dollars are spent on 'counter-terrorism' endeavors. This being the case, why is it then that those who find the United States and its bombing allies culpable in the 'scourge of terrorism' are abruptly dismissed with either silence or angry disdain? More specifically, why is a plan that proposes to attack a whole society with a massive bombardment and warns that 'the political imperative to keep civilian casualties to a minimum will have to be put to one side' greeted with humor, indifference or applause? Why is the plan not openly and universally castigated at least as 'wrong-headed' or, more important, as a morally and politically repugnant strategy of terrorism?

To address these important questions, this inquiry focuses on the theoretical roots of Shock and Awe and the political and moral controversies surrounding the historical use of air power. Throughout, the primary question is: does strategic bombing constitute terror from the skies? But first, to introduce the many issues and controversies surrounding strategic bombing, the inquiry begins with the Shock and Awe experiment of Operation Iraqi Freedom.

THE POLITICAL CULTURE OF 'SHOCK AND AWE'

'Baghdad is burning. ... What more can we say' [16]

Shock and Awe was launched on 21 March 2003. US and British bombs and missiles slammed into Pentagon-designated strategic 'military' targets throughout Iraq, including targets in downtown Baghdad and other cities. With noticeable glee and satisfaction, *Fox News* reported that 'Baghdad took a terrific pounding from Allied missiles, which rained bombs throughout the city. Huge fireballs rocked the heart of the capital, and the sky filled with smoke.'[17] Government buildings in densely populated neighborhoods along the Euphrates River and Saddam Hussein's palaces were bombed repeatedly. Numerous Wal-Mart-like shopping malls and food markets were also 'precisely' hit.[18] Colonel John Warden, a major architect of the 1991 Persian Gulf air war, identified the 3,000-pound penetrating-warhead and enhanced Guided Bomb Unit-27 (GBU-27) 'smart' bombs launched from B-52 and F-117 jets respectively, as the ordnance of choice. Warden also boasted that the United States possessed other bombs that if needed could 'get down as far as the Iraqis can dig. It is probably that simple.'[19]

To the chagrin of the war planners and viewers of the 'light and fireworks show' on live television, in the wake of the initial massive air attack the anticipated collapse of the Iraqi regime did not occur. As ground operations joined the aerial campaign, TV pundits, military media consultants and viewers expressed disappointment that the carnage from the 'precision' application of modern weaponry fell far short of the expectations raised over the previous two months of Shock and Awe hyperbole. Within military circles, the staying power of the Iraqi government and its people renewed the bitter debate about whether or not air power alone could win wars. Army and navy officials noted with obvious relief that once again the claims of the strategic bombers had been proven false. Airpower advocates responded, arguing that Shock and Awe was not a true test of strategic bombing theory as the level of violence was far below that required to 'shock the system' into capitulation. Unfazed, they looked eagerly to the next war, hoping a politically 'unrestrained' aerial attack would finally permit a true test of their theory.

The disappointment in and enthusiasm for Shock and Awe underscore the West's historic passion for the 'technological fix' and a militaristic imperial mentality. At the core of both is callous disdain for 'other' peoples believed to be less sophisticated or not quite civilized. Together, they have produced a military doctrine that assumes modern weaponry will quickly and 'cleanly' crush the enemy's spirit to resist. The experience of twentieth century wars has found this military doctrine wanting and steeped in political and moral controversy. Yet, in planning for the war on Iraq, the architects of Shock and Awe doggedly stuck to this prescription. Success in Iraq simply required upping the level of 'shock' with 'high tech' firepower. The initial targets were the leadership and 'strategic' infrastructure. If necessary, the weapons would then be turned directly on civilians until the 'awed' Iraqis' breaking point was reached. If doing so proved controversial, raising accusations of terrorism from 'adversarial' quarters (whether foreign or domestic), a time-tested system of denial and rationalization, coupled with the 'patriotic media,' would easily silence them. After all, the post-9/11 War on Terrorism was a just cause, requiring 'special tactics.' And international law, embodied in the Hague Resolutions and Geneva Conventions, permitted them to do all things 'militarily necessary' to win. Though the immediate bloodshed would be appalling, morality was on their side, as a quick end to the war would mean saving lives of both friend and foe. Even if victory required a combination of air and ground war, the architects of Shock and Awe were confident that the historically cultivated US callousness toward enemy noncombatants, pointedly reinvigorated with the 9/11 attacks, would sustain the near-rabid public support for the

Bush Administration's 'whatever it takes' approach to any designated enemy. After all, the bombing of Afghanistan had produced high public approval ratings. Thus it was likely 'whereas the tragic loss of life on 11 September 2001 precipitated a blank check for President Bush to hunt down terrorists, and even wage war in Iraq, Americans are not, in turn, willing to grant Iraqis, for example, the same right to indignation and fury.'[20]

Much of the public and official enthusiasm for Shock and Awe stems from the assertion that now, more than ever, air war is amazingly 'high tech.' As the implications of Shock and Awe became clear, Bush Administration officials assured the public and major media that the latest generation of taxpayer-funded weapons were more precise and accurate than ever. Now it really was possible to bomb military targets 'cleanly' while 'minimizing' civilian suffering. The claims of 'precision' and 'minimal' suffering are a constant in bombing lore, as is the military's refusal to define what they mean. The Shock and Awe bombing of Iraq continued this tradition. The new weapons were said to be not only 'smart' but indeed 'brilliant,' with the sensor capacity 'to tell if a spot on the ground is a tank or a farm tractor.'[21] For his part, Deputy Defense Secretary Paul Wolfowitz was delighted with the new technology and the role it played in his military's ability at last to wage a moral war. He asserted, 'This was not a bombing of Baghdad. It was a bombing of the Iraqi regime and it was done with extraordinary precision. We never in history have been able to do it with that kind of precision. As a result we made enormous effort to distinguish between military targets and the civilian population.'[22]

In advance of the bombing, Pentagon officials vowed they were using an 'excruciating amount of time' to do 'everything humanly possible' to keep 'collateral damage minimal.'[23] While adamantly refusing to quantify 'minimal' or 'acceptable' civilian casualties, they did offer some specific measures. For example, any air strike thought likely to cause over 30 civilian casualties would require the personal approval of Defense Secretary Donald Rumsfeld. When the aerial assault began, Rumsfeld rarely hesitated to give his permission to bomb. He authorized fifty such strikes between 19 March and 18 April 2003. Utilizing the Pentagon's own calculations means Rumsfeld's approvals purposely placed approximately 1,500 Iraqi civilians (about half of the total number of 9/11 victims) in harm's way. In most of the strategic bombing there were no such guidelines or 'restrictions.' For example, bombing of 'high value' targets, such as buildings alleged to be housing top Iraqi leaders, even when in heavily populated urban areas required neither Rumsfeld's approval nor verification as to the accuracy of the information.[24]

With reports of mounting civilian casualties, Pentagon officials quietly and without apology backed away from their 'clean' war claims. In reality, they explained, 'air wars are not flawless,' bombs do 'go astray,' 'mistakes are made' and targeting of Iraqi leaders was 'just guesswork.' Indeed, as the war continued, reports surfaced of 'smart' humans making more bombing mistakes, at times resulting in 'friendly force' casualties.[25] When pushed, military officials admitted to targeting civilian facilities, allegedly under Iraqi military occupation, but doing so with 'precision' even though there was limited 'no-kidding, actionable intell.'[26]

After one month of bombing, the Associated Press put the number of Iraqi civilian deaths at 3,240. Reporters wanting to know if the tally met the Pentagon's standard of 'minimal' were forced to endure 'a numbing prattle about the precision of our weaponry, precaution to avoid needless carnage, and promises to investigate possible mistakes.'[27] Rumsfeld and his top commander, General Tommy Franks, bluntly reminded reporters that since the 'fog of war' made accurate counts impossible, 'we don't do body counts.' With no data in hand, Secretary of State Colin Powell issued assurances that civilian casualty figures were 'relatively low.' Central Command spokesman Pete Mitchell echoed Powell, praising the invasion for its 'unbelievably low amount of collateral damage and needless civilian death.'[28] It took a year before senior military and intelligence officials admitted that the 'high value' attacks had been launched with little concern for civilian casualties and all fifty had been unsuccessful and 'some caused significant civilian casualties.'[29] Their admission stirred no adverse media or public reaction, nor apology from the Bush Administration to the Iraqi 'collateral damage' who had paid the ultimate price for their 'liberation.'

CIVILIAN CASUALTIES: WHOSE COUNTING?

'We saw that a truck was delivering dozens of totally dismembered dead bodies of women and children. It was an awful sight. It was really very difficult to believe this was happening.'[30]

Controversy has always swirled around the counting of civilian bombing victims. The Bush Administration's refusal to assess civilian casualties in Iraq while insisting they were low, reflects the effort of the bombing nations to avoid the issue and keep on bombing. This approach is consistent with post-Vietnam US military policy. In Vietnam, 'body counts' of enemy dead became so suspect that they undercut the Pentagon's claim the war was being won. Since then, trying to discern the number of civilian casualties has been left to an assortment of human rights groups, medical personnel, think tanks, reporters and of course the designated enemy. In Iraq, faced with Pentagon inaction and silence, several groups began issuing civilian casualty tallies shortly after President George W. Bush's 1 May 2003 declaration of the end of major combat operations.[31] The preliminary reports, all using Western sources only, offered different totals. They ranged from the Associated Press count of 3,240 to others varying from 5,000 to 10,000.[32] By August 2003, *IraqBodyCount* put the number of civilian deaths, mostly from bombing, between 7,376 and 9,170. At least 20,000 noncombatants had been wounded, with 8,000 in Baghdad alone.[33] Many of the reports attributed the civilian suffering to the dropping of anti-personnel ordinance in the form of cluster bombs. Widely condemned since Vietnam for making civilian life hazardous, cluster bombs are mostly 'dumb' weapons that often miss their targets. On average, they fail to explode 5 percent of the time, becoming deadly munitions that kill and maim civilians for years to come. Experience in the decades since the Indochina War has shown that a large percentage of the victims are children. In the initial Iraq air campaign, the United States and Britain together dropped close to 13,000 cluster bombs (1.9 million bomblets). According to the United Nations Children's Fund (UNICEF), more than 1,000 Iraqi children were injured in the four months after Iraq's government fell. Earlier, *Iraq-BodyCount* reported cluster bombs had killed at least 200 civilians by 6 May 2003. The Pentagon, contradicting its 'we don't do body counts' policy, attributed only one 'unintentional' civilian death to cluster munitions.

By Fall 2004, various studies had put the Iraqi civilian death toll between 10,000 and 30,000. Though three to nine times more than the 9/11 victim tally, the results garnered little official or media comment, let alone sorrow or outrage. On 29 October 2004, the British medical journal *Lancet* published a Johns Hopkins University study: 'Mortality before and after the 2003 invasion of Iraq.'[34] It claimed at least 100,000 Iraqi civilians had died during the invasion and occupation up through September 2004. The researchers estimated air strikes killed the majority of civilians and were particularly deadly to Iraqi women and children. Dr Les Roberts, the leader of the research team, concluded, 'the death toll from bombing suggested a pressing need to alter air strike strategies. ... Violence accounted for most of the excess deaths, and air strikes from coalition forces accounted for most violent deaths.'[35]

In Britain's Parliament, the peer-reviewed report provoked a brief outcry against the government's Iraq policy. Otherwise, the reaction mirrored a historical pattern of denial and dismissal. A spokesman for Britain's Defence Ministry rejected the report claiming, 'No figures that are produced are reliable at this stage.'[36] Some British media pundits derided it for 'flawed research methodology.' True to form, the US government greeted the report with a deafening silence, even refusing to respond to media inquiry.[37] The 'patriotic' US media, rightly outraged by the civilian deaths in the 9/11 attacks, either ignored the 100,000 estimate, or accused the authors of trying to influence presidential politics, or, as in the case of *CNN* and *CBS News*, simply reported the findings without comment, let alone distress. The *Baltimore Sun* and *Washington Post* ran reports challenging the research methodology from the depths of their back pages. In her comparative analysis of major media coverage, Mathilde Soyer notes:

> The study wasn't on the front page of the *New York Times* on Friday, October 29. They merely ran the article published in the *International Herald Tribune*, written by a journalist in France, and put this story in the middle of the news section, rather than on the front page, where such a major story should be expected to appear, especially in a leading national newspaper in a country at war.[38]

The US mantra on bombing and public insensitivity to 'other' civilians dominated what little public discourse there was on the report. A representative sentiment from the Internet callously put it that: 'Our military does not deliberately target civilians; to the contrary, we make every effort to avoid collateral damage wherever we can ... the acceptable number of civilian casualties is the number it takes to get the job done.'[39]

Though met with government silence and media dismissal, the Iraqi civilian death count went on rising. The Iraqi Health Ministry again defied a December 2003 US-orchestrated Iraqi government order to stop counting civilian casualties. It released a study in January 2005 claiming that of the 3,300 Iraqi civilians who died between July and December 2004, US coalition forces killed a little over 2,000.[40] An earlier Iraqi Health Ministry report covering April to September 2004 tallied 3,487 deaths and 13,720 injured, most of them civilians, including 328 women and children.[41] According to Iraqi officials, US air strikes were killing large numbers of civilians. A similar silence engulfed these reports. On 27 February 2005, the announcement that the Iraqi civilian body count was over 106,000 garnered no comment or lament from any panelist, liberal or conservative, on *The McLaughlin Group*, a leading political discussion program. A similar silence engulfed all commentators following the announcement of 'over 111,000' Iraqi civilian dead on the 19 June 2005 broadcast of the same program.

During the entire bombing of Iraq, no one in the high circles of US civilian or military power expressed any outrage at or sorrow for the thousands of Iraqi civilian bombing victims. Officials from nations who had allied themselves with the United States in its 'war on terrorism' also joined in the silence. John Sloboda, of *IraqBodyCount*, says not only is this to be expected from Western leaders, but that US elites know they can count on their allies' silence 'because there is similar blood on their own hands.'[42]

As the war continued and the resistance to foreign occupation rose, support for more violent measures, certain to imperil civilian life even more, became apparent in US civilian and military venues. The six-month 'battle for Fallujah' in 2004 is a poignant example. According to the Johns Hopkins University researchers, civilian casualties were so great in the initial April attack on Fallujah that as a 'statistical outlier' they would skew the results. Thus they were not included in the *Lancet*-published study. The subsequent demolition of Fallujah in November 2004 featured constant 24-hour bombing. Dozens of aircraft were stacked in 'wedding cake' layers awaiting orders to drop bombs or fire rockets on the urban setting. Observers, including the Iraqi Red Crescent Society, described the scene as 'catastrophic'and reported that 'Children and the elderly are dying from infectious disease, starvation and dehydration.' Others detailed 'a shattered landscape of gutted buildings, crushed cars and charred bodies.'[43] Almost daily reports of 500-pound bombs landing on houses were followed by evidence that phosphorus bombs and the notorious napalm were being used. Refugees from Fallujah said aircraft dropped 'these weird bombs that put up smoke like a mushroom cloud ... pieces of these bombs exploded into large fires that burnt the skin even when water was thrown on the burns.'[44] Echoing the classic rationale for strategic bombing, US Air Force Lt. Col. David Staven explained, 'It's better to take the enemy out from a distance than to go face to face with him.'[45]

In military and media circles, Fallujah was hailed as a great victory. To national security correspondent Jack Kelly, the battle for Fallujah was sure to go down in US military annals as 'Iraq's Iwo Jima.' While again refusing to assess civilian casualties, military officials put coalition losses at 53 with a 'terrorist kill' close to 2,000. Fullajah residents reported scores of civilian casualties while the US military commanders 'insist[ed] civilian casualties in Fallujah have been low.'[46] In fact, thanks to US 'precision' bombing, it was extremely difficult to assess Fallujah's civilian casualties at all, should anyone want to do so. Most of the Iraqi medical staff who had provided figures on civilian deaths in the spring assault died when US jets purposely bombed Fallujah General Hospital and the Central Health Center. Both are protected facilities under international law. As Fallujah's civilian refugees returned to sort through the rubble of what once was their home, school, mosque or health clinic, the leaders of the 'family of nations' refused to acknowledge, let alone address, the immediate and long-term price civilians had paid for the 'Fall of Fallujah.'[47] Nevertheless, no matter how rationalized, Fallujah is sure to join Guernica, Stalingrad and Grozny in the legend of modern aerial slaughter.

IRAQI CIVILIAN CASUALTIES: BLAMING THE VICTIMS

Mounting civilian casualties are difficult to ignore, especially with multiple eyewitness accounts, global media outlets and citizens on all sides risking life and limb to assess the death and destruction. In the nations publicly committed to the Bush Administration's 'War on Terrorism,' a few people, all outside the corridors of power, did buck the political correctness of the day and dared to link a bombing policy that guaranteed thousands of civilian deaths to the word 'terrorism'. Those inside elite circles had multiple ways of avoiding doing so.

When US officials did address the issue of Iraqi civilian casualties, they resorted to time-tested rationales and disclaimers. The bombs, they asserted, were not intended for civilians, but were targeted at military installations where civilians happened to be 'in the area' by mistake or because they had become human shields placed there by the odious enemy. The bombing of civilian infrastructure was said to be either accidental, as in the case of Basra's electrical grid, or purposeful because it had been determined to be important to Iraq's military capability. The Iraqi Health Ministry reports of civilian deaths were shrugged off by US military officials with the explanation 'damage will happen.'

As resistance to the US and British occupation grew, the roads became too dangerous for foreign journalists to cover the air strikes. According to British journalist Robert Fisk, this meant the US military's 'fact on the ground' could not be independently challenged or verified. On-the-spot reporting was left to the pool of 'embedded' US reporters accompanying the US military. Senior journalists told Fisk, 'Washington is happy with this situation.'[48] As a result, Pentagon denials of controversial air strikes ever occurring became more frequent. So did the explanation that if 'troubling' air strikes occurred, they were under the direct orders of the newly 'sovereign' Iraqi government.

Other tactics also helped soothe the North American conscience and keep the critics of strategic bombing at bay. As in most wars, the enemy was deemed deserving of ill and harsh treatment. As he stepped up his campaign for war, President George W. Bush had publicly demonized the Iraqi regime. Though the regime had been a long-standing US ally, by October 2002 Bush was describing it as a merciless, deceitful, homicidal, cruel and desperate leader of the uncivilized outlaw world. To Bush, Saddam Hussein was a tyrant, a student of Joseph Stalin, who invoked murder, the 'tool of terror,' to blackmail the world. Plucking the public heartstrings over 9/11 and willing to tally up the Iraq regime's civilian victims, Bush asserted that the regime had 'killed or injured at least 20,000 people, more than six times the number of people who died in the attacks of September the 11th.'[49] The President's words and imagery reaffirmed the Western stereotype of Arabs in general and Iraqis in particular as 'fanatical,' 'towelheads,' 'sand-niggers,' 'thieves,' 'the world's best dodgers' and of course 'terrorists.' Being childlike, they required 'civilizing' and 'assistance' in shaping their future.'[50] Non-lethal weaponry would not work in Iraq, retired Major General Robert Scales Jr insisted to *PBS*'s Margaret Warner, 'because a fanatical enemy simply disregards something that will not kill him.'[51]

As in the past, military parlance highlighted the nobleness of the war and hid the bombing destruction. Thus the invasion was codenamed Operation Iraqi Freedom. Meanwhile the old German Nazi phrase 'Shock and Awe' engendered humor and lighthearted parody, serving to obfuscate the intent to impose 'the non-nuclear equivalent of the impact of atomic weapons ... on the Japanese' on a collapsing civilian infrastructure already reeling from the 1991 air war and twelve years of economic sanctions.[52] The euphemism simply buried evidence of the short- and long-term humanitarian disaster expected from the air campaign.[53] Echoing a UN study on the disastrous effects on Iraqi civilian life from the initial bombing, *Boston Globe* reporter Anthony Shadid concluded that 'A United States-led attack on Iraq would probably devastate its tattered and already overwhelmed infrastructure, severing power to hospitals and water treatment plants, cutting off drinking water almost immediately to millions in Baghdad and possibly elsewhere, and pouring raw sewage into the streets within hours.'[54]

Military jargon, meant to disguise unwelcome realities, dominated military command briefings and media presentations of the invasion. The 'war of liberation' was a 'showdown with Saddam' in which 'coalition forces' conducted 'precise and surgical incursions' against 'pockets of resistance' to 'break the hornet's nest.' Iraqi civilians suffered 'collateral damage' while US and British dead had made the 'ultimate sacrifice.'[55] Aircraft were 'launched' or 'surged' to drop 'precision weaponry' and 'precision-guided munitions' on 'select regime leadership and military targets' in Baghdad and other Iraqi cities.[56] According to retired Major General Scales, 500-pound 'smart' bombs and helicopter-launched missiles are useful in delivering 'discrete fires in urban areas.'[57] By means of such concepts, turns of phrase and objectification of language, the meaningful became meaningless, the politically and humanly problematic rendered opaque. In this way, the 'technological massacre' in Iraq, as Sal Landau refers to it, disappeared from view.

This brief look at the Iraq war, and the Shock and Awe campaign in particular, illustrates the major issues, debates and controversies provoked by the historical question: can air power alone win wars? As will be discussed, the original proponents of air power answered the question with a resounding 'yes!' Wars could be won, they proposed almost from the dawn of the age of aviation, provided air power was used for strategic 'terror' bombing of civilians. This advocacy of terrorism, which became the core of strategic bombing doctrine, was made without hesitation or apology. Since then the moral and political climate has shifted. Concern with terrorism, and specifically the post 9/11 US-led War on Terrorism has produced a political and moral context in which any doctrine advocating terrorism guarantees public controversy, universal condemnation and negative consequences for those who propose and implement it.

Starting in the 1970s the Western industrial nations have monopolized the political and moral high ground of the terrorism issue, reaping political, military and moral advantage along the way. Yet they are the 'bombing nations' who deliberately and increasingly depend on the destructive capacity of air power to prosecute their wars. Whether they compromise their self-assigned exalted moral and political position by doing so should be a question hotly debated in public venues. Instead, among those who constantly bray about their commitment to fight terrorism it has not been an issue and shows no sign of being so, even though nearly a century of strategic bombing has produced millions of civilian casualties. Why it isn't a matter of public debate and more importantly how it is prevented from being so are the major issues in this inquiry.

2

The Origins of
Strategic Bombing

Strategic bombing theory developed out of the problematic nature of trench warfare in World War One and the advent of aviation technology. Principal among its architects were the Britishers Viscount Hugh Trenchard and Basil Liddell Hart, the Italian General Guilio Douhet and the American General William 'Billy' Mitchell. Trenchard and Mitchell are credited as founders of the British Royal Air Force and the Unites States Air Force respectively. Others, particularly British Lt. General David Henderson and Italian pioneer aircraft engineer Gianni Caproni, either before or simultaneously argued in favor of the military use of air power. Yet, it is Trenchard, Hart, Douhet and Mitchell who articulated a theory of strategic bombing and, with the exception of Hart, fought stubbornly for an independent air force.[1]

Strategic bombing theory addresses the question: can air power alone win wars? While there are nuances of difference among them, in general the four 'Prophets', as they came to be called, answered this question with an enthusiastic yes. In the crudest of terms, they proposed that the most effective and moral way to fight and win wars was to bomb the enemy's civilian population centers, cities or what would later be designated as 'vital centers.' The purpose of the terror bombing, as it was often labelled, was to undermine the civilians' political will to resist with the expectation that they will then force the government to surrender.

The bombing was to begin immediately if not before the official declaration of war. Douhet argued that the earlier the air attack began, the better, so as not to give the enemy opportunity to strike first. Trenchard proposed using a large bomber-only force to incinerate the civilian population and force the survivors to flee to an as yet unbombed city. The bombers would then devastate that city, creating a larger refugee population that, having made their way to the next city, would be blasted again. Eventually, and 'by this means alone,' asserted the Prophets, the civilians would quickly lose their will to resist, turn on their own political leadership and force them to sue for peace. In this way, Mitchell argued, air power would democratize warfare. The Prophets predicted fewer casualties would occur in total, resulting in a clear benefit to civilization. Except for Hart, they proposed that since strategic bombing would independently win the war, there would be no need for large standing land and sea forces.

To its architects, strategic bombing was the most moral way to conduct warfare. This view assumed terrorized civilians would very quickly lose their will to fight, immediately rise up and be able to force their political leadership to opt for peace. It also assumed minimal loss of life among airforce bombing crews. Altogether, it was argued, far fewer casualties would result compared to the calamity of set-piece warfare between large military forces as in World War One. In the end, short wars with fewer casualties are moral or, in Douhet's terms, less amoral wars. There is even a hint among some of its proponents that strategic bombing has a deterrent component. Even the most adamant pro-war jingoists, it was said, would hesitate to start a war if they knew they would likely be affected by its 'terrors.' For both critics and proponents of strategic bombing this deterrence potential made its value more political than military.

THE GREAT WAR AND STRATEGIC BOMBING THEORY

It is generally assumed that the most repugnant aspect of the Great War, as it is called, was the massive loss of human life on all sides. Total estimates are by today's standards astronomical: an estimated 10 million dead and 20 million wounded. Yet even before the Great War, European military strategists knew the advances in weapons technology in the middle to late nineteenth century (more explosive small arms and long-range artillery) along with a near-fanatical commitment to 'offensive' strategy, guaranteed great loss of human life on the battlefield. In addition, the central lesson of the Russo-Japanese War of 1903–4 was that the army and national morale were key elements in winning modern warfare. The result, writes Michael Howard, was the proposition that 'readiness to suffer huge losses remained the criterion of fitness to survive as a Great Nation.'[2] Thus, on the eve of World War One, European elites anticipated that large loss of human life could and, as a measure of national greatness, should occur.

For the European (and North American) military strategist, the real problem with trench warfare was its defensive character. World War One began with all sides committed to the offensive thrust. By 1917 the contenders on the Western front were reduced to fighting a defensive war of attrition embedded in mile upon mile of trenches. In doing so, they contradicted fundamental aspects of traditional military strategy and a cherished masculine notion of battlefield virtue. Military historians record a long-standing preference for offense over defense as a strategy for fighting and winning wars.[3] During the nineteenth century, European empire building in Africa and Asia and war in Europe itself reflect this disposition. The offensive mentality was also stressed in the US military's strategy in the Civil War and its pursuit of 'Manifest Destiny,' the drive to extend Anglo-Saxon power across the North American continent and beyond. The aim was to attack, attack and, if required, attack again. The plan was to hit the enemy especially hard initially with a 'decisive weapon', dealing them a crushing blow. Failure to use the full fury of force, especially against the 'fanatics and savages,' as British Colonel C. E. Callwell wrote in 1906, would register as leniency and timidity and give the enemy hope and courage to fight on.[4] Furthermore, the immediate use of the full weight of force was considered more humane as it avoided the certain bloodshed of a drawn-out, full-scale military operation.

Try as they might to stay on the offensive, in the Great War the armies of Europe were eventually forced into a defensive posture. Artillery, thought to be the decisive weapon providing the crushing blow of victory, proved to be dominant but not decisive. With the miles of trenches growing longer and deeper, a soldier's shovel became as important as any other implement of war. Yet, as the soldiers sought refuge in the mud of western Europe, they violated the major military ethos of the day. The ultimate display of courage, military professionalism, and manliness was to stand tall in close order drill, especially in the face of withering fire from enemy guns. Scrambling for cover of any kind, if only lying on the ground, but especially in static entrenchments described as 'poor-spirited and demoralizing' was an act of cowardice and defeat without honor or masculine virtue. Though this mentality was considered strongest in German ranks, the ethos of masculine virtue ran throughout the European military and civilian commands.

This manly commitment to the direct charge left millions dead in World War One. Still, it was the forced retreat into the defensive trenches and the loss of manliness that most concerned the military theorists and their generals. Thus, as the war finally ground to an ignoble end, the central task, indeed the patriotic and patriarchal imperative, was to find a way out of the frustrating impasse that Winston Churchill referred to as 'this frightful bondage' and 'this helplessness' in the art of war. As Churchill put it, 'The chains which held the warring nations to their task were not destined to be severed by military genius; no sufficient preponderance of force was at the disposal of either side; no practical method of decisive offensive had been discovered.'[5]

Yet, as military historian Tom Wintringham recounts, the technology, specifically the airplane, to end this state of helplessness had been present before the Great War. The fault for the deadlock of World War One, he argues, lay with the generals at the top of the command establishment who failed to keep pace with the rapid changes in the machine age and thus 'could not be expected to be pioneers of change' in the art of war.[6]

Out of the mud and blood of the Great War soared the Prophets of air power. Though from three different nations, all four had participated in World War One as military officers. Of the four, only Trenchard and Mitchell were trained pilots. Still, all had a vision about the military purposes of the airplane and, except for Trenchard, wrote extensively about air power and war. Bitter controversy remains over who should be given credit for originating strategic bombing theory, but all four Prophets came to the same conclusion: as the new decisive weapon, air power could recapture the offensive initiative lost in the trenches of World War One. Its use would provide the desired crushing blow that would win future wars quickly, decisively and humanely. Finally, thanks to the reputed skill and bravery of the soon-to-be legendary 'air aces,' who were immediately canonized as the elite of the manly warrior class, air power would restore the masculine ethos of courage and honor to every professional soldier.

Fast-paced developments in aviation technology soon made long-distance strategic bombing of cities possible, if not quite yet practical. Eleven years after the Wright Brothers' 1903 flight, the British Admiralty ordered its first large bomber. The plane had a top speed of 72 miles per hour and carried six 112-pound bombs. Two years later the Handley-Page V 1500 bomber was being readied to blast Berlin with 1,000 pounds of bombs. Though still slow, it was now armed with several machine guns for its own defense.

In 1916, though still in its infancy, Winston Churchill labelled air power as the decisive weapon of future wars. Even though assessments of the

World War One bombing of Germany were mixed, there was no doubt in the opinion of airpower enthusiasts that the future of war would include assaults from the air.

THE PROPHETS SPEAK

Giulio Douhet

The professional career and writings of General Giulio Douhet epitomize the Prophets' deep revulsion for trench warfare and enthusiasm for strategic bombing. In 1914, two years before the British launched their first bomber, Douhet, the impatient commander of the Italian aviation battalion at Turin, ordered the building of bombers. Built without the authority of Douhet's military superiors, the planes would soon carry the name of his close friend, the aircraft engineer Gianni Caproni.

Though there was to be considerable debate over Douhet's place as an airpower strategist, his book *The Command of the Air*, published in 1921, offers considerable insight into the origins of strategic bombing theory. In his assessment, the trench warfare of World War One and the techno-logical development of artillery and the submarine signaled the changing character of both land and sea war. He acknowledged that the World War One militaries were committed to the offensive posture, but argues that new firearms gave the advantage to the defense. In the end, Douhet con-cluded, neither side could launch a 'death blow,' meaning an attack 'which leaves a deep gaping wound and the feeling of imminent death.'[7]

To Douhet, the introduction of air power and poison gas in the Great War necessitated a change in the preparations for future war. In his words, the combination of chemistry and air technology 'makes it possible not only to make high-explosive bombing raids over any sector of the enemy's territory, but also to ravage his whole country by chemical and bacterio-logical warfare.'[8] This 'death blow' from the air, wrote Douhet, is more effective and moral in terms of lives lost than fighting wars of attrition.

But this new kind of war can only be waged if there is no distinction between combatants and non-combatants. The separation of armed forces from civilians – both legally, as established in the pre-war Hague II and IV conventions, and geographically – made the enemy's homeland safe, at least until its defensive lines at the front were compromised. Douhet notes (and World War One confirmed) that this separation meant that war was prolonged as 'the majority (civilians) went on working in safety and com-parative peace to furnish the minority (armed forces) with the sinews of war.'[9] The long reach of air power changed all this. Miles of land defense and water could be flown over. Air attacks on every inch of enemy territory were now possible and for moral and military purposes, desirable. The airplane, the ultimate offensive weapon, changed the character of war as: 'the battlefield will be limited only by the boundaries of the nations at war, and all of their citizens will become combatants, since all of them will be exposed to the aerial offensives of the enemy. There will be no distinction any longer between soldiers and civilians.'[10]

For Douhet and other airpower proponents, the potential return to the offensive character of war and the technological development of a decisive weapon to inflict the 'crushing blow' were exhilarating. Not only was the combination consistent with military tradition, both strategically and in terms of masculine ethos, but it also gave a glimpse into the future of war, one increasingly driven by the technological imperative. The symbiotic relationship between weapons technology and military strategy sparked Douhet's enthusiasm for the airplane as the 'offensive weapon par excellence.' It was also the central factor behind his insistence on the urgent need to comprehend and act on the importance of air power for winning future wars. His conclusion was that nations, in his case Italy, that fail to understand the implications of the technological revolution in aviation and continue to deploy vast army and naval forces will have no defense against an enemy determined to bomb their cities. He specifically warns:

> Victory smiles upon those who anticipate the changes in the character of war, not upon those who wait to adapt themselves after the changes occur. In this period of rapid transition from one form to another, those who daringly take to the new road first will enjoy the incalculable advantages of the new means of war over the old. This new character of war, emphasizing the advantages of the offensive, will surely make for swift, crushing decisions on the battlefield. Those nations who are caught unprepared for the coming war will find, when war breaks out, not only that it is too late for them to get ready for it, but also that they cannot even get the drift of it. Those who are ready first not only will win quickly but also will win with the fewest sacrifices and the minimum expenditure of means.[11]

Douhet insists winning future wars requires absolute control of the air. Preventing an enemy air force from flying is the only way to stop an attack. Only air power has this offensive potential, to be realized by striking first. Once command of the air is accomplished, only the bombing of large targets will suffice. The guiding principle of aerial bombing, Douhet asserts, is that 'the objective must be destroyed completely in one attack, making further attack on the same target unnecessary.'[12] To realize this objective, aerial bombing should target 'peacetime industrial and commercial establishment [sic]; important buildings, private and public; transportation arteries and centers and certain designated areas of civilian population as well.'[13] This comprehensive aerial bombing includes explosive, incendiary and poison gas instruments. Douhet is crystal clear as to the purposes of each type of bomb: 'The explosives will demolish the target, the incendiaries set fire to it, and the poison-gas bombs prevent fire fighters from extinguishing the fires.'[14]

Besides wreaking havoc in the target area, for Douhet the purpose of the first 'death blow' is to demonstrate to 'those of least moral resistance' that unless they quickly capitulate, they face an unopposed and sustained bombing campaign in which there is no separation between civilian and military targets. Unlike his fellow Prophets, Douhet does not specifically identify the urban working class as those whose moral and political will is most easily compromised. It is clear he is talking about the general category of civilians (non-combatants).

In proposing his theory of strategic bombing, Giulio Douhet illustrates an acute understanding of the major political issues of the period following World War One. Aware of the concerns over the costs of military preparedness, he suggests that strategic bombing is not only the effective and moral way to win war, but also the most economical since a national defense system will not require huge sums for land and sea forces. He also sides with those, including Prophets Hugh Trenchard and Billy Mitchell, arguing for an air force independent of the other military services. Finally, his argument for the urgency of adopting the new technology of air power is based on his assumption that a post-war disarmed Germany, with its Prussian dedication to the offensive and its lead in chemistry and mechanics, is most likely to develop new weapons of war. He predicts that the Germans will then seek revenge for their World War One defeat and the repugnant peace conditions imposed upon them.

Hugh Trenchard

The writings of Hugh 'Boom' Trenchard, though sparser than those of his Italian and North American contemporaries, add important nuances to strategic bombing theory. As early as September 1916, he judged that 'the aero plane, as a weapon of attack, cannot be too highly estimated.'[15] As he witnessed World War One bog down into a frustrating stalemate,

Trenchard, who was trained in the British military tradition of offensive economic warfare, proposed strategic air attacks on German industry. The bombing would be decisive, effecting 'the breakdown of the German army in Germany, its government, and the crippling of its sources of supply.'[16] Trenchard's well-earned reputation for pushing the attack, even if it meant great loss of life among his airmen, was consistent with the manly ethos of war fighting. To Trenchard, only those acting on the offensive could achieve moral superiority.

Unlike Douhet, Trenchard rejected the indiscriminate bombing of civilian populations. Instead, he argued that 'precision' bombing of industrial targets would easily undermine the morale of the working class and eventually of the general population. By 1928, Trenchard was even more certain about the effect of bombing what he now called 'centres of communication' in undermining the enemy's political will to resist. He was confident air attacks would 'induce the enemy government, by pressure from the population, to sue for peace, in exactly the same way as starvation by blockading the country would enforce the government to sue for peace.'[17]

William Mitchell

William 'Billy' Mitchell, generally conceded as the father of the United States Air Force, wrote and spoke volumes about air power and its ability to win future wars. In his first flight over the battlefield stalemate, Mitchell grasped the problematic nature of the Great War and the potential of the airplane; as he later wrote:

> A very significant thing to me was that we could cross the lines of these contending armies in a few minutes in our airplane, whereas the armies had been locked in the struggle, immovable, powerless to advance, for three years. ... It was as though they kept knocking their heads against a stone wall, until their brains were dashed out. They got nowhere, as far as ending the war was concerned.[18]

Later Mitchell focused on the dangers of future land wars between industrial nations. In 1926 he wrote: 'it can only end in absolute ruin, if the same methods that ground armies have followed before should be resorted to.'[19] Much like Trenchard, Mitchell thought the salvation was air bombardment aimed at destroying the enemy's 'vital centers;' the major cities and their industrial base that allowed modern nations to make war. Targets would include 'factories, raw materials, foodstuffs, supplies and modes of transportation.'[20] If applied in this way, 'the influence of air

power on the ability of one nation to impress its will on another in an
armed conflict will be decisive.'[21] Mitchell was a bit vague about bombing
civilians directly. On the one hand he argued for attacks on 'the places
where people lived [*sic*] and carry on their daily lives.'[22] Yet in another
instance he called bombing of factories ethical only if the workers had
been given sufficient warning.

It is clear that Mitchell saw bombardment bent on destroying industrial
production as the only means to affect the civilian will to resist. In his 1922
bombing manual he wrote: 'It may be necessary to intimidate the civilian
population in a certain area to force them to discontinue something which
is having a direct bearing on the outcome of the conflict.'[23] Like Douhet,
Mitchell argued that civilian efforts were essential to a nation's war. Thus
it was essential to break their will to resist. This was relatively easy, he
claimed, and did not require directly targeting the populace because
civilian will is very fragile. Much like Trenchard, Mitchell presumed that
raining terror from the skies would create refugees who, unable to find
food or shelter, would quickly cease to resist. For him, air power was 'a
quick way of deciding a war and really much more humane than the
present methods of blowing people to bits by cannon projectiles or
butchering them with bayonets.'[24] It would also be more civilized as it
would 'result in a diminished loss of life and treasure and ... thus be a
distinct benefit to civilization.'[25]

Like his fellow strategic bombers, Mitchell viewed the airplane as the
ultimate offensive weapon, especially when measured against the defensive weaponry of World War One. Echoing Douhet, Mitchell understood
the role technology had played in the trench slaughter and asserted the age
of the bomber was 'also the key to salvation.'[26] More important, it was
Mitchell who envisioned the airplane and the men who flew them as
offering the opportunity to regain the ethos of masculine honor that came
with offensive technology. In his stubborn advocacy for an independent air
force, he insisted that only an airman, a trained and experienced pilot,
should be in command. To Mitchell, 'air-going people' were different than
those who were unfortunately 'earthbound.' As Mark Clodfelter notes
about Mitchell, 'His vision was one of aerial knights engaged in a chival-
rous contest and supported by the population at large. This romantic
notion was both incongruous and appealing after the horrors of trench
warfare.'[27] This sense of personal and professional superiority that was and
remains common among airpower enthusiasts is central to understanding
the context in which strategic bombing theory evolved.

Basil Liddell Hart

The fourth Prophet of air power is Basil Liddell Hart. A British military strategist, he was to become one of the most revered Western military strategists of the twentieth century. Though he staunchly defended the British military's controversial conduct of World War One, with the end of hostilities Hart set out to recapture the dominant place on the battlefield for the offense. His theory of the 'indirect approach' argues that each nation has an Achilles' heel, a vulnerable point not necessarily related to the military forces. If it is discovered and targeted with a quick and powerful blow, the result will be swift and decisive victory. To Hart, the object of war was 'to subdue the enemy's will to resist, with the least possible human and economic loss to itself.'[28]

In both *Paris* and *The Remaking of Modern Armies,* Hart focuses specifically on the potential of air power to bring victory in the prescribed and preferred manner. Sounding very much like the other Prophets, he writes in *Paris*:

> Imagine for a moment that, of two centralized nations at war, one possesses a superior air force, the other a superior army. Provided that the blow be sufficiently swift and powerful, there is no reason why within a few hours, or at most days from the commencement of hostilities, the nerve system of the country inferior in air power should not be paralyzed.[29]

Though bothered by the targeting of civilians, Hart argued that due to its short duration 'terror bombing' would kill fewer people than a drawn-out land war. He also suggested that bombs filled with gas rather than explosives should be dropped on cities to decrease the horrors of strategic bombing. Hart asserts that 'gas may well prove the salvation of civilization from the otherwise inevitable collapse in case of another world war.'[30]

Obviously there are differences among the four Prophets. Still, there is solid agreement on the crucial aspects of strategic bombing theory. All four assert that aviation technology is offensive in character and possesses unquestioned potential to be the 'decisive' weapon of war able to deliver a 'crushing blow.' With the application of air power, the modern battlefield can be rescued from the weapons and tactics of defense employed in World War One. Once again the will and honor of the offensive attack will triumph, serving to re-masculinize or de-feminize the art of war. All four agree that victory means targeting the great industrial cities, the goal being to create such terror, destruction and misery as to undermine civilians' morale and in swift order break their fragile will to resist. Finally, all four

Prophets assume that the dispirited civilians will be able to force the political leadership to negotiate surrender.

Overall, to Douhet, Trenchard, Mitchell and Hart, terror bombing is more effective strategically, less costly economically and more humane and moral than the great land clashes between armies. All are certain that, given the fast-paced advancements in aviation technology, air power and strategic bombing are the keys to success in future conflicts. Speaking for all airpower enthusiasts then and now, Douhet warns that command of the air is not simply preferred but imperative as it 'means to be in a position to win. To be defeated in the air, on the other hand, is finally to be defeated and to be at the mercy of the enemy, with no chance at all of defending oneself, compelled to accept whatever terms he sees fit to dictate.'[31]

CIVILIANS IN WARFARE

From its very inception, two central components of strategic bombing theory stirred controversy. The primary disagreement was over the assertion that air power alone could win future wars. This is an interesting debate, though not the focus here. It is important to note that the historical use of air power – either in the way the four Prophets envisaged or more often in a nuanced form – produced adjustments to the original theory. While those adjustments have influenced the debate over its effectiveness, the purpose here in tracing those adjustments is to determine whether or not strategic bombing, as conceived and practiced in the contemporary setting, remains as it was originally proposed: an instrument of terrorism.

The other aspect of strategic bombing theory that has stirred controversy is Douhet and Hart's support for the purposeful slaughter of civilians and/or the intentional destruction of civilian industrial life as Trenchard and Mitchell proposed. Those familiar with the history of human warfare and the wanton attacks on civilians might wonder why this would be controversial. After all, precolonial and colonial warfare rarely, if ever made a distinction between combatants and noncombatants. A form of limited warfare did arise in autocratic Europe in the eighteenth century that included limiting civilian exposure to the worst atrocities of war. But with the French Revolution came the erosion of autocratic rule and the rise of populace-based nationalism that had military strategists returning to the concept of total war. Most notable amongst these strategists was Karl von Clausewitz (1780–1831). In *On War* Clausewitz advised: 'to introduce into a philosophy of war a principle of moderation would be an absurdity.

War is an act of violence pushed to its utmost bounds.'[32] By the mid-nineteenth century, this spirit had spread to the North American continent. In its conduct of the US Civil War, the Lincoln Administration contradicted its own Lieber Code instruction that civilians should not be targets of war by directing military commanders to ignore the Code at their discretion. The battle strategy of the Union forces, known as the Anaconda Plan, sought to starve the Southern civilian economy with a naval blockade. The Union general William T. Sherman, nicknamed 'Attila of the American Continent' for his devastating march through the Confederate South, defended his war on civilians thus: 'We are not only fighting hostile armies but a hostile people and must make old and young, rich and poor, feel the hard hand of war.'[33]

Despite a return to the theory of total war, three factors limited its practice during most of the nineteenth century. Two of these factors, the minor role of industrial weapons production in warfare and the lack of weapons with the range to hit enemy industrial centers, ceased to exist as the nineteenth century matured. The third factor, which the military historian Gwynne Dyer identifies as 'a genuine reluctance on the part of soldiers to turn their weapons against civilians,' survived from the eighteenth century to be codified in Hague II (1899) and Hague IV (1907), two conventions on the proper conduct of land war. Also in 1907, Hague IX, a similar convention prohibiting naval bombardment of undefended ports, towns, villages, dwellings, or buildings was drawn up. Ratified in 1910, all three Hague conventions prohibit attacks on undefended towns, villages, habitations or buildings in times of war. They reflect an emerging moral taboo against targeting non-combatants in the Western European and North American theaters.

For the Prophets of strategic bombing, however, any hesitation about attacking civilians ended with the rapid advancement in aviation technology after World War One, especially the extended range and load capacity of the bomber. Finally it was possible to reach and inflict heavy damage on the safe havens of urban industrial production. The result, in the Prophets' opinion, was a necessary shift back to the concept of total war in which, in Douhet's strident assessment, 'the entire population and all the resources of a nation are sucked into the maw of war.'[34]

Despite the postwar military support for a strategy of total war, in 1923 another Hague convention was proposed prohibiting 'aerial bombardment for the purpose of terrorizing the civilian population, of destroying or damaging private property not of military character, or of injuring non-combatants.'[35] Though supported by the United States, which was starting to play a larger role in global strategic and diplomatic affairs, these rules failed to be adopted. They were at odds with a powerful European political–military constituency that heeded Hugh Trenchard's warning that 'in the next great war with a European nation, the forces engaged must first fight for aerial superiority ... to destroy the morale of the Nation.'[36] In 1938, the League of Nations nominally ended this tug-of-war over the morality of terror bombing in a unanimously adopted resolution entitled: 'Protection of Civilian Populations Against Bombing From the Air in Case of War.' But by then, the League of Nations was collapsing. Its political impotency, coupled with the bombing of civilians that had already taken place in many contexts including the 1936–38 Spanish Civil War, Japan's air war on China throughout the 1930s, and throughout the colonial world, stymied the League's diplomatic effort to protect civilians from aerial bombardment.[37]

It is important to note that throughout the post-war period when debate over the morality of targeting civilians raged in Europe's military–diplmatic circles, no moral or legal taboo existed preventing European bombs being dropped on colonial populations. During World War One, the British bombed their restless colonial subjects into submission, most notably the Pathans and Mashud of India and Egypt's Sultan of Darfur. In 1919, British bombs pounded the Afghanistan cities of Jalalabad and Kabul. In the same year Hugh Trenchard, allegedly the 'reluctant' strategic bomber, urged Winston Churchill to use the Royal Air Force (RAF) against the rebellious Mohammed Abdille Hassan, the 'Mad Mullah' of Somaliland. Churchill obliged, and from the sky the RAF crushed the spirited revolt with £77,000 worth of bombs. Compared to the cost of a land campaign, the air war was considered a bargain.

The obvious contradiction between a consistent and successful European diplomatic effort, codified in the early Hague Conventions, against the bombardment of civilians, and a willingness to bomb colonial populations raises two important questions. First, and most obvious, why did the power brokers of Europe treat their colonial subjects of Africa and Asia dramatically differently from their own civilians? Second, and most important here, apart from their judgments about effective military strategy, are there other factors to explain the Prophets' enthusiasm – in the prosecution of future wars – for targeting the civilian populations of industrial societies, or for that matter civilians anywhere?

3

Who Is to Be Bombed?
The Self and Other in
Imperial Culture

The concepts of 'self' and 'other' dominated the class, race and gender context of Europe and North America in the late nineteenth and early twentieth centuries. They are pivotal to understanding why, contrary to the Hague Conventions, colonial civilians were bombed and why the Prophets considered that bombing enemy civilians was strategically and morally appropriate in fighting and winning future Great Power wars. In the contemporary context, they elucidate the *why* and *who* of strategic bombing in the so-called 'war on terrorism.'

The notion of 'self' and 'other' is a central construct of the Dialectic of Enlightenment as conceived in critical sociology and cultural Marxism, notably in the writings of Theodore Adorno, Homi Bhabha, Simone de Beauvoir and Edward Said. Briefly stated, in the human condition, individuals are involved in a dialectical struggle between self and other. Defining, classifying and ultimately determining the other develops knowledge of the self and its connection to its environment. Thus the self gains identity and reason for its beliefs and actions. The goal of this endeavor is to find one's place in one's environment through mastery and control, and ultimately freedom.

Several theorists focus on the self/other struggle for identity in the Western cultural context and the role of reason in the search for enlightenment. As Ben Wadham explains: 'Reason, within the cultural enunciations of the Enlightenment became, and so it remains the instrument through which we can legitimate ourselves as truly human, as ordered, as civilized and as truth bearing subjects.'[1] As we saw in Chapter 2, this connection between humanness, reason and civilization was at the core of the Prophets' view of how to conduct future wars. To them, bombing civilians was humane, moral and reasoned – indeed the rational approach to preserving what they deemed as the civilized world.

The search for self/other identity was particularly intense in the decades leading up to the Great War. The determination of the other was a major component of the cultural context of late Victorian life in Europe and in the blossoming imperial culture of the post-Civil War United States. To a great extent it was manifested in the European colonial empire building in Africa and Asia and in the dual colonial/neocolonial expansion of United States' power into South America and the South Pacific. Both experiences produced in all aspects and constituencies of society an imperial mentality, a belief in the goodness of empire.[2]

In this period the liberal concept of national self-determination, the right of nation states to determine their own destiny without outside interference, was taking hold in North America and Europe. Thus, empire building in other parts of the world required a rationalization system. For the imperialists, it was found in the notion of the 'other.' Those outside the core of Western culture were deemed undeserving of or unprepared for self-determination on racial, gender or class grounds. In constructing this aspect of the other, the European and North American collective and individual selves found their identity and place in the world in terms of privilege, dominance and hegemony.

THE RISE OF IMPERIAL CULTURE

During the nineteenth century, Britain, Italy and the United States (the nations that were to produce the four Prophets) all expanded their global power. A new commerce-based ethos of change and progress gave reason and religious missionary zeal to the crusade to conquer forcibly and then civilize the 'unfortunate' colonial subjects. Without European conquest, it was reasoned, 'those people' would never advance, would never be saved from the fires of Hell. With divine blessing, during the Enlightenment the European 'self' had found its place in a new societal order based on the liberal notions of freedom and equality, referred to at the time as the 'rights of man.' Now there was a divine right and indeed obligation to civilize the unfortunate 'heathen savages' of Africa and Asia, to share with them the blessed ways of Western culture even if it took brute force to do so.[3]

Likewise, in North America a perceived divine right of Manifest Destiny drove the Anglo-Saxon experiment to the Pacific coast and beyond. While the North American ruling class ostensibly rejected formal colonial rule, the needs of North American commerce for access to new markets, property and ownership required removal of any obstacle. It was the Native American 'others,' their way of life, their occupation of potentially valuable land and their rejection of the principle of ownership that stood in the way of the expanding commercial interests of the newborn nation. The unwillingness of the 'Indians' to accept the concept of private property, their refusal to sell that which nobody owned, necessitated that they be lied to, cheated and forcibly removed to worthless land or be eliminated. All this was done and defended as part of God's plan for the special Puritan experiment in liberty and constitutional government known as 'Zion in the Wilderness.' As V. G. Kiernan states, 'The US began as a staunchly Protestant nation in an otherwise almost Catholic or pagan New World, and this was bound to impose a sense of superiority, which might suggest a duty to rescue neighbors from their darkness.'[4]

The North American imperial campaign did not end with the slaughter of the Native Americans in December 1890 at Wounded Knee, South Dakota. As Howard Zinn notes, the idea of a North American empire beyond the continental borders was not new and was seen as a 'natural development from the twin drives of capitalism and nationalism.'[5] Zinn argues that this 'ideology of expansion' was by the 1890s firmly established in elite business, political and military circles. Even farmers, who saw overseas markets resulting from expansion, joined the chorus urging the extension of Manifest Destiny to other lands and peoples. In protest at North American expansionist mania, the nineteenth-century political radical Carl Schurz observed that Manifest Destiny was invoked to mark the extension of US power as inevitable.[6]

These imperial beliefs also rationalized both the final 'reservation' of the few survivors left from the 'Indian Wars' and the fortified colonial outposts in Cuba, the Philippines, Puerto Rico, Hawaii, Guam, and Wake Island. With the crushing of the Filipino revolt at the turn of the century, Zinn recalls: 'the taste of empire was on the lips of politicians and business interests throughout the country now. Racism, paternalism, and the talk of money mingled with talk of destiny and civilization.'[7]

Racism was central to rationalizing the European and North American imperial jackhammer. The racist imagery of the time had multiple layers beginning with representations of other peoples as barbarian, savage, lazy, immoral, unreliable, imbecilic and uncouth. In time, deeper and more intrinsic character flaws were identified: the colonized were people without souls or people cursed with being stuck at the development stage of children.

Whatever its manifestation, the point was to plant the notion of the 'unciv-ilized' in contrast to the 'civilized' White world and the need and responsi-bility to civilize (if possible) the other races. For example, the Japanese were portrayed as liars, cheats and swindlers who failed to act properly in affairs of sex and religion. For the British, the Chinese, as Asiatic, were children who needed to be firmly made to do what was 'for their own good.' To Sir Rudolph Slatin, the African 'niggers' were lazy beasts to be forced to work with the feel of the stick.[8] North American whites used all these images and more. In particular, the people indigenous to the continent were specifically portrayed as cunning and fierce, yet without intelligence. Thus they were deemed unworthy of owning the vast continental treasures.[9]

Central to imperial rule was the often-repeated assumption that racial others were brutal people, who only responded to force. The British histo-rian J. F. Baddeley expresses both beliefs when he comments on the proper way to deal with 'Orientals', 'Fire and sword, sacked villages, ravished women, gave the tribesmen "a lesson they thoroughly understood and fully appreciated" since this was how wars were conducted among themselves.'[10] Colonial military philosophy was dedicated to offensive action. Striking hard from the start was seen as imperative since force impressed the fanat-ical savages while leniency gave them courage. For their own sake, indeed as an act of humanity, numerous colonial authorities reasoned, the lower races had to be defeated with decisive force as it brought a quick end to bloodshed and discouraged further resistance. As V. G. Kiernan puts it: 'Those not hypnotized into accepting white superiority had to be made to do so, by processes for which *cowing* was an expression often in English mouths.'[11] Talk of 'nigger shooting' and 'rule via the rod of iron' was rampant whether in relation to British reign in Asia or French and Belgian governance in the African Congo. For the sake of power and the prestige of the imperial order, in dealing with other races all manner of force was to be tolerated. No tactic or instrument of oppression was out of bounds. For example, the Hague Convention of 1899 banned the infamous dum-dum bullet from warfare among the civilized nations. Thus its use was still allowed against the colonial peoples.

Fear of losing a race war fueled the imperial violence of the white world. The exploding hordes of Asia constituted a 'yellow peril'. The British prime minister, David Lloyd George, warned the French against training 'big nigger armies.' Whites were fearful of a 'race war of revenge,' especially after 'dusky Napoleons' proved to be formidable warriors in Zululand and Rwanda. Thus the officer corps of colonial armies remained exclusively white.[12] In North America, fear of black economic and political power joined racial prejudice in brutally enforcing 'Jim Crow' segregation laws and the internal colonizing of African Americans. Fear of another Haiti-type black republic in the Caribbean was behind the McKinley Administration's decision to colonize Cuba once the Cuban rebels won independence from Spain. It was Winston Churchill, fearful of a Cuba under black power, who pointedly advised US leaders that, though defeated, Spain should remain in control of its Caribbean colony.[13]

Talk of race war added the important dimension 'enemy' to the racial image of the other. No matter how childlike the imperial subjects were or how paternalistic the white world felt towards them, they stood in the way of white economic prosperity, civilization and progress. If they could not be persuaded of the correctness and righteousness of the white cause, then as enemies they were to be defeated through force of arms. On this point, the British captain S. Osborn bluntly insisted: 'Our enemy – that is, the enemy of British Progress in China – is he who stands between us and these creatures – the burly, obstinate, over-fed mandarin, thanks to whom squalor, hunger, and misery seemed the general condition of the lower orders.'[14] While the European and North American whites raced each other to conquer the world, when it came to any serious colonial rebellion, as in India in 1857 or the Boxers of China in 1900, the often bitter white rivals unified against the common enemy. As Kiernan records, by the end of the nineteenth century: 'Europe had grown more solid than in its earlier day of chronic colonial wars, and better able to come before the world as one civilization.'[15]

Issues of class and gender also factored into the representation of the colonized other. European class-consciousness and bias produced images of the colonized common man as beasts of burden that, unlike the 'decadent' colonized upper classes, were 'submissive to authority in a degree that must render them excellent subjects.'[16] Class analysis was also at the core of the European militarists' push to develop the most advanced weapons of war regardless of the cost. According to science historian Robert Routledge, winning the high-tech arms race was imperative since history recorded that 'in ancient times opulent and civilized communities could hardly defend themselves against poor and barbarous races. ... In our day it is the poor and barbarous tribes who are everywhere at the mercy of the wealthy and cultivated nations.'[17]

Throughout the colonial world, class-conscious Europeans utilized existing caste, racial (skin tone) and aristocratic tribal distinctions to pacify and eventually govern their subjects. It was impossible for colonial rulers, who depended heavily on the cooperation of native 'blue blood' in the daily operations of empire, to ignore class divisions within the ruled. Conversely, divided by their class positions in European society, a class notion of 'indefinable aristocratic ascendancy' united white settlers. The civilizing of the colonial other as expressed in class and racial terms, gave identity to all Europeans as a brotherhood united in blood, both white and blue.

Empire also meant a gendered image of the other. Colonial expansion and the wars accompanying it were defined as masculine adventures, whose dangers and actions were appropriate for men only. The European women, wives and kin of the male empire-builders, were summoned to their male's side only when the colony was safe for the allegedly weaker sex. The patriarchal mentality and practice of the North American and European male conqueror meant native women suffered increased hardship under both formal and informal empire. As patriarchal property, they were subject to rape and multiple forms of sexual violence such as debauchery, torture and humiliation that often ended in death. The violent fury of the male conqueror was also a rejection of the matrilineal and matrilocal forms of precolonial society in which women held status and voice equal to men. Deemed a threat to the supremacy of male power, any memory, legacy or, most important, champion of these 'abnormal' or 'godless' forms of society must be wiped out. In other cases, as in the genocide against the indigenous North American population, because of their primary role in reproduction women were singled out for sexual violence and murder. To destroy a people, the North American general and subsequently President Andrew Jackson believed, a disproportionate number of women, as carriers of future generations, required killing.[18]

The construction of the gendered other, like that of race and class, took on multiple and nuanced forms throughout the colonial world. Yet every-where native women faced common conditions of invisibility and less value. They had no role or voice in the affairs of the colonial state, in the spheres either of governance or of production. Until uncovered by recent feminist research, little was known of the plight of colonized women, taken by European men not only to 'perform domestic work but to service their sexual needs, psychic well-being and physical care.'[19]

In the sexual division of labor, fathers, husbands, brothers and sons worked the fields and mines of colonial enterprises and at times were appointed to government positions under the auspices of the supreme colonial authority. Native women's visible sphere was relegated to providing less valuable but necessary goods for the family, both in the home and in the fields. Their common condition of 'less value' was expressed in their status as property, not to be educated in the affairs of human endeavor as native men were. They were to be bought and sold as property. They were 'taken' or 'used' until they wore out physically and psychologically, only to be discarded. Their colonial masters' view of them as prizes and sex objects, in either the exotic or erotic sense, defined native women as less than human, as playthings or quaint cultural objects existing only for economic or physical exploitation. Even when native women resisted the gendered rules of patriarchy, they suffered invisibility and decreased value. Prohibited behavior such as dancing or going naked resulted in their continued invisibility before colonial authority. Native men were held responsible and called upon to answer for the 'childlike' actions of 'their' women.

The European and North American imperialists' image of the colonized gave identity to the colonizer. Civilizing the savage was a noble cause, thus the imperial self was noble. As the other was deemed inferior and worthless, the self was cast as worthy and superior. At the core, the colonized other is less than human; the imperial self, given its self-appointed task of attempting the impossible, of humanizing the inhuman, of civilizing the uncivilized, is anointed as superhuman. Failure at these tasks did nothing to undermine this superior place. As often expressed in the justification for imperial expansion and domination, the most elementary, achievable and noble goals of this 'splendid adventure' were liberation of the savages from the chains of cultural stagnation and the enforcing of order on chaos. The very presence and dominant position of imperial forces amongst and over the colonized was enough to manifest and sustain the contrast between the noble, civilized, rational colonizer and the ignoble, yet to be civilized savage.

Imperial mentality was obvious throughout imperial Europe and North America. Yet the greatest enthusiasts for empire were found among the professional military and among upper-class European women. As Kiernan details, building empire gave males from every class greater opportunity for a professional military career.[20] This was particularly true of working-class and middle-class males for whom a military commission was not available as a matter of heredity. As professional soldiers, they played the essential role in subjugating (in imperial terms, liberating) the colonized and then enforcing discipline and order on a daily basis over them. Thus, regardless of their class origin or military rank, they were certain of the nobleness of their cause and by identity their self.

Apparently the cause of empire was most important to those, both officer and enlisted alike, who, because of class, ethnic or national status, had a history of being identified as other. Scots from the lower classes rose within the ranks in the British military more than others, it was said, due to a 'hunger for success.' Scottish commanders, in pursuing their military duties against the colonized, consistently displayed a taste for brutality bordering on sadism. Likewise, 'Anglo-Irish officers, far more still, had imperialism in their blood and bones.'[21]

The same was true of upper-class European women who by the late nineteenth century were fighting against patriarchy in their own society. In championing the expansion of women's lives into the public arenas of power, they were often outspoken advocates for 'strenuous imperialism.' Among the British in India, it was upper-class women who openly advocated the strongest application of force and discipline against the colonial subjects. Florence Nightingale, daughter of a British general and crusader for a noncombatant role for women on the battlefield, was renowned for her distaste of peace-loving women and her enthusiasm for war as the enterprise of heroic virtues.

In all cases, imperialism abroad placed those seeking equality of status within their own national ranks in common cause with the very constituency of white upper-class males who saw and treated them poorly. Like with the ambitious and successful social climber or those newly converted to religious belief, it was in the interest of their own sense of superior self that the 'inferior' character of the colonial subject be reinforced through harsh words and brutal deeds.

The widely held notion of the colonial other within the European and North American societies in general, and the high circles of political and military power in particular, helps to explain why air power was invoked against colonial populations at a time when international resolutions against the bombing of civilians had been adopted or were under discussion within those same circles. In the British case, the decision of Churchill and Trenchard to bomb civilians in colonial Somaliland at the very moment they were cautioning against the direct targeting of European civilians evokes no hint of awareness of contradiction from them. Likewise, neither the British bombing of colonial India in 1915 and Egypt in 1919 nor the French and Spanish 1912–1913 bombing of villages and marketplaces in their respective parts of Morocco sparked hand-wringing over these violations of the Hague Conventions. The point was to do 'whatever it takes' to subdue the imperialized, particularly in cases where they were resisting the noble mission, disrupting the imperial order or being ungrateful for their liberation. Air power, the new technology both of demonstrating power and taking decisive measures, became the obvious instrument of imperial subjugation.

THE IMPERIAL CENTER:
BOMBING IN THE GREAT WARS OF THE FUTURE

As originally articulated, strategic bombing theory was about winning the future wars among the Great Nations in the imperial center. Events and influences in Europe and North America thus played the central role in the Prophets' formulations of strategic bombing doctrine and its application in the mid-1930s and beyond. The most important aspect was construction of a rationalization system that determined who in the imperial center would be bombed and why.

The journey from the nineteenth into the twentieth century was a period of transition for both Europe, in particular Britain, and the USA. Rapid industrialization and the dynamic development of weapons, in particular, played an important role in the prosecution and outcome of World War One, which influenced the origin of strategic bombing theory. The rise of Prussian power in continental Europe and the emergence of the USA on the world stage also decisively changed the strategic environment in which the Prophets theorized about the future.

These transitions were important, but the domestic context – rife with class, race, and gender consciousness and conflict – also heavily influenced the Prophets and fashioned their view of the human condition. It shaped what role they, as professional military officers, could play in defending the highest virtues of civilization within the imperial center. At the heart of their view is a self/other identity that permitted them to justify the bombing of civilians in the imperial center as rational, humane and moral.

The nineteenth-century rise of social Darwinism had dramatically influenced European and North American power elites, particularly as they attempted to deal with rapid industrialization and the social tensions it produced in the imperial center. For the upper classes, Charles Darwin's thesis of the survival of the fittest explained their place at the top of the social ladder as well as the situations of those on the rungs below. For power brokers in the United States such as John D. Rockefeller, a vigorous exponent of this explanation, the struggle that brought 'men like himself to the top, was indispensable to progress.'[22] In Britain, Herbert Spencer and other powerful students of social organization espoused this theory. On the other hand, Marxism, the other major school of nineteenth-century social theory, interpreted social Darwinist theory in terms of class struggle. By the last decades of the nineteenth century, the influence of Marxist ideology had led to the emergence of 'socialist organization' in the form of working-class trade unions and political parties. The result was a dramatic increase in social tensions, as the conservative upper class, sure of their deserved Darwinist superiority, sought to mitigate the gains of the undeserving classes below.

Within general social theory, the character traits of those 'below' were articulated in specific class terms.[23] In Victorian Britain, where 80 per cent of the population was working-class, the upper class portrayed working-class people and areas as akin to colonial places and peoples. Travel literature pictured the trip from the civilized city center to the 'poor man's land' as a journey down into the dark, strange, forbidding and dangerous 'unknown lands' of the London slums – not unlike a journey to the colonies. Once in the 'netherland' of working-class life, one was subject to the filth and animalism of the lower classes. In contrast to bourgeois Victorian culture, in which cleanliness was next to godliness, working-class people were portrayed as 'dunging in the street' out of choice and normal practice. As a result, it was said that smell separated them from respectability. Due to 'excessive sexuality,' marriage was assumed to be rare and incest common among the 'out group.' From 1834 on, when prime minister Benjamin Disraeli declared poverty a crime, the working class was described in the language of criminality and anti-social behavior, as products of their own immoral, fraudulent nature. Like the colonized peoples and other racial groups in the imperial order, the working class was portrayed as irreligious with only 'a rude idea of the creation.' To social theorists such as Herbert Spencer, A. R. Wallace and Charles Lyell, the working class was uncivilized, immature, impulsive, indeed stuck at the development stage of a child.[24]

In the USA, the liberal concepts of freedom to choose and equal opportunity combined with the westward drive for Manifest Destiny to support the myth of a society based on 'liberty and justice for all.' Yet class-consciousness and class stratification, though not as apparent or rigid as in aristocratic Europe, were evident, particularly as North America shifted from being an agrarian to an industrial society. Waves of Italian, Greek,

Jewish and Russian immigrants, like the earlier German and Irish 'Anglo-Saxon' poor, were piled on top of each other in the teeming ghettos of the industrial cities. In upper-class opinion, the North American working class was stigmatized with the same traits as Europe's workers. White workers, who made up the bulk of the poor, were not considered as purely 'animalistic' as the black or 'Yellow' segment of the working class. Still they were viewed as of low intelligence, dirty, lazy, loud and violent. They were said to be products of inbreeding with a religious zeal evoking a fundamentalist and superstitious, rather than rational, mindset. This legacy remains today in stereotypes of 'rednecks' and 'white trash.'[25] As in Britain, poverty was a crime: the punishment for being poor was institutionalized in the workhouse and in the army of private and public guards who policed an unofficial system of forced labor. In short, the degradation of the poor and working classes gave the European aristocracy and North American upper class identity as rational beings, superior in human and moral terms and, as creators and guardians of progress, deserving of all their riches.

Three other factors of class, all products of rapid industrialization, were part of the context in which strategic bombing theory was conceived and practiced. One was the growth of the bourgeois middle class for whom the othering of the working class was of great importance in creating and sustaining their new identity, Within middle-class consciousness, disdain for the working class, a willingness to believe the worst of the 'out group,' was more strident than in the aristocracy. Though they were in the center of the class structure, middle-class Europe and North America directed their attention and their loyalties to the political, social and cultural aspects of upper-class life. It was where they wanted to be. When they did look downward, it was from a position of superiority marked by 'contagious snobbery' that made scapegoats of those below.[26]

Class conflict increased with industrialization. As organized resistance to capitalist exploitation grew, particularly in the form of a socialist agenda, fear of the power of the teeming masses – now seen as a political enemy – emerged within the middle and upper classes. Working-class gains threatened the traditional and new privileges of both segments. In the Darwinist context, working-class militancy threatened human progress. The forces of light were ranged against those of darkness, the rational versus the superstitious, the civilized world against residents of 'netherland.' In the view of the rich and powerful, open class warfare was being waged against them. Since the enemy from below had instigated the war, and, being irrational, only understood force, all the implements of state and society were to be mustered to save civilization.

Spurred by working-class militancy, economic depression and, in the case of the USA, waves of immigrants, the European and North American upper classes brought all the instruments at their command, including the courts, public and private military forces and political concession, to bear against their enemy class. As a result, at the end of the nineteenth century, class antagonism, and at times outright class warfare, dominated industrial life on both continents.

One other product of capitalist industrialization was the inclusion, as a matter of economic necessity, of large numbers of women into the industrial workforce. The reality of women under capitalist patriarchy will be attended to later. Here, it is sufficient to say that the fact that women were forced into the industrial labor force added one further element to the class identity of the late Victorian age.

In Europe, the class-consciousness of social Darwinism also extended to the nation-state system. As noted, when judged against the rest of the world, all of Europe was considered the apex of civilization. Yet divisions based on class and racial distinctions, between high and low Europe, rich and poor Europe, Anglo-Saxon and non-Anglo-Saxon Europeans were common. In Victorian Britain, these rankings were based on a national identity of British superiority and a dim view of their second-class European relatives. As Newsome says, 'The Victorians had a natural pecking order for European countries, too. Germany, because of the kinship of common stock, was unquestionably at the top; Switzerland and the Low Countries were in the second rank, with the Latin nations coming at the bottom.'[27] Class distinction among European nations was in part based on success at empire building. While the continent as an entity benefited in terms of wealth from colonialism, the polarization between rich and poor nations, between the advanced British and French and 'retarded' Spain and Portugal increased.[28] In the national hierarchy, the Anglo-Saxon nations epitomized excellence, a notion that spawned and sustained efforts at building 'an English speaking peoples' league of God for the permanent peace of this war-torn world' which by the end of the nineteenth century consisted of North America and Britain.[29]

The Victorian mindset also applied race distinctions to Europe. Throughout the nineteenth century the doctrines of polygenism, a theory proposing separate or unequal human creations, and phrenology, the belief that skull structure could place racial groups at different places in the evolutionary process, gained considerable ground in scientific and commercial literature. Both reinforced the existing notion of a world divided between civilized (white) and the uncivilized (non-white) races that was a central part of imperial mentality and the mission of empire. In industrial Britain, belief in racial superiority and inferiority and its accompanying prejudices were applied to black, yellow and brown peoples, but also to the Irish and Jews. Irish immigrants and most persons of color were poor and working-class. Labeling the Irish as irrational, childlike, intemperate, believers in religious mumbo-jumbo (Roman Catholicism), possessed of a ghetto mentality, and living in the squalor of 'rookery' housing would seem to be a distinction of class rather than of race. After all, they are white. Yet, according to polygenism and phrenology, the permanent poverty of the Irish (both as a national condition of Ireland in comparison with other European nations, and as a fact of their life of the Irish in Britain), reflected their lower place on the evolutionary ladder.[30]

As Ruth Frankenburg writes, 'Whiteness refers to a set of locations that are historically, socially, politically, and culturally produced and, moreover, are intrinsically linked with unfolding relations of domination.'[31] As the dominant power of Europe, if not the world, the British were in position to define 'Whiteness' and in doing so set 'a standard by which all other forms of humanity have been measured.'[32] For the Irish, as well as the populations of the 'low European' nations who just happened to have swarthy complexions, it was the British construction of race that mattered. Armed with racial consciousness, the British defined the white Boer settlers of Dutch heritage who fought against British power in South Africa as 'exactly like the Chinese, impressed only by strength.'[33] Likewise, in preparing for and prosecuting World War One, the British played the race card as 'the passions and prejudices long worked up against other races were diverted against a new target, with the Germans in the role of "Huns" ... once again civilization confronted barbarism.'[34] As Chalmers Mitchell wrote in his 'Biological Review of Our Foreign Policy,' 'Here is the first great racial struggle of the future.'[35]

In the USA, the Civil War abolished African American slavery but did not end institutionalized white racism or racial violence. This has been well chronicled in numerous ways; notably the housing and labor ghettoizing of 'free' Blacks, laws institutionalizing racism under the myth of 'separate but equal'; the rise of white vigilante groups such as the Ku Klux Klan, and the wholesale violence and intimidation against people of color and 'out' ethnic groups. As in the push for working-class rights, the cause of racial justice, especially when supported by white 'race traitors' or led by fiery black orators such as W. E. B. DuBois, constituted a threat to white privilege. As efforts to organize 'nigger power' increased in the closing decades of the nineteenth century, they were met in various and imaginative ways, including unofficial and official violence, to 'legally' disenfranchise the other race, politically and economically.[36]

Gender was also important in the Victorian development of a self/other identity. Though under challenge within upper-class circles, for most men and women the rigid patriarchal gender roles were intact. Men occupied the institutions of public power, where they debated and decided the affairs of state. They were also the final voice of authority in domestic life. Women faced a common condition of invisibility in the realms of public power and less value in terms of their life role and contributions to society. Young girls were raised in preparation for their 'traditional' (patriarchal) role as wife, childbearer and domestic laborer. Once married, they became the property of or lost any right to an economic life independent of their husband. Where these gender roles were not enforced in the law, either secular or religious, or by social custom, they were sustained through patriarchal mentality, a set of ideas about the appropriate gender roles of men and women.[37]

By the close of the nineteenth century, the rising influence of social Darwinism had reinforced patriarchal images of women as the weaker sex, inferior in physical strength and intelligence to men. They were characterized as overly emotional and irrational and therefore unsuited for responsibility beyond domestic life. Herbert Spencer and Patrick Geddes argued that feminine and masculine characteristics, starting with the very lowest forms of life, were divided into a nurturing anabolic nature (feminine) and an active, energy-releasing katabolic (masculine) nature. In this view, woman's biological reality of pregnancy, menstruation (viewed as a debilitating illness) and child rearing left her with little energy for other activities. She needed to stay home to conserve her energy. Man's capacity for abstract reason and attachment to the notion of social justice, both evidence of a highly evolved status, and his limited role in procreation – viewed as solely fertilization – made him suited to and required by his energized nature to pursue other activities. Accordingly, the social structure of patriarchy was biologically determined: polarized between an emotional, passive, childlike woman, weaker in body and in mind, and an energized, courageous, rational, independent, cerebral and adult man. In Victorian England and North America, patriarchy was determined to be natural and, as the Bible asserted, the Christian God's Will, indeed a moral ordering of human life.[38]

But as already mentioned, like class and race issues, in nineteenth-century liberal industrial society, gender was contested terrain. Low wages for husbands in combination with the spinster status of many poor females had forced many women into the industrial workplace. Liberal feminists, mainly from the upper class, proposing that equal opportunity and freedom of choice applied to women as well as men, fought for property rights within marriage, educational opportunities, the right to vote, and freedom from a life of domestic labor. In both economic and political terms, what was assumed to be the very basis of the natural and moral patriarchal order was under a challenge of revolutionary proportions. For advocates of patriarchy, the fight for gender equality was powerful proof of the irrational, emotion-driven, immaturity of woman 'the child.' Feminists were doing the sinister work of the Devil and were the enemy of all God-fearing people. Feminism's impact on society's moral decay, Henry Mayhew and W. T. Stead complained, was obvious in the general increase in prostitution and child prostitution everywhere but most evident in the streets of London. Giving women the vote, opined Lord Salisbury, would lead to socialism.

The power brokers of Victorian society (the 'gentlemen' of the aristocratic and professional classes) felt that feminists had opened another front in the war on their privileged position. In both the public and private arenas, their personal power was at risk. Much like their confrontation with other races and classes, the powerful of Victorian Britain and North America saw the feminist challenge to patriarchy as an attack on civilization itself. Viscount Wolseley, who attributed positive value to the 'impulse' of war, thought the very manhood of the state and thus civilization itself were at stake since 'effeminacy ... destroys nations as well as individuals.'[39] In the USA, according to historian Gail Bederman, the future US president Theodore Roosevelt was openly disdainful of the emerging Victorian notion of manliness according to which 'male power was growing murky'; and he championed a return to a world in which 'the white man's power, the power of civilization, was crystal clear.'[40]

Moderate legislative success, growing feminist militancy and female participation in the working class added 'woman as enemy' to the patriarchal other. In the last stages of the Victorian age, the dominant class, race and gender mindset was expressed in multiple ways. Its most poignant statement may have been at the 1893 World's Columbian Exposition in

Chicago. Intended to 'demonstrate American civilization's astonishing progress toward human perfection' the White City, centerpiece of the exposition, celebrated the accomplishments of the civilized self, the white, male, upper-class kings of commerce and science.[41] The products of the uncivilized barbarians were vividly displayed on the exposition's Midway Plaisance. As originally conceived, the exposition stood as a monument to the visibility of men and the invisibility of women in the human endeavor. Only after a group of North America's most prominent women pressed hard within the corridors of power was a Women's Building 'added on' to the White City. Their larger effort to integrate women's achievements alongside the male-dominated displays in other venues ultimately failed.

THE MILITARIZED PROPHETS

Class, race and gender identity and the turmoil it sparked defined, both at home and in the outposts of empire, the social context in which the Prophets attained manhood and professional stature. Other factors of identity influenced their outlook as well. By the end of the nineteenth century, a belief in the uniqueness of the British and American experiments held sway in the political and social circles to which Trenchard, Hart and Mitchell belonged. The British empire was at its zenith, resulting in a strong sense of the 'rightness' of anything British and a wholesome contempt for all else. This included their European rivals, most notably the Germans. In North America, the continental expansion of white Christianity under the aegis of Manifest Destiny had reached the Pacific Coast, dismissing Native Americans along the way. Already, the 'special American experiment' was spreading to foreign parts. British and North American elites were supremely confident their nations would rank at the top of the twentieth-century power league. Italy, home to Giulio Douhet, was belatedly emerging as a player in Europe, its frustrated elites anxious to return Rome to imperial status. In 1911, Libya joined Somalia and the port of Massawa in Ethiopia, as Italy's colonial conquests. Though World War One ended in ignominious defeat for Italy, the rise of fascism afterwards quickly built a militarized Italian state bent on restoring the glory of Rome.

As military professionals, the Prophets benefited from a militarized culture that gave them exalted status. In a militarized society, all things military or connected to the military are privileged. To question or criticize the militarized culture is deviant, seditious, even sacrilegious behavior. Historically, the soldier has been admired, but in a militarized society his status becomes almost that of an icon. Citizens who choose a military career or don the uniform temporarily, especially those who risk life and limb in battle, are exalted as the 'nation's finest.' In the patriarchal culture of the military, they are the 'manly men' or 'the warrior class.'[42]

The militarization of European and North American culture intensified dramatically in the decades before the Great War. In this highly charged nationalistic context, the stature of the military grew not merely because of its traditional role in national security, but also as a symbol of national power, pride and civil virtue. Central to this process was the popularity of the complementary notions that war was a natural and unavoidable state of man and that conflict was endemic to advanced civilizations. Within the dominant conservative upper-class circles, war was seen as a test of the nation, of race (the lighter the skin the more prowess and courage) and of masculinity. Indeed, for social Darwinists, it was an instrument of God's divine laws of evolution from which emerged the highest stage of civilization. The measurement of people as 'martial' and 'non-martial' was commonplace, with unqualified respect for the former. In Britain, plans for the conscription and training of the nation's male youth in matters military, which was Robert Baden-Powell's basis for founding the boy scout movement, were offered as the antidote to an increasingly feminized male youth and a society gone soft in the pursuit of luxury and ease. Increasingly popular were Viscount Wolseley's patriarchal sentiments that 'national training keeps healthy and robust the manhood of the state' and 'the drastic medicine of war alone can revive ... former manliness.'[43] Even for British liberals, war functioned to spur the nation's imagination, with victory in war invigorating otherwise dull lives. Indeed, as Britain prepared to fight the Boer War, jingoism, defined by J. A. Hobson as 'that introverted patriotism whereby love of one's own nation is transformed into the hatred of another nation, and the fierce craving to destroy the individual members of that other nation,' rose in popularity. Jingoism was a manifestation of I. S. Bloch's influential treatise that future wars would depend on the social resilience of civilians.[44]

All these factors raised the position of the European military, especially the British and French, the greatest of the imperialists, to new heights within their respective societies. For the British military, they also confirmed their tactical, strategic and technological superiority over all other military traditions. This was especially true relative to those 'paper-pushing' German Prussians, their new European rival. In the highly gendered culture of Britain, military officers were designated as 'Victorian gentlemen,' an exalted status due to their chosen profession rather than aristocratic birthright.

Likewise, though the USA faced no external threat, in the late nineteenth century a militarized jingoistic political culture emerged. It was consumed with fighting and winning future imperial wars. Recent popular military overseas successes, dramatic advance in seapower technology, and a strong commitment to rehabilitating the Army officer corps, had freed the US military and political establishment from the ghosts of the Civil War.[45]

Other factors relate more directly to the age of aviation and in turn to the emergence of strategic bombing theory. In Victorian Britain and the United States, a century of imperial wars had produced both new weapons and a strong belief in the decisive role of advanced technology in military victory. Thus, strategic thinking about the military application of air power was to be expected. In addition, the dawning of the age of aviation made more acute the fear of invasion, a possibility that consumed the energies of British military strategists for decades. In 1909, a Home Ports Defence Committee, for the first time fearful of both naval and air attacks on the island homeland, specifically from a militarizing and technologically modern Germany, recommended the creation of the Royal Flying Corps. Also before war broke out, a view emerged in Britain nominating air power as the perfect instrument to control restless colonial peoples. Among its foremost champions were Winston Churchill, David Lloyd George and Air Marshal Hugh Trenchard.[46]

Across Europe the rise of futurism, known as the 'cult of the modern' in the arts, science and philosophy, dramatically affected culture and enhanced the power of the bureaucratic state. In the futurist world-view, revolutionary change and chaos are marks of modernity in which the machine takes on godlike qualities. Futurism instigated a sense of urgency and an aggressive celebration of the 'barbaric' in the rapidly industrializing capitalist world, In the Britain of Trenchard and Hart, the futurist influence, though milder than in France and Italy, helped undermine positivist individualism and bolster the militarist view of the benefits of war. The British form of futurism, coupled with the rapid industrial pace, helped to justify the rise of a strong centralized bureaucratic British state whose primary role was to conduct the business of peace and war. Within this powerful militarized bureaucracy, Trenchard and Hart, in conjunction with their white male aristocratic mentors, were positioned to define what was moral and rational. From Britain's hegemonic global position, they were also able to enforce a standard of humanity consistent with their beloved upper-class Victorian values.

In Douhet's pre-World War One Italy, a furious brand of futurism bent on destroying the existing world order rose and added fuel to the fire of Italian capitalist-backed imperialism. Subsequently a disappointing performance in the Great War and the threat of an Italian socialist political Left provoked futurism's embryonic forms of fascism and imperialism into full expression under the leadership of Benito Mussolini and his banker-funded fascist Blackshirts. In 1922, a year after his *Command of the Air* was published; Giulio Douhet accepted Mussolini's invitation to join his futurist-inspired fascist government as Commissioner of Aviation. Though Douhet stayed in the fascist bureaucracy for only two years, his stature as the pre-eminent airpower strategist in Italy positioned him to influence directly the course of future war.[47]

The futurist connection to fascism played a role in the emergence of strategic bombing theory after World War One because it promoted the exalted status of the aviator. Colin Cook explores this important relationship in his article 'The myth of the aviator and the flight to fascism.'

> Man/machine presented one vision where aviation, Futurism and Fascism merged to resolve the dilemma of nineteenth-century individualism and the revolts against it. These ideas converged during the opening years of the twentieth century at the same time powered flying machines took to the skies. It was over the maelstrom of the First World War trenches that these winged men became the mythic symbols of a new tomorrow.[48]

The celebrated 'myth of the aviator' insists that 'no machine requires so much human concentration of soul and will power as a flying machine' and that control over the new technology means 'the positive ideals of heroism, adventure, sacrifice and masculinity became invested in those who could, quite literally, get above it all.'[49]

Not all early aviators were fascists, but many were. They and their supporters envisaged aviation as a symbolic 'rebirth,' blending heroism and corporate responsibility with new technology to create a new society. Fascist or not, at the end of the Great War the newly crowned 'aristocrats of the air' were not only credited, as in the British case, with raising the morale of the trench-bound foot soldiers, but celebrated as architects of a rejuvenated future in which reason would triumph over nature. Thus, with the aviation age came another dimension to the self-and-other identity. To airpower enthusiasts, particularly those trained as pilots like Hugh

Trenchard and Billy Mitchell, people shackled to the earth became the objectified other. In contrast, those in the skies above were free and superior. As World War One air ace Cecil Lewis put it: 'The earth so far below! A patchwork of fields ... Men! Standing, walking, talking, fighting there beneath me! I saw them for the first time with detachment, dispassionately: a strange, pitiable crawling race, to us who strode the sky.'[50]

BOMBING CIVILIANS TO WIN

The Prophets possessed a unique status within the militarized culture. As aviation specialists, they were masters of a new technology with both civilian and military utility. In advocating air power as the decisive weapon of offense that would end the defensive, feminized deadlock of trench warfare and provide a strategy to win future wars, they set themselves against their celebrated military colleagues. In the exalted military universe, their star was rising fast. As military professionals, the strategic bombers also had a strong sense of the other, most poignantly structured in the identity of the enemy. In military parlance, the world is polarized, divided between black and white, us and them, good and evil and, most important, friend (self) and foe (other). In the post-World War One context, the essential role of the industrial home front in the Great War meant renewed enthusiasm for total war. For the Prophets, the key strategic constituency of the other had become the enemy's civilians, and civilians were once again seen as a component of the enemy. For the Prophets, to whom targeting of civilians was and is the recipe for winning war, this expanded notion of enemy was essential in overcoming the moral qualms at the purposeful targeting of innocent civilians. Another problem they faced was that historically women are the largest segment of the civilian population. Thus for military strategists looking to preserve the masculine character of war, it was and is imperative that the civilian target be stripped of any feminine qualities.

In this endeavor they had a formidable task. The historical distinction between combatants and non-combatants had grown out of the patriarchal notion that the art of war was a manly endeavor. It was the most masculine of men who did the fighting: the male-only warrior class confronting the male warrior class of the enemy on the battlefield to decide the fate of the nation, if not civilization. All other citizens are non-warriors (non-martial and non-combatants), disqualified from the field of battle because they possess a characteristic preventing them from being the manly man.

Obviously the disqualifying characteristic for women is their sex and for children their youth. But non-combatant status is also assigned to males who due to old age or some physical or psychological infirmity are deemed incapable of soldiering, and to 'deviant' males, possessors of a 'feminine gene' or consciousness, who are unwilling or thought unable to perform the manly responsibility. Regardless of the reason, all are defined as inferior to the warrior class. As weaker members of society they are in need of protection. As non-combatants, they perform non-martial (civilian) tasks that, while necessary for society, are apart from and less important than the military tasks of preparing for and fighting war. The division of labor and space is the basis of the notion of civilians as innocent. They are neither responsible for nor culpable in the political or military affairs of manly men. It is civilian innocence that provokes the moral issue, if not qualms, when non-combatants are targeted in war. In classical and contemporary terms, it is at the core of what is deemed to be the immorality of terrorism.

In the historical reality of war, the combatant–noncombatant distinction is an artificial one. In Women and the War Story, Miriam Cooke, in noting the invisibility of women in the legends of war, addresses this reality: 'Maybe it has always been the case that all are involved in war though few are acknowledged.'[51] Even though artificial, the distinction is important for patriarchal societies as it helps sustain the privileged position of all things masculine, especially the idea of the manly man and war as the province of men. Conversely, it supports the idea of women as the weaker sex in need of protection.

But events of the nineteenth century exposed this dichotomy as problematic, if not false. For many military strategists, especially Douhet among the Prophets, both the industrial revolution that produced weapons of war greater in range and killing power, and the central role of the industrial home front in the Great War had rendered the combatant-non-combatant distinction obsolete.

In the case of the so-called 'reluctant' bombers Trenchard, Mitchell and Hart, their race, class and gender consciousness and the profile of the civilian population as 'enemy' combined to quash any remaining moral qualms about the targeting of civilians. The 'reluctant' bombers' advocacy of 'precision' bombing of urban industrial capacity and working-class populations has a clear class, race and gender bias to it. The Prophets' socialized view of industrial workers as inferior, indeed a threat to the standard-bearers of civilization of their own class, meant that those newly designated enemy combatants who kept industrial production humming, were dispensable cannon fodder. War upon them, while maybe not quite moral, was at least less than totally amoral. It was certainly less amoral than dropping bombs on middle- and upper-class neighborhoods and businesses. The fact that a growing number of industrial workers were members of racial minorities and women on whose behalf the champions of racial and gender justice were making increased claims against the privileges of the white male provoked even greater antipathy toward this segment of the enemy. Most important, the deep-seated opinion concerning the various weaknesses of the childlike other, in particular the alleged inferior constitution of women, the working class, the 'darker' races, the infirm, aged and young, are at the heart of the strategy that assumes civilians will quickly succumb to terror from the skies. Their will and capacity, in military parlance known as 'cost tolerance,' to resist the hell rained from above on their daily life was said to be demonstratively weaker than those of men. This made them, in Liddell Hart's terms, the 'Achilles' heel' of the nation. Besides, like the colonial savages, working-class people and inferior racial and ethnic groups only respond to force.

Without these core beliefs, the targeting of civilians makes no strategic sense, as it is an indirect way to achieve surrender. According to the Prophets' scenario, the ruling class, under assault from the easily demoralized civilians, will decide when and how to sue for peace. Conversely, if it is assumed that the elite's political will to resist is the same as or less than that of the classes below them, wreaking destruction on upper-class neighborhoods and workplaces would be a more direct way to force them to a decision. However, the Prophets and their upper-class mentors were not prepared to turn their class-conscious evaluation of themselves and others on its head.

Though silent on this issue, the Prophets' assertion that bombing industrial areas will influence the enemy elite to sue for peace reveals other layers of class-consciousness. First, attacking the enemy's industrial working class where they labor and live could potentially undermine the morale of the 'cannon fodder' of the enemy's warrior class. After all, it is the families of the common foot soldier who are enduring the aerial assault. Whether they are in the barracks or at the front, affecting the enemy foot soldier's will to resist adversely undercuts their war effort. Second, partial or wholesale destruction of the enemy's productive forces and facilities will also influence the enemy elite. The greater their command over the productive forces is threatened, the more likely the upper classes, to preserve their post-war class position and control, are to negotiate with 'their own kind' a way out of their dilemma.

In addition to being a winning strategy, to the Prophets bombing the working class was also a more moral way to conduct war since it was assumed that fewer casualties would occur. Their calculation was based on the amount of total losses. But they also acknowledged a shift in the identity of the casualties. Here again class and gender consciousness is apparent. Under the strategic bombers' proposed scenario, aerial bombing would bring a quick end to the conflict with few of the 'warrior class,' the most valued members of society, falling in battle. Those warriors who did pay the ultimate price would be the heroic pilots of an independent air force, the 'aristocrats of the air,' the 'best of the best' of their class. As sole conquerors of the enemy, the airmen's privileged place in society would be secure, as would the class and gendered bias accompanying such privilege. Creation of an independent air force would make obsolete the standing armies of the sort that slugged it out in World War One, thereby sparing both human and material resources. With fewer total casualties, with the expendable citizens of both sides bearing the brunt of war's horror, and with a select warrior elite heroically responsible for protecting the weaker majority, the moral order of society, defined in patriarchal, aristocratic and racist terms, is preserved.[52]

The Prophets' assertion that strategic bombing was superior in moral and rational terms over alternative war-fighting strategies was in part based on the class, race and gender biases dominating their day. Indeed, well in advance of the post-war articulation of strategic bombing theory, these biases influenced the limited application of air power during World War One. A few examples will suffice. In the aftermath of Germany's initial use of airships against England in 1915, Kaiser Wilhelm II issued an order enthusiastically endorsing the air war against a broad range of industrial 'military targets.' But he also ordered, '... no attack is to be made on the residential areas of London, or above all on royal palaces.'[53] The Kaiser insisted on his class-conscious command despite knowing that the Zeppelin airship had no capacity for precision bombing. For their part the British, under the advice of Trenchard, Air Commander Edgar Ludow-Hewitt and Wing Commander Arthur Tedder, specifically rejected bombing all civilians indiscriminately. They all argued it was politically, morally and militarily counterproductive to do so. Yet Trenchard, based on his analysis of the impact German bombing had on London, advocated a massive aerial assault on German industry to undermine working-class morale. Other high-level British military officials, such as Sir Frederick Sykes, knew that such precision bombing was impossible and urged 'area bombing,' the wholesale attack on densely populated industrial centers. Lord William Weir went one step further, advocating daylight use of incendiary bombs 'when the people are out at work, and perhaps only children left to look after the house.'[54] In all three scenarios, targeting the working class or their offspring while purposely avoiding any attack on the enemy upper class was at the heart of the strategy.

To sustain the distinction between themselves and the other Europeans, the Anglo-Saxon nations also played the race card. At the same time as they were bombing Berlin's workers, the British characterized the German army's attack on French civilians as further evidence of the savagery of the 'bestial' Huns. Likewise, newspaper headlines such as 'GREATEST OF ALL AERIAL FLEETS TO CRUSH THE TEUTONS' rallied North American audiences to the racial virtue and purpose of air power.[55]

LIVES OF THE PROPHETS

The personal and professional biographies of the Prophets lend weight to the analysis contained in this chapter. As a group, they were inculcated with the values and impacted by the experiences of their time. All were white and male, indeed in militarized gender terms manly males. Their class origins were similar, ranging from the upper-middle strata (Hart, Trenchard and Douhet) to upper-class (Mitchell). All enthusiastically chose the patriarchal military as their profession and did so, with the exception of Liddell Hart, well before World War One. All had battle experience: Hart beginning with the Great War; and Trenchard, Mitchell and Douhet rising through the ranks in service to the imperial ambitions of their nations well before the guns of August 1914 blazed away.

These factors shaped their outlook and accorded them privilege in the societies of their day. They also qualified them to gain access to persons with higher-class standing and positions of power, a status all four achieved relatively early in their career. As such, like their colleagues and mentors, their mentality was imperial, their values aristocratic, racist and patriarchal. Moreover, inclusion in the power circles of their respective societies meant that their ideas or ruminations did not go unnoticed. They would at least get a fair hearing and when championed, as they were by a powerful constituency within the ruling class, play a pivotal role in twentieth-century Western national security doctrine.

Many of the character traits identified here show up in each biography. Hugh Trenchard, though born into a middle-class family, had an aristocratic heritage. His class-conscious yearning to re-establish his aristocratic connection earned him a reputation as a notorious social climber. He was described as a dull, but hard-working Walter Mitty-type man determined to get to the top of the landed class. In his ambition he befriended a young Winston Churchill for life. Later he counted the influential Field Marshal Lord Kitchener, Sir William Robertson and Sir Douglas Haig among his colleagues. He was the 'manly man,' his patriarchal mentality expressed through his zealous commitment to the manly arts of sport and war. A bout with illness left him acutely intolerant of those with physical weakness. Finally, his advocacy of using air power against the colonial peoples and his assertion that in a bombing war, the French would 'squeal' before the British, expressed his racial consciousness.[56]

Liddell Hart, the other Britisher, was the son of a Protestant minister. His biographer John Mearsheimer describes Hart as an upper-middle class Edwardian boy interested in sports, military history and aviation.[57] When the Great War began, Hart joyously joined the military, where he served in the front lines in France on three occasions. A heart problem forced him into retirement from the military after which he built a towering reputation as a military strategist. Eventually he was called the twentieth century's von Clausewitz. His hero worship of Britain's oft-maligned World War One generals and his offensive-minded approach found favor with and brought him access to the most powerful political and military luminaries of North America and Europe. Among them were Lloyd George, Sir Ian Hamilton and Colonel Edward M. House. Hart's close friendship with the well-known fascist and anti-Semite General J. F. C. Fuller and his accommodating posture toward Hitler's Third Reich raised speculation about possible fascist and racist leanings. The views he expressed in an article, 'Woman wanders – the "World Wavers" or Woman and the world-quake,' left no doubt as to his patriarchal commitments and his distaste for the feminist movement.[58]

The personal histories of Douhet and Mitchell show similar traits. Both were admirers of Mussolini and his fascist agenda. As noted, Douhet accepted a post in Mussolini's initial government. Mitchell, after meeting the Italian president, praised him as a man possessing the 'greatest powers for constructive government that exists in the world today.'[59] In word and military deed, both Douhet and Mitchell demonstrated a vigorous commitment to empire. They also possessed aggressive, independent personalities, so much so that at their respective courts martial they were found guilty of insubordination. Mitchell, the grandson of the most powerful banker and railroad magnate in the Upper Midwest and the son of a United States senator, was well acquainted with the values and class interests of powerful economic and political circles. In concert with opinion at the time, he also held racist attitudes, as expressed in his prediction that eventually 'the white and yellow races will be brought into armed conflict to determine who shall prevail.'[60]

To summarize, the analysis here suggests that the 'morality' of identifying civilians as bombing targets, and the theses of a fragile civilian will and the savior stature of airforce pilots are all products of a political socialization process steeped in class, race and gender bias. It is these biases, along with a militarized imperial culture, that structured the Prophets' identity. In their search for a strategic doctrine in which air power would be, not just effective, but the decisive instrument in winning future wars, they had to rationalize the jettisoning of the Hague Conventions' restriction on targeting civilians. Their socialized biases, a commitment to the technological imperative and a belief in the concept of total war provided just the rationalization needed.

4

Strategic Bombing
Comes of Age

BOMBS FOR THE COLONIAL MASSES

Between World Wars One and Two, the Europeans and North Americans began to rely on air power to thwart the rising tide of national liberation or to extend empire.[1] The bombing of colonial peoples was not quite what the Prophets had envisioned. Air power was used in support of the other services, rather than as the sole, let alone decisive instrument of war. Increasingly, as aircraft and bombing techniques developed, aerial assaults on civilians became an essential component of that support task.

The British had bombed their rebellious subjects in India and Egypt before and during the Great War. With their empire in crisis and lacking the financial resources to employ armed forces on a permanent basis, after the war the British were 'forced to rely instead on bombing to guarantee the collection of taxes and the enforcement of some kind of order.'[2] They used air power in concert with the army and navy as the new and indispensable instrument of 'civilization and liberation.' In this context, raining terror from the skies had both military and political benefit. It returned to the British the technological advantage lost during World War One when their colonial subjects gained access to new rifles. It also exposed the despotic power of the British state to the colonized. The airplane became the regulator 'of the broad parameters of permissible behavior by bombing tribes who were "out," rebelling against the government, or those which refused to pay taxations.'[3]

In 1919, under the command of the future and controversial airpower chief Arthur Harris, the British bombed the Afghanistan cities of Jalalabad and Kabul. In the same year, they employed Trenchard's RAF to quash the Egyptian demand for independence. In addition to the bombing of Somaliland, in 1920 British planes struck the Iranian town of Enzeli and civilian populations in Transjordan. Also in 1920, the British began using bombers in innovative ways to enforce their new imperial strategy of 'control without occupation' in Iraq. The practice of bombing entire areas was inaugurated for what were labeled 'pacification' purposes. Aerial attacks on whole villages were used to soften up civilians before the arrival of the tax collector. Any small hint of revolt and planes were dispatched preemptively to set fire to crops. The practice of night bombing also began in Iraq and proved to be extremely successful as 'villagers were caught returning home after hiding from daytime raids.'[4] Reports of Iraqi women and children dying at the hands of British aircrews, now dropping high-explosive bombs around the clock in the middle of villages, disturbed even Air and Colonial Secretary Winston Churchill, a bombing enthusiast. He finally asked to be spared the details of British air raids against civilians. Air squadron leader Arthur Harris had no such qualms, asserting, 'The Arab and Kurd now know what real bombing means: within 45 minutes a full-sized village can be practically wiped out, and a third of its inhabitants killed or injured, by four or five machines which offer them no real target, no opportunity for glory as warriors, no effective means of escape.'[5] Despite (or because of) its savagery, the 'air policing' of Iraq provided the blueprint for future bombing as the technological and financial advantages to British rule made it 'the backbone of the whole organization.'[6]

In 1922, and again in 1925, 1930 and 1932, British bombs fell on the upstart Hottentots of South West Africa. The bombs falling from a height of 100 feet completely overwhelmed the Hottentots. In 1932, massive British bombing of villages failed to subdue nationalist rebellions in Burma and northwestern India. The effect of the air terrorism on civilians was appalling. British soldiers who entered the devastated towns reported 'pariah dogs are already at work eating the corpses of the babies and old women who have been killed.'[7]

Spain, France and Italy also bombarded colonial peoples in the interwar years. In an effort to subdue the Moors, Spain began bombing Morocco in 1924 with explosives and poison gas. In a cruel campaign lasting years, the attacks killed many civilians. For Spain and its future dictator Francisco Franco, the French bombers' destruction of the Moroccan city of Chechaouen – constitutionally a part of France – in 1926 was a seminal event. It violated the political taboo against wielding foreign air power against one's own citizens and The Hague convention provisions against the targeting of defenseless civilians. In 1925, the French employed their air force to crush anti-colonial rebellions in Syria. Massive bombardments of villages in the Druze region were followed by attacks on the towns of Hama and Suwayda. Subsequently, more than 2,400 civilians died in bombings of Damascus and its surrounding neighborhoods, with uncounted more dead in attacks on rural areas.

From December 1935 to May 1936, Italy dropped tear gas, mustard gas and explosives on Ethiopian civilians, forcing the government to capitulate. In his unsuccessful appeal to the League of Nations, the Ethiopian emperor, Haile Selassie, protested the Italian fascists' air war in which 'soldiers, women, children, cattle, rivers, lakes and fields were drenched with this never ending rain of death.'[8]

As diplomats debated the propriety of strategic bombing of 'civilized' Westerners at The Hague, the European bombers rationalized their reign of terror against the imperial subjects in class, race and gender terms. To the *Johannesburg Star*, the bombing of 'the little yellow men' of the southern African Hottentot tribes, who were at the mercy of the airplane, was simply another case of a race coming to its natural end. In the interwar years fictional accounts of air power and the expected development of atomic power, the 'ultimate' weapon of the white world to be dropped from the clouds, were full of racist imagery. The atomic 'superweapon' was deemed the 'protector and savior of the colonies.'[9] Popular English novels, such as Frank McIlraith and Roy Connolly's *Invasion from the Air*, echoed Trenchard's prescription for bombing 'the dangerous classes' on the ground that, like rats, they easily panic and will force the bourgeois government to sue for peace. The British use of phosphorus bombs, timed bombs and liquid fire on Iraqi civilians brought no condemnation at The Hague. In RAF headquarters killing Iraqi women was excused with the opinion that, unlike their European civilian counterparts, in Iraqi society they were viewed as a piece of property, the same as a cow or a rifle. Japan's massive bombing of Chinese civilians throughout the 1930s drew no comment, let alone condemnation, from the British until 1937. In that year they complained bitterly when the British diplomat Sir Hughe Knatchball-Huggesson was wounded in a bombing that also killed hundreds of Chinese civilians. Citing international law and the 'conscience of mankind,' an indignant British Foreign Office charged that attacks making no distinction between combatants and noncombatants were both illegal and inhumane.[10]

The French, claiming that in Syria they were conducting a 'police action' against 'bandits', invoked two popular theories to exclude their terror bombing from the constraints of the laws governing war. They first argued that international law had no jurisdiction over the non-European and un-civilized Syrians. They also claimed that French 'guardianship' over the 'underdeveloped' Syria gave them a 'mission to civilize.' Thus the bombing was a domestic issue, also outside the purview of international law. To the Spanish, and Franco in particular, the terror bombing of Morocco was perfectly appropriate since the Moors were 'like children who needed a father's firm hand.'[11] Fascist Italy's bombing of Ethiopia 'showed how greatly the application of science to war had widened the gulf between the forces of civilized and uncivilized nations.'[12] Among the Italian pilots involved were the fascist leader Benito Mussolini's sons Bruno and Vittorio. The latter described Galla tribesmen as 'bursting out like a rose after I had landed a bomb in the middle of them.'[13]

In the two decades after the Great War, aerial bombing was used exclusively to 'civilize and liberate' the imperial other. Whether it be in Libya, Iraq, India, Morocco or Syria, the colonized civilians 'provided a laboratory where the military high-technology of the post World War One era was first tried out and where the textbook on the aerial bombardment of civilians was written.'[14]

TOTAL WAR IN THE IMPERIAL CENTER: THE SEARCH FOR RULES

From the start of the interwar period the Prophets' vision of future wars pitting the air forces of the civilized nations against each other in a fight to the finish, preoccupied the European and US military commands. As they scrambled to build bomber fleets, efforts were under way to establish the rules of total war. Britain and the USA, which were soon to dominate both the theoretical and the practical sides of strategic bombing, were particularly active in these efforts. For instance, at the end of World War One, a demand was made for the German pilots who had bombed Britain to be prosecuted for war crimes under the Hague Conventions. In a secret report, Hugh Trenchard's British Air Ministry rejected the proposal, arguing that applying Hague Conventions to air power would severely restrict the effectiveness of bombardment in future wars. Instead, they recommended a public relations campaign emphasizing the possibility of precision bombing of military targets. This would disguise 'the truth that air warfare has made such restrictions obsolete and impossible.'[15] By 1924, an argument ensued at The Hague between Britain and the USA over the targets of air power. The British proposed limiting bombing to military objectives. This concept was so broad and undefined that, as the experience of World War One had already demonstrated, essentially anything could be targeted. The USA wanted air power to be limited to a 'combat area;' meaning that the target would have to be within the firing range of artillery or a specified distance from the front lines. The unresolved debate left only a 'moral' restraint against indiscriminate bombing. In reality the bombing nations were free to define military targets as they pleased.

By the 1930s, Douhet's notion of total war dominated European high commands, and the distinction between combatants and non-combatants had effectively collapsed. In 1932, few British military and political authorities objected to senior government member Stanley Baldwin's statement that 'the only defence is in offence, which means that you have to kill more women and children, more quickly than the enemy if you want to save yourselves.'[16] With a wary eye on Germany and fascist Italy, the British prepared for a future war in which civilian casualties would be of mammoth proportions. In 1935 they rejected Adolf Hitler's proposal to limit bombings to an area no more than 100 kilometers behind the front. By 1937, the British government had decided against providing insurance for losses incurred in air attacks and issued one million extra burial forms. On the assumption that British civilian morale and thus civil order would collapse under the duress of fascist bombs, 17,000 army regulars and 20,000 reserve constables were organized to reinforce the police.

THE FASCISTS BOMB REPUBLICAN SPAIN

The fascist bombings of the republican areas in the Spanish Civil War (1936–39) was the first test of post-war air power in Europe. Again, class, race and gender biases were in play. Initially, little if any objection was raised in European liberal capitalist circles to the bombing of Spanish civilians. Government officials either denied reports of civilian suffering or dismissed it as the deserved destiny of Spain's citizenry.

In April 1937, the fascists bombarded Guernica, the center of Basque culture but a city of no military significance. The city core was virtually destroyed, while the two military targets on the outskirts were left untouched. In marked contrast to their previous stance, the bombing of Guernica drew expressions of ire from the liberal capitalist states. Now, they proclaimed, civilized Europe was under attack from German barbarian Huns and swarthy Italians of 'lower Europe,' both of whom had succumbed to the political disease of fascism. Similar to the cancer of communism in the Soviet Union, if left untreated this totalitarian disease would surely eat away at the body politic of the enlightened Anglo-Saxon democratic states.

In Anglo-Saxon opinion, Guernica proved the thesis that unlike 'democratic' generals, fascist and communist dictators were prepared to use aerial terrorism in their search for quick and easy victory. For example, in early 1938, two editorials in the *Charlotte News* of North Carolina condemned Franco for bombing the heart of Barcelona, including churches filled with children. The church attacks, screamed the editors, proved Franco's allegiance to the fascist 'Douhet theory' of bombing. Yet the same voices were silent about the tons upon tons of German and Italian bombs that fell on the working class in Spain's industrial towns and cities. In his eyewitness account of the war, the journalist Henry Buckley reports that British authorities allowed German aircraft to refuel at Gibraltar on their way to bombing the working-class districts of Seville. He also records the class-consciousness of a British official: 'The important thing is to remember that it is about a civil conflict and it is very necessary that we support our class.'[17] Unlike Guernica's innocent, who are rightly memorialized in Pablo Picasso's painting, the working-class victims of Durango, Bolivar, Arbadeque, Guerricalz and many other towns, remain unnoticed to this day. The massive bombings of Barcelona and Madrid also received little attention compared to Guernica.

The use of air power in both Republican Spain and against colonial populations raised the profile of strategic bombing to new heights. Yet, in neither was it the sole instrument of winning war, and thus the Prophets' strategic bombing theory was not truly tested. The Spanish experience found air power unable to provide decisive victory. It also was ineffective in undermining civilian or military morale, thus prolonging rather than shortening hostilities. The bombing, moreover, proved to be highly inaccurate, making the notion of precision targeting both laughable and cruel. Yet, a strong commitment to strategic bombing remained in Europe, particularly in Britain. In part this was because strategic bombing enthusiasts convincingly argued that the fascist bombing was tactical rather than strategic. More important, the lessons of World War One preyed on British minds. As Michael Sherry notes, 'a profound anxiety over exposure to aerial attack fused with an equally powerful sense of England's limited moral and material resources for conventional combat' fueled British enthusiasm.[18]

In preparation for the next total war, the bombing nations began to set up separate stand-alone air forces, but they also retained the competing branches of the military and their air components. Thus, for the foreseeable future, wars would not be fought or won with air power alone. The diplomatic failure at The Hague to enforce a distinction between combatants and non-combatants and the continued bombing of colonial populations did, however, reinforce the Prophets' theory of total war. As world war again approached, all the world's industrial powers, fascist, communist and liberal democratic alike, were either terrorizing civilians from the sky, as Japan was doing to the Chinese, or preparing to do so. The sole question now under debate was whether to bomb indiscriminately as Douhet and to some degree Hart proposed, or on a class and race basis as Trenchard and Mitchell desired.

THE UNITED STATES ENTRY INTO STRATEGIC BOMBING

The USA's air power experience after the Great War was initially limited to scouting and reconnaissance 'air services' for Army counterinsurgency efforts in Latin America. The history of US military aerial operations actually began in 1916 in Mexico. The First Aero Squadron provided General John 'Jack' Pershing with communication and reconnaissance support in his effort to track down the rebel leader Francisco 'Pancho' Villa. Though Villa was never caught, the new air arm of the Army flew over seven hundred sorties and recorded the first 'kill' of a rebel leader from the air. Beginning in 1919, the US Army began employing air force units against the often rebellious citizens in its Latin American 'sphere of influence.' In the Dominican Republic and Haiti, Marine pilots refined their 'air service' tactics. During his stint in Haiti, Lieutenant L. H. M. Sanderson invented the 'dive-bombing' technique, for the purpose of boosting the accuracy of aerial bombing. In 1927, the very first dive-bombing attack was conducted when Marine aircraft swooped down on Sandino rebel forces in Ocotal, Nicaragua. Also in the late 1920s, a Marine aviation squadron flew 3,818 sorties in support of US forces during the civil war in China.[19]

Despite the USA's limited experience with air power, beginning in the 1930s the US military took the lead in refining the Prophets' strategic bombing doctrine. In a formidable challenge to Douhet and his disciples who preferred the wholesale terror bombing of civilians, students at the Billy Mitchell-inspired Air Corps Tactical School (ACTS) argued for a strategic bombing doctrine that emphasized the 'vital links' or interdependent nature of modern industrial societies and precision bombing. Lt. Colonel John MacMullen credits the ACTS theorists, known as 'the Bomber Mafia,' with the concept of the industrial web in which, 'A nation's industry was believed to be a series of interconnected activities in which one relied upon the other, like links of a chain.'[20] The 'vital links' among the industrial, economic and social structures of a modern industrial state are essential to both 'the production of weapons and supplies for the armed forces and provision of services to sustain life in that highly industrialized setting.'[21] Precision strategic bombing of these vital links would disrupt or destroy at the same time the enemy's capability to fight and the civilian population's will to resist. In short, the ACTS 'bombing mafia' asserted, victory would come if the vital links of civilian life were destroyed. If civilian resistance continued, the bombers were to attack the cities until urban life was untenable.

According to Neville Jones, by the end of the 1930s ACTS had successfully changed the 'working definition' of strategic bombing to:

> the direct attack against the most important elements of an enemy's warmaking capacity, for example, his industries, communications, and the morale of his civilian populations, as opposed to the units and equipment of his armed forces. The object of such bombing, which is the product of an age in which the distinction between soldier and civilian has disappeared, is to undermine the enemy's war effort.[22]

In both ACTS 'vital links' theory and orthodox strategic bombing doctrine, the core purpose remains the same: to undermine the will of the civilian population. The two major differences between them are on the issue of how this is to be done. The Prophets' answer was immediate and sustained bombing of all civilian or working-class targets with explosive, incendiary and chemical weapons. For ACTS theory, the strategic bombing of the total urban setting is a last resort. Second, in attacking cities, ACTS theorists oppose indiscriminate destruction of people and structures. Acting on Trenchard's World War One's plea for precision bombing, they suggest the enemy's will to resist can be undermined by means of more selective targeting of urban industrial life.

As the bombing in World War Two would demonstrate, the differences between orthodox strategic bombing and ACTS theory are minor and essentially meaningless. The common goal of both is the undermining of the civilian will to resist. The urban population is targeted either directly or indirectly with the expectation that massive suffering will occur and that victory will go to the side inflicting the greatest amount of pain on the enemy's civilians. Because of its plea for 'selective' or precision targeting and direct bombing of civilians as a last resort, what ACTS theory does is make strategic bombing more politically palatable to its perpetrators, especially those attempting to convince themselves and others of the morality of their cause and actions.

Leading up to World War Two, United States military strategists were preparing to practice what they preached in the Asian and European theaters. The plan for the total destruction of Japan's cities was based on Billy Mitchell's analysis of the Tokyo earthquake of 1923 in which the accompanying firestorm devastated the largely wood-and-paper city. Indiscriminate incendiary bombing was expected to do the same to Japan's cities and towns. A 1939 ACTS targeting exercise that 'bombed' the vital infrastructure of New York City preceded AWPD-1, a secret report that was drawn up before the US entry into the European conflict. It proposed an all-out aerial attack on the civilian population of Berlin. From his research on pre-war bombing plans, Mike Davis concludes, 'counter-civilian or "morale" bombing had never been excluded from US war planning against Germany.'[23] In short, by World War Two, both orthodox and ACTS theories of strategic bombing openly projected that terrorism, in this case bombing civilians, worked and was the most effective strategy to assure victory. Michael Sherry notes that as World War Two drew closer, the popular conception that only fascist dictators were enthusiastic bombers of civilians ended up concealing 'the Anglo-Americans'' developing interest in strategic air war and muting their concern about the morality of that interest.'[24]

Two further developments helped overwhelm any remaining US qualms about bombing enemy civilians. One was Japan's 'sneak' attack on Pearl Harbor, an event for which US elites sought righteous revenge. The second and subtler phenomenon was the influential argument Alexander P. de Seversky made in his futuristic and highly promoted 1943 book (and Disney film) *Victory Through Air Power*. Sounding what would become familiar Cold War rhetoric about the benevolent purpose of the United States as guarantor of global law and order, de Seversky proposed that air power's destructive capacity and inaccuracy were in fact moral virtues. Visualizing the enemy in animal terms as a prey to be captured alive or destroyed, he opted for complete elimination of the enemy as the only way to return the world to normalcy. In short, argued de Seversky, wholesale bombing in a 'war of elimination' was the effective and virtuous path to restoring moral order to the world.[25]

STRATEGIC BOMBING IN WORLD WAR TWO

The Allied nations' application of strategic bombing during World War Two demonstrates both the commonalties and differences between its strategists. It is not the intention here to evaluate the World War Two experience in detail.[26] Yet it should be noted that class, gender and race considerations were important in guiding the bombing of Germany and Japan. In these cases, race and class issues are the primary focus as, when bombing civilians, the gender bias is a constant. As a number of feminist researchers assert, 'war is an integral part of capitalist patriarchal culture, it silences and disempowers women, excludes them from decision-making processes, ties their rights to nationalist objectives and demands a misogynistic masculinist culture of emotional steel from both men and women.'[27]

The British Bombing Campaign

Britain's World War Two strategic bombing came closest to following the prescripts of the Prophets. Hugh Trenchard's influence remained substantial but indirect. In 1942, his disciple Arthur Harris replaced him as head of the Royal Air Force (RAF). The British approach to bombing cities, now officially designated 'area bombing,' invoked the central precept of orthodox strategic bombing. The dual goals were the simultaneous terrorizing of the population and the destruction of industries. Following the prescription of Trenchard and Douhet, the use of incendiary bombs on cities of occupied Europe and Germany, notably at Caen in Normandy and later Lübeck, Hamburg, Dresden and Berlin, had the desired effect of creating massive firestorms that sucked the air and life out of the tortured urban populations.

Beyond a theoretical predisposition, political factors fueled the British government's decision to bomb urban areas indiscriminately. Hugh Trenchard, the architect of the concept, and Harris, who was more enthusiastic about area bombing than even his mentor, were close to or in powerful institutional positions. Their official standing, coupled with Prime Minister Winston Churchill's reverence for air power and the 'demonstration' effect it was to play in his post-war anti-Communist agenda, gave them political advantage over their rivals. The German Luftwaffe's bombing of Britain's cities from September 1940 to May 1941 had generated an immediate and angry demand among the populace for revenge, thereby strengthening the strategic bombers' political position.

British terror bombing was rationalized within a race- and class-conscious context. The British imagery of the barbaric German Hun, dominant during World War One, remained powerful twenty years later. With his 1936 book *War Over England*, British Air Commodore L. E. O. Charlton had already become an important voice in the pre-war construction of the 'barbaric Hun' and the threat of air war. With German bombs landing on England, his racist imagery became even more poignant. To Charlton, British air terror on Germany was justified, indeed necessary. The 'barbaric races,' among whom, he noted, the Germans had a unique thirst for vengeance and blood, were prepared to terrorize Britain from the air. Charlton's advocacy of strategic bombing was also based on his class-conscious contempt for the industrial working class. Subjecting them to aerial bombing, which experience had proved to be indiscriminate, would be highly successful. Workers, he argued, were hard to control and prone to dismay and stampede.[28]

Joining Charlton in advocating class-conscious bombing was Churchill's close advisor Lord Cherwell (F. A. Lindemann). Fearing Germany retaliation against the British upper class, he rejected targeting the mansions of Nazi elites. To Cherwell, even bombing German middle-class homes was a waste of ordnance because they were not packed closely together. He urged strongly that the 'bull's-eye' of British bombing be the squalid quarters of the German working class. Responding to the urgings of Trenchard, Harris and Cherwell, in mid-1940 Churchill expanded the definition of military targets to include industrial areas and working-class neighborhoods. This was area – or in Churchill's earlier parlance 'extermination' – bombing, which sought to level everything around a given target. British aircrews were explicitly instructed that the target was 'the morale of the civilian population and in particular of the industrial workers.'[29] In September 1940 the German Nazis responded with their own terror from the skies over Britain. The Luftwaffe's nine-month bombing campaign left 40,000 British civilians dead.

In 1942, Directive 22 was issued to the British Bomber Command. It called for the purposeful targeting of residential neighborhoods. The specific targets were designated as 'the morale of enemy civil population, in particular industrial workers' and '[the] aiming points [were] to be built-up areas, not for instance, the dockyards or aircraft factories.'[30] A month later, 'Bomber' Harris ordered the incendiary bombing of residential neighborhoods in Lübeck, Rostock and Cologne, Germany. As he wrote in his memoirs, Harris was convinced air power alone could win the war if the RAF were allowed to bomb the working class into open revolt against the Nazis. From then on, British bombing of Germany, particularly during the night when targeting was completely dependent on radar, was purposely indiscriminate with the intent of terrorizing the civilian Huns into political revolt or flight.

If any doubt remained about the strategic purpose of Allied bombing, it ended in early February 1943 at the Casablanca Conference. From the combined British and United States Chiefs of Staff came the instruction to their air commands stating: 'Your primary objective will be the progressive destruction and dislocation of the German military, industrial and economic system and the undermining of the morale of the German people to a point where their armed resistance is fatally weakened.'[31]

As British pilots targeted the industrial base and working-class homes of German-occupied Europe and Germany, they consciously avoided, with some success, upper-class neighborhoods. Trenchard's influence was obvious. Their actions followed his prescribed path to victory of destroying the industrial workforce while leaving intact the upper-class leadership to negotiate peace. Effectiveness aside, by late 1942 Churchill gleefully told President Franklin Roosevelt 'about the heroic quotas that the RAF had pledged to produce: nine hundred thousand civilians dead, one million seriously injured, and twenty-five million homeless.'[32] Meanwhile, the British bombing of German-occupied Europe, particularly in the preparation for the Normandy invasion, was done carefully and 'under proper orders' with a purposeful distinction between military and civilian targets. This extremely difficult task had two goals; bomb the industrial sites important to the German war effort, yet keep the civilians under German occupation, like the French workers at the Paris Renault plants, alive and supporting the Allied cause.

The imagery of self and other helped to rationalize what Churchill labeled the 'moral bombing' of non-Britishers. Only when he realized all that would be left was an 'utterly ruined land' did he call for a review of the 'acts of terror and wanton destruction.' British officials insisted that their high moral purpose of defeating the treacherous enemy guided their bombing of Germany. Initially the military command resisted the Churchill government's insistence on bombing civilians to undermine their morale. But military considerations overwhelmed their moral qualms when it was clear bombing enemy civilians was the only way to attack

Germany with effect.[33] From then on, British officials effectively excused their 'terror' bombing by arguing that systematic bombardment of German homes was not in violation of international humanitarian law. Meanwhile, in their public statements in the House of Commons, British policy makers denied they were wantonly bombing the women and children of Germany, a claim they made even after the purposeful and well-documented fire-bombing of Dresden in 1945. Yet from July 1942 onward the British had defined all area bombing targets as 'military'.

US Strategic Bombing

Until its attack on Dresden in early 1945, US strategic bombing policy in Europe followed the prescription of ACTS theory. Targeting what soon were to be known as 'vital centers' of industry, the US political elites initially rejected the British practice of indiscriminate area and night bombing. In practice, the difference between the two nation's bombing strategies was more imaginary than real. By the time of the Dresden attack thousands of European civilians had already been killed in US bombing raids over occupied Europe, notably in France and Belgium, and then in Germany.

Precision bombing may have been the intent and desired goal. But generals Curtis LeMay and Leon Johnson, who were responsible for putting North American planes into the air over Europe, acknowledge that United States aircrews were poorly trained. In addition, bad weather too often made daylight bombing completely dependent on rudimentary radar technology.[34] It is also evident that some North American air commanders, notably General Henry Harley 'Hap' Arnold, a staunch advocate of the Douhet theory of strategic bombing, considered any restraints on civilian bombing repugnant in times of war and were not committed to them. And, as noted earlier, by the end of the 1930s the United States was already planning to target urban areas and their populations. In 1943, the theoretical became reality when the Chemical Warfare Corps built mock German and Japanese working-class neighborhoods in the Utah desert. Exact replicas of the working-class 'rent barracks' of Berlin's densely populated 'Red' (socialist and communist) districts and the industrial towns of the Rhine were built. They were then bombed and studied in excruciating detail. Armed with the test results, including proof of the utility of the new anti-personnel M-69 napalm ammunition, the Allies bombed 'into rubble more 1920s socialist and modernist utopias than Nazi villas.'[35] With Britain's Operation Gomorrah and the 1943 firebombing of Hamburg, US support for indiscriminate incendiary bombing grew. Among its enthusiasts were President Franklin Roosevelt, Assistant Secretary of War Robert Lovett and Air Force Commander Curtis LeMay. A rising military star, LeMay advocated indiscriminate firebombing in every war zone.

In practice, for most of the war in Europe, United States' air power policy followed the class and racial prescripts of Trenchard and Mitchell. As incorporated into ACTS theory, the North American strategic bombing approach, anointed as 'precision bombing with democratic values,' was intended to undermine the morale of the enemy industrial class. But at least politically and theoretically, the United States left the purposeful indiscriminate bombing of European civilians to the British. This all ended in February 1945. Under Operation Thunderclap, US pilots joined their British counterparts in the saturation bombing of Dresden and other Germany cities.

The US air war in the Pacific was a different story. From the start, the Roosevelt Administration purposely targeted Japan's major cities. In the six months before the August 1945 atomic attacks, North American planes dropped incendiary and chemical (napalm) bombs over 178 square miles, killing untold thousands of Japanese civilians. Unlike its image of the enemy in the European theater, racism was at the core of the North American view of the Asian adversary. Following Mitchell and de Seversky's script, saturation bombing was deemed essential to a war of annihilation against a Japanese 'prey' said to be at the core of a general 'yellow peril' facing Anglo-Saxon civilization. The Japanese were depicted in racially contemptuous terms as animals, among which jungle rats and apes were the favorites – as 'yellow monkeys' and 'little yellow dwarf slaves' who were even 'below the standards of Italians'. Though German behavior was judged more maniacal, it was the image of Japanese fanaticism that held sway in US civilian and military circles. Also common were testimonies to Japanese racial inferiority in the art of war, openly expressed in North American soldiers' disappointment in the Japanese as a worthy enemy, especially when compared with the German military man. Japanese pilots were alleged to be incapable of shooting straight because of their eye slits. Other racist caricatures in popular Anglo-Saxon writings and pictures depicted the Japanese as having a bestial nature, being 'particularly slow brained' and indifferent to life.[36] This virulent racism toward the 'treacherous Japs' intensified with the 'sneak' attack on Pearl Harbor. It made revenge rational, if not virtuous, and the strategic bombing of Japanese civilians 'the ideal vehicle – savage in consequences but impersonal in method.'[37]

Class-consciousness also guided US aerial assaults on Japan. Bombing workers' residential areas was seen as necessary in order to destroy 'a vast feeder system of home shops and cottage industries.'[38] Air Force Commander Curtis LeMay, now in charge of the air war on Japan, explained that in good weather, priority 'military' targets were hit, but 'If we weren't sure of the weather, we would go after the industrial areas' where accuracy was not required.[39] In preparation for air attacks, members of the Joint Target Group suggested that bombing working-class slums while avoiding upper-class neighborhoods could provoke greater hostility among Japan's classes.

On 10 March 1945, Operation Meetinghouse dropped 2,000 tons of incendiaries on Tokyo's working-class district of Asakusa. An estimated 100,000 civilians died in the attack. In his public report, Air Force Chief of Staff Lauris Norstad avoided any discussion of civilian deaths, but counted 1,200,000 factory workers homeless, over 100,000 man-months of production lost and 369,000,000 square feet of highly industrial land destroyed.[40] Echoing the Prophets, General LeMay explained: 'We knew we were going to kill a lot of women and kids when we burned this town. Had to be done ... For us, there are no civilians in Japan.'[41] As with occupied Europe, cities under Japanese occupation in China and Formosa were bombarded with 'careful precision.' Bombing Hankow, China, however, LeMay casually noted, was done with 'a little experimental work with the incendiaries.'[42] Obviously, many other Asian civilians met the same fate as the incinerated Japanese.

Construction of the Japanese other in class, race and enemy terms permitted a righteous and vengeful North American Anglo-Saxon nation to plan for and then rain terror upon Japan's tinderbox cities and its occupied populations. Thanks to the test bombing of replica Japanese housing in Utah and Florida, as well as British advice on city-burning techniques and the experience gleamed from Operation Thunderclap, the United States air command was well equipped, both psychologically and materially, to perform the massive conventional incendiary attacks on and then the atomic bombing of Japan's civilians.

News reports of the massive fire bombing of Japanese cities were met with vengeful satisfaction if not glee in the United States. Still, like British officials, to maintain the high moral ground the Roosevelt Administration attempted to manage the news and rationalize the attacks. The hellish horror caused during Operation Meetinghouse was kept from the public for three months. When it was eventually reported, the military command told the public and high administration officials alike that the bombing was precise 'with city-block accuracy'. Unknown to the US public, by July 1945 all of Japan's cities of above 50,000 people had been largely destroyed. Only four cities remained as possible targets for the atomic attacks, two of them being Hiroshima and Nagasaki. To this day there is little public awareness in the USA of the air terror dropped on Japanese cities or the political impact it had on the Japanese leadership. The atomic bombings, and the justifications for them, have overshadowed all that came before.

In the Pacific campaign, the arguments of the Prophets dominated North American elite opinion throughout. The massive firebombing of Japan was moral, it was asserted, since it would bring a quick end to the war.[43] The same moral claim was made for the atomic attacks on the civilians of Hiroshima and Nagasaki. Despite contrary evidence, in North American political culture it was and remains the gospel truth that the atomic incineration of these two Japanese cities was necessary; brought immediate Japanese surrender and saved at least one million North American soldiers' lives. Indeed, the atomic decision was applauded for preserving the warrior class, the most virtuous members of North American society and Anglo-Saxon civilization. Little sympathy was wasted on the annihilation of the racial, class or gendered Asian civilian. In the militarized culture of World War Two, Giulio Douhet's earlier defense of bombing civilians made moral and political sense: 'All human lives are equally valuable but ... a soldier, a robust young man should be considered to have the maximum individual value in the general economy of humanity.'[44]

The Anglo-Saxon populations came out of World War Two with an 'objectified' view of strategic bombing as a 'clean' and moral way to wage modern war. Michael Sherry notes in his discussion of postwar attitudes that even before the USA turned its revenge bombing on the yellow peril in Asia, the destruction of Berlin and other major German cities brought no debate concerning the morality of the bombing or the bombers. Indeed, Sherry concludes, 'Shaped by culture, politics, geography, and the nature of air war, the distance from which Americans viewed the bombing not only enhanced its attractiveness in the immediate struggle, but blinded awareness of future perils.'[45] The subsequent bombing of Korea provided the first evidence of the correctness of his conclusion.

5

Cold War Strategic Bombing: From Korea to Vietnam

The *United States Strategic Bombing Survey* (*USSBS*) is the most comprehensive assessment of the terror bombing and its place in winning World War Two.[1] The authors of the survey, who were all white males from the upper reaches of the North American corporate, financial, academic and legal professions, did not validate the Prophets' prediction that air power alone could win wars. But they did conclude that strategic bombing, including the atomic attacks, did play the most valuable role in the Allied victories in the European and Pacific theaters. While disappointing to the most ardent champions of strategic bombing, for air-power enthusiasts in general it was a ringing endorsement with important ramifications. It encouraged them to push for an independent air capability separate from the other services. It validated the indiscriminate nature of atomic bombing, thereby relaxing any precision or accuracy requirements. In doing so, it offered the possibility that air power could deliver the long-yearned-for decisive blow. Thus, the authors kept alive the debate over the efficacy of strategic bombing and reserved the high moral ground for the bombers rather than their victims. In short, the *USSBS* secured a prominent place for air power in future wars.

US COLD WAR BOMBING DOCTRINE

Under the cover of a rigid Cold War posture, the USA assumed a hegemonic role in the Western capitalist world. The rapid decline in European, most notably British, imperialism paralleled the rise in North American Anglo-Saxon power. It was now left to the US military and civilian authorities, particularly those on the payroll of the newly created independent

US Air Force, to search for an appropriate strategic bombing doctrine for the new terrain of Pax Americana.

This task was undertaken within a legal and moral context advantageous to the strategic bombers. First, they were free of any legal restraints. Throughout the short history of strategic bombing the imperial nations had consistently excused their bombing of colonial and European civilians from the legal charge of 'crimes against humanity.' In the London Agreement, signed in the few days between the bombing of Hiroshima and Nagasaki, the triumphant winners of another war exonerated themselves once again. Prosecutor Telford Taylor determined that 'air bombardment of cities and factories has become a recognized part of modern warfare, as practiced by all nations.'[2] With one sweep of the pen, the Hague Convention of 1907 was declared null and void. In addition, the United States and Britain successfully exempted conventional and atomic bombings of civilians from the Geneva Convention of 1949. Absent any new legal judgement, if militarily necessary the bombing of civilians was again lawful.[3]

Second, the favorable *USSBS* assessment enhanced the US Air Force's ability to compete effectively with the other military services for funds and political attention. Cold War tensions meant that the development of aviation and weapons technology, both conventional and nuclear, proceeded at fever pitch. Civilian militarism, the recruitment of the scientific and corporate community to the national security effort and the cause of air power, had begun in earnest during World War Two. In the permanent Cold War against communism, it became an essential component of the North American national security state.

The rise of a scientific elite that grew up within airpower research groups such as the Rand Corporation and Caltech's Jet Propulsion Laboratory, focused on 'the perfection of technique rather than the enemy.'[4] This left most of the moral and ethical issues of bombing either trivialized or rationalized away. A culture of 'scientific objectivity' pervaded researchers and bombing crews alike, cementing the notion of bombing as 'a cut and dried mechanical affair.'[5] Production of aircraft that flew fast, far and at great altitude further enhanced the heroic pilot's objectification of the invisible civilian enemy far below. The US Air Force was increasingly home to those with a 'godlike feeling of power that emerges when one can easily and playfully destroy others from a unreachable position on high.'[6]

Despite the indiscriminate wartime firebombing of Germany and Japan, the ACTS doctrine of daylight precision bombing developed in the

1930s still dominated political and public discussion. Improvements in the technology of bombsights and bomber range were heralded as producing the morally superior and politically desirable 'clean' war. As in the past, both unabashed reverence for new bombing technology and Great Power political machinations obscured the moral and legal issues that strategic bombing advocates would otherwise have faced in political and public discourse. They would and could be counted on to do so in the future.

As the intensity of the Cold War increased, whatever hesitation existed about strategic bombing evaporated as the imagery of 'Red fascism' was presented to a war-weary Western public, imagery that purposely linked the new scarlet peril to the just-defeated European and Asian black-coded fascists.[7] The Red enemy was portrayed as a bestial monster, striking outward with its octopus-like tentacles intent on strangling the lifeblood out of the God-fearing Free World and imposing its messianic atheist ideology.[8]

The Cold War imagery used to depict the communist enemy relied heavily on race, gender and class stereotypes. The dull, unimaginative repressive life of working-class stiffs under 'collectivist' communism was contrasted with the Free World worker, said to be at liberty to utilize his own talents, make a life for himself and his family, and own his own home and eventually his own business. Bill Levitt claimed that 'no man who owns his own house and lot can be a Communist, he has too much to do.' Levitt was responding to criticism that his Levittown was a communist enterprise of 'little boxes on a hillside out of tickytacky and they all look the same.'[9] The popular notion of a communist–Jewish conspiracy combined both race and class. With the 1949 triumph of the Red Army in China's civil war, the perceived threat of the 'yellow peril' now had racist and ideological roots, much akin to the racism directed at the Russians as 'quasi-Asiatic' during World War Two.[10] Federal Bureau of Investigation (FBI) director J. Edgar Hoover intimated that anyone who believed in racial equality was probably a communist.[11]

The feminization of communism was a popular theme, illustrated in a *Look* magazine photograph of a large Russian wrestler with the subtitle 'Many tough-looking communists are crybabies in defeat.'[12] In turn, in the so-called Free World rigid patriarchal roles were pushed as instrumental to the thwarting of the Red Menace. The 1950 'Educating Our Daughters' campaign urged women students to wed and have at least three kids, as it was their duty to fight 'the drift toward totalitarianism.' *Atlantic Monthly* reminded women of their primary role 'as mother ... to restore security in our insecure world. ... Let him know you are tired of living alone, that you want him now to take charge."[13] Any resistance to the forcing of women out of their wartime factory jobs and back into the home, any renewed support for gender equality was seen as part of a subversive communist plot to undermine the North American way of life and God's will.

Political elites in the Anglo-Saxon nations were responsible for the imagery supporting Cold War policy. Winston Churchill's vision of the Iron Curtain clanging down to divide Europe and President Harry Truman's announcement of a world polarized between 'us' and 'them,' of democracy versus totalitarianism, created powerful political imagery of a polarized landscape. Both garnered support for a Free World containment/liberation policy. The rigidity of this bipolar construction was cemented in the 'you are either for our way of life or for the other' choice offered to nations anxiously seeking escape from a drama threatening global annihilation. Soviet power, wrote George Kennan, was so entrenched and so single-mindedly bent on world domination that only its complete removal could save the god-fearing nations of the West, if not civilization itself.[14] Only the United States, with its vast untapped resources, industrial capacity and superiority in conventional and atomic air power was in a position to perform this task.

The rigid Cold War climate spurred US enthusiasm for air power in another way. Not only the USA's emerging global economic interests, but also its self-assigned task of saving Western civilization from communism meant that US military power and presence would spread around the globe. As it did, direct contact and confrontation increased between the neoimperial nation and its by now familiar subjects: peoples of color, populations of lower socio-economic status and societies with rigid patriarchal structures and practice. As Zillah Eisenstein documents, in this new context a more robust, racialized, class-conscious and gendered virulent strain of the 'other' was bound to develop.[15]

Meanwhile, under the radar of Cold War hysteria, the victorious but war-weary European allies were desperate to counter the rising tide of national self-determination that threatened their colonial empires. Looking for 'victory on the cheap,' they quickly returned to bombing the imperial populations with improved aircraft and bombing ordnance. As Europe celebrated peace in May 1945, French bombers destroyed over 40 Algerian towns, killing a large but uncounted number of civilians. Thus began the long French campaign to save their empire, dropping terror from the skies on civilians in Syria, Madagascar, Tunisia and Vietnam.

Beginning in 1947, for nearly two decades British warplanes, armed now with chemical defoliants, carpet-bombed rebellious subjects in Aden, Malaya and Kenya. But contrary to strategic bombing theory, this havoc wreaked from the skies on allegedly inferior colonial peoples was not decisive against their strong urge for independence.

TOTAL WAR: THE ATOMIC STRATEGIC BOMBING SCENARIO

For the USA, it was the Soviet-led communists who most threatened its postwar imperial ambitions, if not Western civilization. In all likelihood eliminating this threat would require total war. Fresh from the instant 'success' over Hiroshima and Nagasaki, the Truman Administration held the enviable position of sole possessor of the decisive weapon of mass destruction. For the US political and military elites, waging total war meant the atomic bombing of Soviet cities. To this end, in 1946 the Strategic Air Command (SAC) was designated a separate military branch. With the development of the B-36 intercontinental bomber, SAC had the capacity to carry out what many view as a horrifying fantasy.[16]

Yet, the Cold War architects of atomic strategic bombing were deadly serious. In plans wrapped in tight 'national security' secrecy, there was no pretense of 'precision' or 'clean' bombing of vital centers or industrial areas. Wholesale civilian death and suffering were and remain at the core of US strategic nuclear policy. According to the initial 'massive retaliation' or, in Pentagon parlance, 'massive pre-emption' war plan, the strategic bomber would deliver the decisive instrument to win World War Three. In 1948, Operation Trojan called for the bombing of 70 Soviet cities, anticipating that tens of millions of civilians would die. The next year, Operation Dropshot targeted 100 Soviet urban areas with 300 atom bombs.

Clearly US policy makers were convinced of the winning potential of strategic atomic bombing and possessed the political will to order it. Five times between 1946 and 1948 the USA threatened to respond to communist 'provocation' by annihilating Soviet civilians from the sky. The assumption was that, as in the Japanese case, quick surrender would ensue. By 1949, as Western Cold War lore has it, the devious communists, unable to figure out the complexities of the atom on their own, with the help of the local communist–Jewish conspiracy managed to 'steal' the atomic secret from the Free World. Then, somehow the Soviet Union was able to arm itself with the weapon of mass destruction. Now the scenario Douhet and Mitchell had predicted decades earlier, of bombs raining down on the civilians of the civilized world, became a sure bet given the assumed evil nature and maniacal intentions of the communist enemy.

But what was the expected effect of the atomic bombing? Again, self/other identity dominated strategic bombing discourse and policy. Atomic bombing of the inferior communist civilians would, as in the vision of the Prophets, be so devastating as to compel surrender. Conversely, the inferior enemy's rain of atomic terror inflicted on the superior civilians of the Free World would not only be survivable, but would harden their resolve to save civilization. The Free World's civil defense policy prepared the civilian population for both scenarios. Civil defense literature urged citizens to 'love the bomb, it is your friend but not the enemy's.' While the Free World's bombs were retaliating with total destruction of the enemy, European and North American populations could protect themselves from the ravages of atomic attack in a variety of ways and with little effort. A handkerchief over the face would prevent inhalation of radioactive mist. Standing in a doorway and covering up with a blanket would be adequate protection. 'Ducking and covering' under furniture or retreating to a homemade backyard bomb shelter would bring one safely through the bombing, prepared to fight another day. Newspaper accounts of 'mock' bombings of North American cities such as Syracuse and Buffalo New York, presented this scenario in vivid imagery and detail.[17]

In sum, for Free World populations, the Cold War meant learning to live with the atomic bomb, believing in its strategic capacity to wage a holy total war against evil while the civilized world survived. Since in this extremely militarized environment there were no innocents and no battle-fields in the traditional military sense, everyone was a soldier. For the initial Free World planners, atomic terror from the skies became the *sine qua non* of winning, quickly annihilating the enemy with an 'acceptable level of loss' on the Free World side. Meanwhile, the Soviet elites constructed their own, largely mirror self/other imagery of the Cold War context. They came to see the strategic bomber loaded with atomic ordnance as their salvation from the evils of the imperialist capitalist enemy.

A RETURN TO CONVENTIONAL STRATEGIC BOMBING

As nuclear stockpiles grew and the number of vulnerable targets increased, winning at the nuclear strategic level became impossible. According to Pentagon documents, under SAC Basic War Plan 1956, launching a first-strike nuclear attack by either side meant and still means committing suicide. A strategic stalemate existed as both sides, in a retaliatory second attack, could exterminate the first-strike aggressor.[18]

The strategic nuclear stalemate and the development of the tactical nuclear weapon meant that airpower doctrine at the sub-strategic nuclear and conventional level again preoccupied war theorists. Of chief concern was the Prophets' premise that bombing civilians, in particular the working class, would break their morale, causing them to rebel against their government. So far strategic bombing had not done so. In some cases it had actually hardened civilian resolve, a conclusion ACTS theorists had reached about the 1930s bombing of Barcelona, Madrid and China. The *USSBS* report on the effects of World War Two bombing added further doubt. It concluded, 'Bombing thus succeeded in lowering psychological morale but its effect upon behavior was less decisive. ... The German controls remained relatively untouched, and thus repression and coercion kept an increasingly defeatist population from overt acts of opposition to the conduct of war.'[19] *USSBS* authors also found that despite massive fire-bombing of Japan's cities, civilian morale was not decisive in the eventual surrender. Bombing, they concluded, did play a role in fortifying the position of those within the Japanese political elite who sought a way out of the conflict.

Though troubling to strategic bombing purists, these conclusions did not undercut the US commitment to air power or strategic bombing. They did cause a shift in strategic bombing doctrine from its affecting the people's will to resist as the ultimate goal of war to a central aim of severely damaging if not destroying the enemy's ability to make war. This shift began a debate within the US Air Force between members of the Joint Chiefs of Staff (JCS) and the SAC, dominated by General Curtis LeMay. The JCS advocated 'vertical bombing,' targeting key systems of industry such as transportation and electricity. Based on the incendiary and atomic attacks on Japan, the SAC commanders espoused 'horizontal targeting,' the bombing of cities where military and industrial facilities are located.

In political terms, the shift from purposely targeting civilians could be important, particularly as terrorism and the moral issues it provokes came to define the Cold War and post-Cold War landscape. In practice, the shift is less significant. Indeed for two important reasons, it is a distinction without meaning. First, the interdependence of modern industrial society, so central to the efficacy claims of orthodox and ACTS strategic doctrine, continues, and since World War Two, the internal 'industrial webs' have become more complex, their global threads now tying together the nations of the world. Given the precision, speed and mass destructive power of modern weapons, the industrial and post-industrial society and the people who live in them are more vulnerable than ever before to disruption at multiple points.

Second, in the Cold War and global context of Pax Americana, the populations to be bombed are the racial, class and gendered other. Allegedly, their morale is easily crushed, moving them in their panic to force their government into surrender. In short, to the strategic bomber, the modern target range is even more inviting than in the Prophets' time. As Lt Colonel John MacMullen asserts: 'Even within this slightly altered paradigm, the targeting priorities did not shift significantly from those of pre-WWII doctrine. Industry, raw materials, transportation, and electricity remained at the core of the targeting doctrine.'[20]

In the rigidly hostile climate of the first two Cold War decades, US strategic bombers practiced their trade and tested their theory on those portrayed as a communist 'yellow peril' in Korea and Vietnam. They did so with the enthusiastic blessing of civilian political authority. Whether it was done vertically or horizontally, undermining Asian civilian political will was a central goal of both air wars. Thus, Asian civilians and their livelihood remained the primary targets of strategic bombing. Among political leaders, this was of little concern or consequence as the moral and political issues surrounding terrorism had not yet taken take center stage in Western discourse. Besides, the attitude of 'it serves the bastards right' dominating Western public discourse at the end of World War Two was quickly applied to the new communist enemy.[21]

THE BOMBING OF KOREA

The first test of Cold War air power was on the Korean peninsula. On 25 June 1950, in the country the two superpowers had artificially divided at the 38th parallel, the armies of North and South Korea turned their minor military skirmishes along the border into a major ground war. Thus began a three-year test of the US Cold War containment/liberation policy.

In the Truman Administration there was immediate and great hope among civilian policy makers that air power, if quickly applied, could effectively reverse the communist 'rule of force' and install the 'Free World's rule of law.' Two days after the North Korean push across the border, President Truman authorized unrestricted bombing in South Korea in an effort to change the military situation on the ground. The bombing decision was largely symbolic as military advisors told the President they doubted air power could reverse the situation. Still, Secretary of State Dean Acheson argued that politically and psychologically 'it was important for us to do something even if the effort were not successful.'[22] Two days later, Truman expanded the bombing to North Korea. Fearful of drawing China and the Soviet Union into the conflict, thus sparking World War Three, he forbad any bombing of border areas close to China and Manchuria. SAC drew up plans for 'horizontal bombing,' proposing Japan-like incineration of five North Korean cities. The plan included deployment of nuclear-capable aircraft in case the JCS accepted soon-to-be President Dwight Eisenhower's vigorous urgings to resolve the crisis quickly with atomic bombs 'if suitable targets could be found.'[23]

Under pressure from civilian command in Washington, General Douglas MacArthur rejected the SAC proposal in favor of ACTS-inspired vertical bombing. This meant bombing urban military facilities with high explosives. He rejected the vertical bombers' request to drop leaflet warnings to the civilians in North Korean cities. Echoing the past as he forecast the future, MacArthur soothed the moral qualms of his bombers with the sentiment: 'If you miss your target and kill people or destroy other parts of the city, I accept that as part of war.'[24] In what he later described as a plan to win the war in ten days, in December 1950 MacArthur submitted a list of targets he wanted to destroy with 34 atomic bombs. A JCS committee had already recommended atomic bombs as a decisive factor against Chinese encroachment or for enforcing a *cordon sanitaire*. The civilian authority did not approve MacArthur's plan or General Matthew Ridgeway's May 1951 request for 38 atomic bombs. Still, strategic atomic bombing of Korea and later Manchuria were in the foreground and under constant review during the entire war.

With complete aerial supremacy, US air power was used to support the army on the ground and for 'interdiction' purposes. The bombardment of the North began on 13 July 1950, over Wonsan. During the next two months, 30,000 bombs were dropped. By October, the US Air Force had run out of targets and North Korean industry was, in the words of Far East Air Force commander Lt General George Stratemeyer, 'paralyzed.' In early November, MacArthur ordered that a 'wasteland' be created between the front and the Chinese border, destroying from the air every 'installation, factory, city, and village' over thousands of square miles.[25] In mid-December, the Air Force hit P'yongyang with 500-pound bombs, napalm and 175 tons of delayed-fuse demolition bombs. In early January 1951, assuming bombing would be decisive against Chinese intervention, MacArthur decided to attack North Korean cities with incendiaries. General Ridgeway ordered two firebombings of P'yongyang with the 'goal of burning the city to the ground.' New 12,000-pound 'Tarzan' bombs rained terror on Kanggye.

By the end of January, Air Force pilots reported they had again run out of targets. All the major cities of North Korea were virtually destroyed and thousands of civilians were dead. Fighter-bombers, flown by 'cheery' pilots with 'a kind of gay moral imbecility' then began the bombing of 'enemy-occupied' towns and villages as though they 'were playing in a bowling alley, with villages for pins.'[26] A few shots fired from a village meant, in official policy terms, that the town was enemy-occupied. Any distinction between combatants and non-combatants ceased to exist. Pilots were free to unleash 'saturation' terror from the sky on entire villages. As in the bombing of Japan, napalm, the new antipersonnel chemical developed at Harvard University, was the instrument of choice to deal with the Korean 'yellow monkeys' or 'gooks.' Eyewitnesses from the *New York Times* and the British Broadcasting Company reported the effect on thousands of village inhabitants. Dropping the sticky chemical goo meant peasants 'throughout the village and in the fields were caught and killed and kept the exact postures they had held when the napalm struck.'[27]

In May 1951, under Operation Strangle I, the US Air Force began bombing transportation targets. In August, Operation Strangle II attacked the North Korean rail system. Both bombing campaigns were aimed at depriving the enemy of any offensive capability. The ultimate goal was to convince the Koreans and Chinese they could not win the war and should sue for peace. By early 1952, it was clear that the Strangle bombings would not be decisive. In fact they were leading to a deadlock and 'trading of coolies for aircraft at an uneconomic rate.'[28] In May 1952, the Air Force, in a 'shift in emphasis' away from supporting the defensive posture of the army, went on the offensive. Bombers began applying 'air pressure,' a campaign 'to inflict maximum possible damage on military-related facilities perceived as essential to the civilian population's well-being.'[29]

Consistent with ACTS doctrine, the goal of the expansion of the scope of military targets was to have 'a deleterious effect upon the morale of the civilian population actively engaged in the logistic support of enemy forces.'[30] From then on, the aerial reign of terror that targeted the political will of civilians was the principal instrument utilized to force surrender. As Defense Secretary Robert Lovett asserted, 'If we keep on tearing the place apart, we can make it a most unpopular affair for the North Koreans.'[31] The entire capital city of P'yongyang was declared a military target and was directly bombed again and again. Under the 'air pressure' campaign, in late June the bombers hit North Korea's hydro-electric plants for the first time. After four days of bombing, 90 percent of the electricity generation capacity was shut down. By summer 1952, eye-witness accounts, such as that of William O. Douglas, Chief Justice of the United States Supreme Court, detailed the bombing effect on civilian life:

> I have seen the war-battered cities of Europe, but I had not see devastation until I had seen Korea. Cities like Seoul are badly mangled; but a host of towns and villages, like Chonwon on the base of the Iron Triangle, are completely obliterated. Bridges, railroad, dams are blasted. ... Misery, disease, pain and suffering, starvation – these are all compounded beyond comprehension.[32]

As in the past, bombing failed to have the desired decisive effect on civilian morale or the North Korean leadership. As peace negotiations dragged on, new targets and goals were assigned to the 'air pressure' campaign. The September 1951 bombings of Radio P'yongyang and North Korea's military academy were more for psychological impact than military, intended to undermine the 'image of control.' With the January 1952 presidential inauguration of Dwight Eisenhower, the JCS proposed the use of tactical nuclear weapons to 'force a settlement.' President Eisenhower decided against his military command's plan. He did authorize renewed air bombardment of Yalu River hydroelectric plants and a search for new targets. The Far East Air Force Target Committee recommended and General Mark W. Clark agreed to bomb the dam system that controlled the irrigation water for North Korean rice production. The goal was to flood the rice fields and destroy the crops, giving 'the enemy a sample of the totality of war ... embracing the whole of a nation's economy and people.'[33] Consistent with the Prophets' scenario, the starving civilians who survived the bombs and floods were expected to force the North Korean political leadership to capitulate.

The Korean War ended in an armistice signed on 27 July 1953. Assessments of the impact of air power on the final outcome are conflicting. Some, like General Otto P. Weyland, strongly argued the offensive posture of the 'air pressure' campaign was decisive in forcing peace and undermining civilian morale. Others, including Mark Clodfelter, are not

convinced bombing alone was responsible. Still others, such as SAC commander Curtis LeMay, argue that had the Far East Air Force been allowed
to unleash the kind of air attack on Korea that had been successful in
bringing Japan to its knees, the war would have been over in short order.
In LeMay's estimation, the bombing of Korea was not a test of strategic
bombing theory since the US Air Force, because of political restrictions,
was not allowed to hit strategic targets. Indeed, to LeMay the lesson of
Korea was 'How not to use the strategic air weapon.'[34]

LeMay's lament aside, the air campaign against North Korea met
important criteria of ACTS strategic bombing theory. First, three years of
indiscriminate bombing in which everything in North Korea became a
military target left every city 'a collection of chimneys' and millions of civilians dead. Estimates of civilian deaths range from two to five million. It
wasn't as though air power went unused or was ignored. Even with his criticism, Curtis LeMay admits the bombing eventually killed around 20
percent of the Korean population and 'burned down every town in North
Korea.'[35] For him, the ACTS vertical killing just didn't happen quickly
enough to bring victory. Second, as aerial destruction of the vital centers of
a largely agrarian society proved ineffective, civilians and the infrastructure they directly depended upon, such as electrical plants, dams, communication and transportation facilities, became the targets of choice, or in
ACTS terms, 'militarily necessary.' Utilizing a wide array of incendiaries
and explosives, they were bombed with the specific goal of undermining
civilian morale. In turn, it was assumed the demoralized North Koreans
would pressure their political leadership into making concessions at the
stalled peace talks.

LESSONS OF THE FORGOTTEN WAR

The Korean War would soon be known as the 'forgotten war.' But for the
high command of the US Air Force, there were important lessons to be
learned or relearned and not forgotten in the prosecution of the next war.
In assessing the failure of air power to be decisive, two familiar refrains
were offered. First, there was the lament that due to civilian political
restraints imposed primarily by the State Department, the Air Force could
not unleash its full fury on the civilian population. Operationally there
were other restraints. The Air Force was primarily used for tactical interdiction in support of ground forces. Thus, the claim went, valuable
resources were unavailable to conduct total war from the sky. As a result,

Air Force chiefs asserted, Korea, like the Spanish Civil War and World War Two before it, was not a true test of strategic bombing theory.

Once again, however, the conclusion that air strategic bombing, while not decisive, was an important contributing factor to the eventual outcome sustained the US elite's commitment to air power. In fact, in the post-Korean Cold War, Western security was seen to be singularly dependent on responding to communist provocations with a massive atomic bombardment of Soviet cities. In conventional terms, ACTS doctrine remained intact, if not reinforced. As presented in *Air Force Manual 1-8*, 'Strategic Air Operations,' the goal remained the disruption of 'an enemy nation to the extent that its will and capability to resist are broken.[36] The target was the nation rather than the armed forces. The goal was to diminish the civilian will to resist. In a tip of their hats to LeMay and his criticism of Korean air policy, the authors of *Manual 1-8* asserted that only 'weighty and sustained' bombing could accomplish the desired win. In effect, after Korea the US air power strategy was under the heavy influence of Curtis LeMay. The LeMay doctrine 'SACerized' the Pentagon, 'establishing offensive doctrine strictly directed against strong, industrialized enemies.'[37]

As a result, one lesson from the Korean War went unheeded and resonates today. Both orthodox and ACTS strategic theory assume future wars will be conducted within an interdependent industrial context in which civilian comforts, if not life itself, are highly vulnerable to massive and immediate disruption. Indeed, Clodfelter argues that the authors of *Manual 1-8* were so focused on developing bombing strategy for 'modern' society that they 'equated "modern" with "all".'[38]

But the Korean air war, like the earlier bombings of colonial and neo-colonial civilians, was conducted against a primarily agrarian society. In the absence of any vital centers or key links, a few precision strikes were unlikely to cause massive disruption of civilian life. In this setting the only option left to affect civilian morale is indiscriminate bombing that produces levels of agony and death few humans can endure.

There is nothing precise about the area or carpet-bombing strategy applied against those now labeled Third World peoples. When tried by Europeans and the US against imperial subjects, the historical record shows it failed to snuff out the flame of independence. By 1942, even strategic bombing advocate Alexander de Seversky questioned the effectiveness of air power to win total wars in agrarian areas. Yet, the 'civilized' bombers had ways to deny or rationalize their failures: for them, as for many military strategists of the past and present, technology, if applied correctly will always triumph over the human spirit. In industrial settings, the failure to undermine civilian morale could be laid at the feet of politicians or military commanders who limit attacks on the kind and number of vital centers to be hit. In the agrarian context, as in Korea where vital centers were virtually nonexistent, the doctrine loses its plausibility, and in the wake of massive bombing, what gains increasing credibility is the conclusion that the imperialists' assumptions underlying the race, class and gendered identity of the Third World 'other' are highly suspect, if not dead wrong. In particular, what appears problematic are the sequential and comforting convictions that the enemy responds only to force and will submit to aerial terror. Despite their experiences in the Korean War, the Anglo-Saxon elites were not prepared to consider this verdict. To do so would have meant challenging and possibly abandoning the central psychological, political and cultural components of their carefully constructed worldview.

Meanwhile, despite fueling a million-plus air attacks to bomb a Third World enemy into submission, US Air Force commanders and their civilian champions retreated into self-serving rationales. The failure led not to a re-evaluation of their worldview but to the conclusions of LeMay and his coterie at SAC that an air power strategy that causes slow, agonizing death to Third World people will not be successful. In moral and efficacy terms, it is a failed policy. In the tradition of the strategic Prophets, they forcefully argued that only immediate massive amounts of the 'technological fix' of strategic bombardment would bring a quick and decisive win. Like those before them, they were determined to prove the civilized world's view of the unsophisticated 'other' was correct.

In the tense climate that followed the Korean War, the atomic and conventional bombing enthusiasts enjoyed great political clout in the military and civilian hierarchies of the two Cold War antagonists and their industrial allies. They were able to thwart any attempt, such as that by the International Red Cross, to re-establish the combatant/noncombatant distinction in international law. The Cold War rivals, scrambling to build their nuclear arsenals, much preferred the assessment of Douhet, according to which no such distinction could or should exist. This guaranteed that the next generation of bombers, particularly those of the Free World colossus in Washington DC, would again test the assumption of the Prophets and their ACTS offspring that terrorizing civilians from the skies could win wars.

BOMBING INDOCHINA

A decade after the Korean War ended, the United States entered into another Asian conflict. This time it was in Indochina, principally Vietnam, where again the issue of air power came into play. Within the US Air Force, the LeMay doctrine continued to guide atomic and conventional strategic thinking. In other elite military and civilian circles, political power had shifted from the first-use nuclear posture of massive retaliation to a second-strike stance labelled Mutual Assured Destruction (MAD). This nuclear terror doctrine assumed that holding the Cold War protagonists' civilians hostage to the threat of annihilation would prevent strategic nuclear war. For conventional war, the ACTS vital centers doctrine held sway within the JCS and John F. Kennedy Administration. By this time a slight, but significant, indeed necessary, modification in their view of Third World peoples was in fashion. They proposed that Third World leaders are extremely protective of their country's industrial infrastructure. No matter how limited, they were assumed to value it as a matter of extreme national pride and 'as necessary components of modern war, but also as fundamental features of twentieth century social order.'[39] Thus, if their 'treasure' was threatened with destruction, the Third World enemy would easily succumb. Of course, air power was assumed to be the instrument to force this decisive decision.

Until the Tet Offensive of 1968, the Vietnam conflict was a guerrilla war fought primarily in the jungle terrain of South Vietnam. From then on, until its end in 1973, the war was fought with conventional forces. Throughout, air power was considered central to achieving the various and shifting US goals. From 1961 to 1965, after the Johnson Administration decided to expand military involvement in Indochina, it was used primarily in support of the South Vietnamese army and to defoliate the jungle, thereby depriving the National Liberation Front (NLF) guerrillas of their leafy cover. In February 1965, the bombing of North Vietnam began under Operation Rolling Thunder; it continued until 1968. The goal was to convince the North Vietnamese to end their support of the NLF insurrection in the South and to stabilize the South Vietnamese regime. After the Tet Offensive, the Operation Linebacker One and Two bombing campaigns were intended to convince the communists they could not win the war.

As in Korea, debate raged over how to use air power to achieve US goals. In their initial survey, the JCS listed only eight industrial targets in all of North Vietnam worthy of bombing. The strategic bombers saw the situation differently. The US Air Force, still dominated by Curtis LeMay, promised that a Japan-like incendiary bombing that blasted North Vietnam back into the Stone Age would end the conflict in ten days. The chairman of the JCS, Army General Earle G. Wheeler, seeking a 'sudden, sharp, blow,' offered a revised list of 94 North Vietnam targets. Civilian authorities rejected both plans.

Much to the frustration of the SAC-dominated Air Force, the plan Operation Rolling Thunder called for B-52 close support bombing in the South (code name 'Arc Light') and tactical bombing of the North's limited industrial base. Fearing Soviet and Chinese intervention, the civilian command insisted on restricting bombing close to the Chinese border and the centers of Hanoi and Haiphong. In line with ACTS vital centers doctrine, targets included transport systems, oil storage facilities, electric power plants, cement and steel plants, and a number of water dams. Based on the assumption that the North Vietnamese highly valued their meager industry, the goal of the bombing was to wreck North Vietnam's industrial base and its capacity to prosecute the war in the South without threatening the nation's survival. The expectation was that with their industrial base under siege, the North Vietnam leaders would call off their insurgency. As Army Brigadier General William C. Depuy, infamous for his willingness to call in air strikes in highly populated areas of South Vietnam, asserted: 'The solution in Vietnam is more bombs, more shells, more napalm ... till the other side cracks and gives up.'[40]

Operation Rolling Thunder lasted for nearly three years to no avail. The North Vietnamese continued to support the NLF in the South, enduring the bombing with heightened morale and greater levels of material support. Throughout the campaign, US Air Force chiefs were extremely exasperated with the restrictions imposed on their air war. In 1969, Seventh Air Force Commander General William W. Momyer registered the frustration when he wrote: 'We had the force, skill, and intelligence, but our civilian betters wouldn't turn us loose. ... If there is one lesson to come out of this war, it must be a reaffirmation of the axiom—don't get into a fight unless you are prepared to do whatever is necessary to win.'[41]

One of the restrictions the US Air Force chiefs allegedly accepted was to avoid the wanton bombing of 'the man in the street.' Pursuant to the ACTS strategic bombing agenda, Rolling Thunder was geared at hitting military targets near population centers, without direct targeting of civilians. The goal was to destroy North Vietnam's capacity to fight with a 'minimal' loss of civilian lives while making the civilian survivors cringe in fear. By 1967, with 200,000 tons of bombs dropped, the CIA totaled the number of civilian death and injury from bombing at 29,600. Defense Secretary Robert McNamara put the civilian death count much higher at 1,000 per week.

When Rolling Thunder ended in 1968, 643,000 tons of bombs had been dropped, destroying 65 percent of North Vietnam's oil storage facilities and 59 percent of its electric power plants and major bridges. US officials proudly reported that out of a population of 18 million, only 52,000 civilians had died in the bombing. From their perspective, there were plenty of civilians left alive who would flinch from the hell poured on their precious industry in future bombing campaigns. At the time, in the attempt to prove their point, they were secretly dropping bombs on the civilians of Laos.

In 1969, Richard Nixon came to the presidency determined to 'Vietnamise' the war in the South while making a 'peace with honor' in the North. Air power was at the heart of his Indochina strategy. From 1969 to May 1972, as defoliation efforts continued in South Vietnam and the secret bombing of Laos continued, air power was used to interdict men and material along the Ho Chi Minh Trail. It was also used for 'protective reaction strikes' in the North. In March 1969, the first stage of Operation Menu – the secret 'area,' now known as 'box' bombing – of Cambodia began.

Frustrated with peace negotiations and looking to bolster the morale of the South Vietnamese, Nixon unleashed Linebacker One from May to October 1972 and Linebacker Two for ten days in mid-December 1972. Much like Rolling Thunder, the strategic bombing of Linebacker One was aimed at what remained of North Vietnam's industry. Fearing world condemnation, Nixon prohibited 'direct attacks' on civilians. Yet, as Linebacker One continued, geographical restrictions close to the cities of Hanoi and Haiphong disappeared. Area bombing of railyards and storage facilities with 500-pound 'iron' bombs and the new laser-guided 'smart' bombs was authorized. Military officials expected that civilian casualties would occur, but would be limited to the desired 'minimal' level. What minimal meant went undefined. Overall, the US Air Force was given the authority to attack any 'valid military' target. According to General David A. Burchinal, bombs were dumped in 'an area of 100-yards wide or 1,000 yards-wide and thousands of yards long.'[42]

On 18 December 1972, President Nixon, furious at North Vietnamese intransigence, unleashed Operation Linebacker Two. For the next ten days, US Air Force jets and B-52 bombers relentlessly slammed North

Vietnam night and day to 'inflict the utmost civilian distress.'[43] The array of military targets nearly matched those proposed by the Air Force strategic bombers in the mid-1960s. They included targets in and around central Hanoi, such as the downtown Bac Mai communications center, and Haiphong. The bombing of Haiphong ended on 27 December 1972 when the Air Force announced no 'suitable targets' were left to attack.

The North Vietnamese and North Americans signed a peace agreement in early 1973. The Air Force chiefs were ecstatic, crowing that when finally left to conduct the war on their terms, air power had been decisive. Even Curtis LeMay, while again stressing the decision had come years too late and that a few more days of bombing would have produced an outright win, was very pleased. Finally, his bombers had been allowed to conduct a 'real' strategic bombing campaign. Outraged anti-war critics called the Christmas 1972 bombing 'a crime against humanity' and 'the most savage and sense- less act of war ever visited, over a scant ten days, by one sovereign people upon another.'[44] The criticism failed to sway the unabashedly gleeful strategic bombers. For them, Linebacker Two vindicated their long-term commitment to strategic bombing, especially the expected crumbling of the civilian will to resist under heavy bombing. According to Air Force Major Paul G. Niesen, the only remaining mystery was 'why the powers that be chose a defensive position as the name of an offensive operation.'[45]

The efficacy claims of the US Air Force strategic bombers did not go unchallenged. Some argue it was the vertical 'war of attrition' conducted over time that finally brought both sides to a peace agreement. Others, notably Air Force Academy Professor Mark Clodfelter, suggest that the influence of numerous 'anomalies' such as developments in the ground war were a fundamental part of the military and diplomatic context of the Vietnam War.[46] Thus, the debate over the efficacy of bombing continued.

ASSESSING THE CIVILIAN CARNAGE

The strategic bombers' lamented that up until the last month of the war they were prevented from punishing the people of Indochina in a way that would bring them to their knees. Given what Indochina's civilians endured during the air war, this is difficult to fathom. If the bombers' premise that these Third World peoples lacked a strong will to resist was correct, they should have capitulated in the early months of Operation Rolling Thunder. Instead, they persevered through a decade of US air terror applied in various ways and in multiple places.

It began in 1961 with Operations Trail Dust/Ranch Hand, the herbicidal warfare program intended to defoliate the jungles and destroy the crops of farmers alleged to be NLF supporters in South Vietnam. When halted in 1971, the US Air Force had dumped over 19 million gallons of 'Rainbow' poisons, code named Orange, Green, Pink, Purple, Blue and White, on an area equal to 30,305 square miles or 10 percent of South Vietnam's countryside. Seventy-six percent of the total was sprayed between 1967 and 1969.[47]

North American officials claimed the herbicides were harmless to humans. Military strategists called the infamous Agent Orange, the most widely used of the herbicides, a benign, life-saving 'prototype smart weapon.' This view was contradicted in a 1967 RAND study, but sustained in the Department of Defense sponsored 'independent' 1974 National Academy of Science study. Amid complaints from Vietnam veterans experiencing various maladies and the birthing of their severely disfigured children, a multitude of other studies contradicted the Pentagon's position. Teams of international scientists now assert that the allegedly benign Agent Orange contains TCCD, one of the most toxic strains of dioxin poisons known. In 1982, two hospitals in Ho Chi Minh City housed Agent Orange children with genetic malfunctions. Western eyewitnesses report children born without eyes or brains and others with mangled and deformed limbs. In the 1990s, the US Department of Veterans Affairs sponsored an Institute of Medicine study that found direct links between the Rainbow agents and soft tissue sarcoma, non-Hodgkin's lymphoma, Hodgkin's disease, chloracne and a long list of virulent cancers. By 1995, in the southern part of a reunited Vietnam dioxin levels from Agent Orange spraying were still 900 times higher than in the north. In total, due to the herbicide war, its indiscriminate nature, thousands of the US warrior class and hundreds of thousands of Indochina's civilians suffered the effects of herbicide aerial spraying. As of 2003, 1,250,000 Vietnamese civilians living 'on the ground' during the war and their offspring have died or remain alive but scarred for life because of it.[48]

As in Korea, 'swept' Vietnamese villages and hamlets suspected of 'sympathy for the Viet Cong' were routinely and indiscriminately bombed with B52s and napalm-loaded jets or strafed by helicopter gunners. One Navy pilot describes bombing villages at 500–600 miles per hour as 'electronic warfare,' 'all business' and 'strictly professionalism' with no time for personal thoughts. Echoing the sentiments of past air aces, another Vietnam-era pilot asserts, 'Flying a fighter plane is ... a macho thing, maybe

– an extension of your manhood ... we're basically patriotic, conservative people. ... And we're blameless.'[49] Still another pilot stresses: 'You never see the people ... occasionally see the houses when bombing around or in a village ... never heard explosions ... you never saw any blood ... any screams ... it was very clean. You were doing a job. You're an expert at what you do. I was a technician.'[50]

Former Pentagon official Daniel Ellsberg reports that in the aftermath of helicopter attacks on civilian housing in the Mekong Delta 'the count of captured enemy weapons accompanying these "enemy kills" was – as at My Lai – strikingly low, in fact negligible, and the provincial hospitals overflowed with civilian wounded.'[51] The favorite incendiaries were napalm and white phosphorus. In Vietnam, 'nearly three quarters of all napalm victims were burned through to the muscle and bone (fifth-degree burns). The pain caused by the burning is so traumatic that it often causes death.'[52]

The B-52 and B-57 bombers, operating at undetectable altitudes in their 'restricted or limited precision' attacks, dropped 8 million tons of bombs on Vietnam between 1965 and 1973. The tonnage was over three times that of the World War Two strategic bombing. In addition to conventional explosives and incendiaries, the US Air Force employed new anti-personnel devices, including special plastic bombs such as the Pineapple. It was designed to demoralize the enemy by maiming rather than killing its victims, thus overwhelming enemy health services. According to the Pentagon, 285 million of the now infamous cluster bombs (CBU-24), containing shrapnel and flammable agents, were dropped on Indochina. Released from high altitude, many fell to the earth without exploding. Like landmines, they went undetected for years only to explode when disturbed. Three decades after the war, the bright yellow 'toys' are still terrorizing the children and parents of Indochina.[53]

Claiming to minimize civilian casualties, the US Air Force box-bombed rural Indochina. James Gibson, in *The Perfect War*, describes the basic carpet-bombing technique thus: 'They often first dropped explosive bombs in order to "open the structures," then napalm to burn out the contents, and finally CBU-24s to kill the people who came running to help those who were burning.'[54] The three-part scenario matched the suggested bombing sequence of the Prophets Douhet and Hart's perfectly.

Assuming that cities in the North would be the primary targets of Operation Rolling Thunder, North Vietnamese officials ordered civilians to leave Hanoi for the countryside. But only a small percentage of residents evacuated the city because until Operation Linebacker, the B-52s' wholesale box-bombing of North Vietnam's rural areas made them more dangerous than the cities. According to William Shawcross, much the same was true of the secret bombing of Cambodia. Several pilots testified during the pounding of the peasant-occupied landscape during various stages of Operation Menu that 'almost anything in Cambodia constituted a legitimate target.'[55]

Defenders of the bombing campaigns claimed that a new generation of smart bombs, named Remotely Piloted Munitions, allowed the US Air Force to hit military targets close to highly populated areas precisely and with minimal civilian casualties. If so, then based on eyewitness accounts of the destruction, hospitals and other medical facilities, schools, churches and pagodas, and civilians in extremely isolated villages had all been designated as military targets. According to Abraham Behar, a member of the four Commissions of Inquiry conducted by the 1967 War Crimes Tribunal, all were 'precisely' hit as though they were the primary targets.[56]

Other aspects of the bombing campaign undermine the air commanders' professed commitment to precision bombing. Throughout the war, B-52s flying at high altitude, often in bad weather and increasingly at night to avoid enemy fire, did the bulk of the 'precision' bombing with 'dumb' ordnance. Air Force commanders said that, though not intentional, casualties – or, as they began to be termed, 'collateral' damage – were a certainty. It was, they explained, a regrettable but unavoidable by-product of air war. After 1965, the same commanders advocated nuclear bombing. They, along with General William C. Westmoreland, the top military official in Vietnam, were clearly prepared to drop all pretense of a lack of intent to target civilians.[57] In the end, political, rather than military or moral reasons prevented them from completely having their way.

The determination of minimal is subjective and highly political depending upon whose civilians are among the casualties. For instance, in the North American mindset the 9/11 attacks on United States' facilities and civilians are correctly labeled terrorism. Indeed, because close to 3,000 'civilized' civilians died, the 9/11 attacks have been described as constituting a 'catastrophe that changed the world.' In contrast, US officials always refer to Vietnamese and Indochinese civilian losses as minimal. For example, United States' officials determined the 58,000 Vietnamese civilian casualties of Rolling Thunder to be minimal or acceptable. Other estimates of civilian dead from the Vietnam War are higher still. In April 1995, the Vietnamese government reported that four million of its civilians had died in the war. In this case, the claim of 'minimal' meant Vietnam alone lost over ten percent (four million of 38 million)) of its population to the war.[58] In his 22 April 1971 letter to the *New York Review of Books*, Daniel Ellsberg says a United States congressional inquiry counted between 125,000 and 150,000 Vietnamese civilian casualties (between 25,000 to 35,000 dead) in 1970 alone. The authors of *Peace Aware Factsheet* estimate in waging the Vietnam War with modern 'smart' technology, alleged to 'minimize collateral damage,' 340,000 total casualties were Vietnamese civilians compared with 56,000 dead US GIs or 85.74 percent of the combined civilian/GI total. This was double the percentage of civilian deaths in World War Two and four times greater than that in World War One.[59] Finally, during the Linebacker II Christmas bombing, Air Force commanders fretted over the loss of a few planes and their air warriors to Vietnamese anti-aircraft fire. Meanwhile, they calmly if not gleefully hurled terror on the civilians of Hanoi and Haiphong in what 'other' people viewed as 'a crime against humanity.' In sum, while the calculations differ they all agree that more civilians died in the Vietnam War than on 9/11. Yet, no US official has ever said Vietnam's or Indochina's civilian casualties constituted a world-changing catastrophe.

OBJECTIFYING INDOCHINA'S VICTIMS

The standard of minimal or acceptable civilian casualties also depends to a great extent on the view constructed about the enemy. In general military parlance, as 'the enemy' all North Vietnamese and their supporters in the South were expendable. Other assumptions and imagery helped soothe the consciences of North Americans as they ravaged Indochina and its people. Among the political and military elites, well schooled in the racist notion of the 'yellow peril,' few if any objected when General William Westmoreland declared: 'the Oriental doesn't place the same high price on life as does the Westerner. Life is plentiful ... life is cheap in the Orient. As the philosophy of the Orient expresses it, life is not important.'[60] President Nixon continued bombing during the summer of 1971 because in his mind the Vietnamese communists only understood strength. Previously, top Johnson Administration officials and the JCS bombed away assuming 'the other side is not that tough ...' and 'never imagined that their Third World enemy could withstand even a limited bombing campaign.'[61]

Gendered imagery was a central factor in the mindset of top leaders. Any strategy that demasculinized the enemy was considered a winner. As President John Kennedy had 'cut his balls off' (referring to Nikita

Khrushchev in the Cuban Missile Crisis), President Lyndon Johnson, having secured congressional approval to escalate the war, reportedly boasted, 'I didn't just screw Ho Chi Minh. ... I cut his pecker off.'[62] Meanwhile, the 'puppet-like Viet Cong,' of whom North Vietnamese leader Ho Chi Minh was alleged to be the master string manipulator, were portrayed in North American cultural venues as rapists, their thirst for sex virtually unquenchable.[63]

Other North American officials saw the Vietnamese as human but child-like, their minds equivalent to 'the shriveled leg of a polio victim,' and their 'power of reason ... only slightly beyond the level of an American six year old.'[64] The infantile Vietnamese were portrayed as needing the guiding hand of a strong adult. According to General William Westmoreland, 'Vietnam reminded me of a child ... the developing of a child. The laws of nature control the development of this child. The child has to sit up before it crawls. It has to crawl before it can walk. It has to walk before it can run.'[65]

President Johnson was known to characterize the ancient Southeast Asian peoples as 'yellow dwarves' and their societies as 'young and unsophisticated nations.' Just as in past Western imperial philosophy, Vietnam was the woman that the masculine West needed to protect.[66] In Cambodia, 'les autres' (the others) were thought of 'as shadowy, insubstantial, inconsequential, wraiths almost, inhabiting that unknown, fearsome world.'[67] In congressional testimony, top officials such as General Maxwell Taylor tagged Vietnam 'Indian country,' an image and terminology US troops quickly adopted. Vietnam was said to be 'infested' with 'termites' or diseased by the cancer of communism. 'What does Vietnam look like?'– a Navy pilot rhetorically asked in response to a young Catholic schoolgirl's question – '... if it wasn't for the people, it was very pretty ... the people over there are very backward and very primitive ... they just make a mess out of everything.'[68]

The tradition of Anglo-Saxon racism toward Asians dominated the US psyche. As in the Korean War, the 'yellow monkeys' of Indochina were derisively dubbed 'gooks,' with 'slants', 'dinks' and 'slopes' added for good measure. Dead Vietnamese were 'body counts,' products of the military strategy of 'meat grinding.' US legal authorities further dehumanized the Vietnamese, applying what they called 'the mere gook rule' to all Vietnamese who, if dead, were counted as Viet Cong combatants.

Class mattered as well. Tailoring the bombing to the ACTS agenda of industrial vital centers meant that Vietnamese working-class bodies and political will were specifically targeted throughout the air war. Finally, gender consciousness was rampant, as noted, at the highest political levels. Like the European occupier of the colonial past, to US males the women of Asia were at times exotic, other times erotic and always compliant and inferior. Among the writings of US combat veterans 'Asian women were mirrored as whore or whore-with-a-heart-of-gold, or inscrutable lover, or will-less mistress.'[69]

In prosecuting both the Korean and Indochina Wars, the US empire builders exhibited clear signs of racism, class-consciousness and gender bias that sustained their long-held identity as a superior people and permitted them once again to dismiss the Asian people as unimportant or deserving of their fate. For the political and military establishment, Korea and especially Indochina, were classic cases that 'might is right.' It was assumed that the white world's superior technology would win over crude implements of war, especially when wielded against pajama-clad, slant-eyed peoples of color. The idea that an inferior and sinister ideology held the Asian populace hostage only elevated US righteousness. If anything would free the wretched souls of Korea and Vietnam from the chains of their cultural heritage, would demonstrate the spiritual and psychological inferiority of the yellow race, and would cause them to rise up against their communist masters, the civilized world's gift of aerial bombing would be it.

Despite such sentiments, the conduct of the Indochina War was heavily criticized. In the decades to come, debate over how to avoid another 'quagmire' would be at the center of US foreign policy. Talk of a 'Vietnam syndrome' and what it meant dominated public discourse. To some in the top military and civilian establishment, the concept pointed to a need for sober reassessment of US power and purpose in a changing world. To others, the need to avoid the Vietnam syndrome meant overcoming hesitancy to use the full force of power regardless of the circumstance or enemy. But both sides of the debate, in planning for the future, deemed that air power was the 'clean' way to push the values and interests of the 'civilized world' while avoiding another messy quagmire. Indeed, in the decades ahead, it would be affirmed again and again that, as anti-war activist H. Rap Brown observed, 'bombing is as American as cherry pie.'[70]

6

Terrorists in the Bombsights

THE POLITICS OF TERRORISM

Four months before President Nixon ordered the December 1972 Christmas bombings of North Vietnamese cities, a terrorist tragedy struck the Munich Olympics. Members of Black September, a splinter group in the Palestinian movement, murdered eleven Israeli athletes. It was a watershed event in the Cold War and beyond. Before Munich, concern over anti-Western terrorism, particularly related to the Arab–Israeli conflict, barely registered in Western public opinion. True, in the late 1960s and early 1970s several airplanes had been hijacked, causing some concern about air travel. Officials of the imperial West, faced with wars of national liberation, had tagged a few anti-colonial movements, such as the Mau Mau of Kenya, the Irish Republican Army (IRA) in Northern Ireland and the Palestinian Liberation Front (PLO), as simply small groups of Soviet-backed terrorists. Still, in the capitalist West, terrorism held few people's attention or caused much alarm. The Cold War issues of communist aggression in Indochina, the specter of nuclear war and the New Left, black militant and feminist challenges to Western white, patriarchal, middle-class life remained the chief concerns of Western policy makers and their constituencies.

But in Munich, a few ski-masked terrorists captured the rapt attention of millions of people and held hostage their revered attempt at global friendship. Glued to their televisions, Western viewers witnessed first hand, and many for the first time, how vulnerable the industrial world was to a single act of terrorism.

Western governments moved quickly to monopolize the discourse on terrorism for their political advantage. Media coverage of a rash of hijackings, bombings, kidnappings and assassinations in Western Europe, the

Middle East, Africa and Latin America allowed them to hype the terrorism threat. By the time of the 1975 hostage crisis at the Organization of Petroleum Exporting Countries (OPEC) meeting in Vienna, led by the now infamous Carlos the Jackal (Illich Ramirez Sanchez), the specter of terrorism had begun to penetrate the Western psyche.

Over the remaining years of the 1970s, a 'terrorism industry' – academic researchers and security analysts in service to the US, British and Israeli governments – constructed a politically loaded conventional wisdom focused on the what, why, where and who of contemporary terrorism.[1] At the heart of their 'ideology of terrorism' was the general assertion that terrorism had become the exclusive tool of the West's Cold War enemy. Specifically they argued that: (1) Terrorism is primarily a strategy of revolutionary groups or individuals directed against the state; (2) state terrorism is solely the instrument of totalitarian (fascist and communist) governments; (3) terrorism is primarily a strategy of the political Left in theory and in practice.[2]

In the Cold War climate in which 'peace-loving' democracies were touted as morally superior to 'violence-prone' communists, Western terrorism experts and their government clients easily convinced the public to view terrorism as the most evil of deeds and the work of morally corrupt and irrational 'crazies.' Conversely, they and their political mentors asserted that the industrial West must monopolize the instruments of violence if the terrorists were to be defeated.

For millions in the United States, this view of terrorism was validated in November 1979, when Iranian 'students' took fifty-two US citizens hostage and held them over the entire course of the 1980 presidential campaign. In the words of Claire Sterling, who soon became President Ronald Reagan's favorite terrorist expert, this long drama became 'America's trauma in Fright Decade I.'[3] In purposeful fashion, the Reagan presidential campaign used the Iranian hostage crisis to validate the highly politicized 'ideology of terrorism' to defeat President Jimmy Carter and push a revitalized Cold War agenda. Under the constant glare of television lights, the Reagan campaign hammered at Carter's inability to free the hostages, accusing the leader of the world's most powerful nation of ineptitude and incompetence when faced with a 'few crazies.' The release of the hostages on the very day Reagan took the oath of office raised his status to new heights as a champion of counter-terrorism.

The new administration moved quickly to capitalize on the President's exalted status and the public frenzy over the terrorism threat to the United

States and its Western allies.[4] Only weeks into his tenure as Secretary of State, Alexander Haig announced that terrorism was the primary threat to human rights and thus to US foreign policy. President Reagan followed with his image of an 'evil Soviet empire' in control of an international terrorist network bent on undermining the Western industrial democracies. Terrorism industry experts jumped to fill in Reagan's network imagery. They asserted that wherever terrorism occurred across the globe it was the world of the Kremlin. Allegedly this was the case whether in Afghanistan, Nicaragua, Latin America or the Middle East, and whether the work of the IRA or the African National Congress, or of individuals such as Carlos, or the soon-to-be infamous Abu Nidal and Mehmet Ali Agca.[5] In sum, national security experts Samuel Francis and Dr Ray Cline said, through their vast array of terrorist clients the Soviets had launched World War Three against the Free World.[6]

The Reagan Administration's 'counter-terrorism' posture reaped political dividends for it and its friends. It immediately provided the political rationale for Israel's June 1982 bombing of Beirut, Lebanon, in which over 17,500 civilians are reported to have died. Like previous bombers, Israeli military leaders claimed they had conducted 'surgical' bombing, ' hitting exactly what they had targeted. Eyewitnesses agreed, claiming that Israeli jets, dropping phosphorus, vacuum and cluster bombs 'went out of their way to destroy hospitals, schools, orphanages, school buses – and any other place where children collected in large numbers.'[7] Robert Fisk, the British *Independent*'s Beirut-based journalist, reported that the Israelis blasted residential areas with '50 shells at a time ... slaughtering everyone within a 500 yard radius of the explosions.'[8] Israel, claiming it was targeting PLO terrorist leaders and their sympathizers, demanded the PLO terrorists leave Beirut before it would stop bombing. At the United Nations, the Reagan Administration supported the Israeli position by vetoing Security Council resolutions 512 and 513 which called for respect for civilians and repudiation of all acts of violence against civilians.

Throughout the 1980s, the Reagan Administration wrapped its own foreign policy efforts in the garb of counter-terrorism. This initial North American 'war on terrorism' included the anti-Soviet effort in Afghanistan, the Contra war against Nicaragua's Sandinista government, the US military interventions in Lebanon, Grenada and Libya, and the US sponsorship of the wholesale terror of Latin America's 'national security states,' most notably El Salvador, Argentina, Guatemala and Chile.

Western leaders were not alone in playing politics with the terrorism issue. As the Cold War heated up anew, Soviet leaders constructed a mirror-image international terrorist network. For millions of people loyal to the Soviet cause, terrorism was the exclusive instrument of a 'capitalist evil empire' housed in Washington DC, its imperialist agents using terrorism to defend the corrupt capitalist system and thwart the progressive march toward socialism.[9]

Throughout the New Cold War of the 1980s, the issue of terrorism was the preeminent instrument of political polarization. Constant attention was drawn to the other side's use of terrorism to victimize innocent civilians. Conversely, any civilian death or injury resulting from 'counter-terrorism' was 'regrettable but unavoidable.' The point was to divide the world between their terrorists and our freedom fighters, stake out the high moral ground and doggedly cling to it. The advantages of being on the 'right' side of the terrorism issue became so obvious during the 1980s that, throughout the world, leaders of diverse political stripes raised the specter of terrorism against their adversaries in the attempt to manipulate issues to their advantage.[10]

With the end of the Cold War, the United States became the sole architect of the post-Cold War political order. Even before the demise of the Soviet Union, Washington's security establishment went in search of a new 'aggressor' to justify a global military presence. Collaborating through the *United States–Soviet Task Force to Prevent Terrorism*, the security agencies of the former Cold War antagonists identified a 'new face of terrorism' they said threatened the emerging post-Cold War landscape. No longer was the center of the international terrorist network located in Moscow or Washington. With Iraq's 1990 invasion of Kuwait, the terrorism network allegedly had moved its headquarters to Baghdad.[11]

Since then, all US administrations have invoked the terrorism/counter-terrorism mantra to polarize the global community between 'good' and 'evil'. Utilizing what is labeled here the jingoist model of terrorism and its central premise that a terrorist is 'an enemy of the Western establishment, somebody who stands in the way of the realization of Western aims,' they have leveled the charge of terrorism at all adversaries who threaten the 'American way of life.'[12] Conversely, by labeling their various military endeavors counter-terrorism they have stymied their critics and roused the Western 'family of nations' to their cause. In the 1990s, this unqualified support came even as the US, NATO, Israeli and Russian strategic bombing of Iraq, Kosovo, Lebanon and Chechnya respectively sent thousands of civilians to their deaths. But, even in the decades before 9/11, linking terrorism with Western policy, particularly that of the USA, Israel or Britain, was simply not to be tolerated, condoned or even debated in Western discourse.

THE NEW WORLD ORDER:
KEEPING TERRORISM AT A DISTANCE

The US effort to mobilize public support for its 'counter-terrorism' policy has relied heavily on the imagery of 'terrorism-at-a-distance.'[13] Two general assertions combine to produce this representation. The first contends that terrorism occurs 'over there,' that it is a product of foreign cultures and a sinister act of foreign adversaries bent on victimizing North Americans who live in or travel to far-off lands. A companion premise, vigorously asserted before 9/11, instructed that though the USA had been spared the horrors of contemporary terrorism, it was only a matter of time before its global pursuit of freedom and democracy and its open society made enemies of foreign terrorists. Western terrorism experts warned that unless foreign and domestic preventive measures were taken, the stage was set for the terrorist 'victimization' of the USA.[14]

In arguing that the concept of terrorism has been useful in 'sanitizing' US foreign policy, Richard Falk writes: 'This process is aided by locating "terrorism" in the foreign other, a process that can build on the racist convenience of non-Western challenges.'[15] The Western terrorism industry experts well understood how locating terrorism in the foreign other had served the political interests of the West during the Cold War. Thus, for them, the terrorism of the New World Order would still be located in the foreign 'other,' mostly from Third World societies of color. Now state-sponsored terrorism was the work of 'rogue' states, namely Cuba, Iran, Iraq, Libya, Syria and North Korea. Over the course of the 1990s, the center of the international terrorist network remained on foreign territory, moving first from Moscow, to Baghdad and then after the Persian Gulf War to Teheran. In August 1998, President Bill Clinton announced that the network's headquarters was somewhere in the hinterland of Afghanistan, now under the complete control of former US-backed 'freedom fighter' Osama bin Laden.

Non-state terrorism is said to be multi-faceted and as always, is imaged with a foreign face. It includes newly 'orphaned' leftist groups, set adrift by the demise of their Soviet parent, who now search the political landscape for 'foster' parents to supply them with the materials of terrorism. Islamic terrorism and narco-terrorism both survived the end of the Cold War to threaten once again the Western world in general and the United States in particular. Islam continued to be portrayed as a monolithic menace, an image built upon historic stereotypes of 'Islamic militancy,' of an 'Islamic mentality,' of 'Islamic fundamentalism' or 'the Shi'a penchant for martyr-dom.' These historical stereotypes had already provoked the fervently hostile Western response to the 1979 Iranian hostage crisis. Commenting on the imagery of Islam in that crisis, Edward Said wrote:

> We were back to the old basics. Iranians were reduced to 'fundamentalist screwballs' by Bob Ingle in the *Atlanta Constitution*, Claire Sterling in the *Washington Post* argued that the Iran story was an aspect of 'Fright Decade I' while Bill Green on the same pages of the *Washington Post* wrote of the 'Iranian obscenity' aimed directly at the heart of American nationalism and self esteem.[16]

In the 1990s, the Persian Gulf War, the 1993 New York World Trade Center bombing, the Hamas–Hezbollah challenge to the US-sponsored Middle East peace process, and the terrorism tied to Osama bin Laden and his Al Qaeda colleagues all helped to sustain the anti-Islamic frenzy. The re-emergence of the 'Iranian threat' and the constant media and academic drumbeat warning of the more generalized 'Islamic menace' or a 'clash of civilizations' further fueled fear and hatred of this foreign and 'other' religion.[17]

Now in need of financial resources following the demise of the Soviet Union, the modern terrorists were alleged to be seeking to 'enjoy the huge profits of illegal activities' (that is, narco-terrorism).[18] Though the United States is the major drug market, narco-terrorism has foreign origins, either in the Islamic 'fundamentalist' regimes of Iran, Iraq and Libya or in the drug cartels operating in South America, Asia and the Middle East.

In August 1995, terrorism industry experts 'identified' an alleged new form of foreign-instigated terrorism plaguing North America and its "family of nations'.' In this 'decentralized' or 'ad hoc' model, '"specialist" guerrillas are only brought together to commit a specific act and then quickly disbanded and returned to their current country of refuge.'[19] Allegedly Moslem extremist groups including those who bombed the New York World Trade Center in 1993 were first to adopt the new *modus operandi*. Also, a new terrorist operational design having no clear patterns, associa-tions or traditional 'cell' structures as in past terrorist organizations was allegedly in place in Argentina, the UK, Egypt, France, Algeria and Israel.

In both its Cold War and post-Cold War constructs, the imagery of terrorism-at-a-distance advantages United States foreign policy makers and their 'counter terrorist' agenda in multiple ways. First, insisting that terrorism is the dastardly deed of foreigners reinforces the high moral opinion North Americans generally have of themselves, their society and their benevolent role in the world. In their eyes, since US foreign policy is on the firmest of moral ground and defensive in orientation, its foreign initiatives are to be supported with vigor if not righteous fervour. In this climate, the assessments of foreign policy analysts, particularly terrorism experts, are held in high esteem as they make 'moral' sense. Terrorism industry expert Brian Jenkins's distinction between 'moral bombing' and 'cowardly bombing' is typical of these 'moral truths.' For him, dropping US bombs on Iraqi cities at 20,000 feet or lobbing 16-inch shells into Druse and Shi'ite Lebanese towns from the battleship *New Jersey* for six months is moral behavior. On the other hand, the suicidal car bomb terrorist who killed 241 marines in Beirut is guilty of shameful cowardice.

Typical also was the climate of official and public moral outrage displayed in February 1996 when Cuba shot down two private planes belonging to Brothers to the Rescue, a Cuban-American anti-Castro organization. The group's planes had been violating Cuban airspace and dropping anti-communist leaflets over Havana for nearly a year. Yet for most North Americans, Cuba's status as a US-designated state sponsor of terrorism and the alleged innocence of the 'humanitarian' Brothers to the Rescue overrode Cuba's claims to national self-determination. In the end, thanks to Clinton Administration officials and media efforts, the crimes of the Brothers were sanitized. In turn, the tightened US embargo and United Nations censorship of Cuba were deemed appropriate political and moral responses to the 'terrorist' 'rogue' regime.

Second, the imagery of terrorism-at-a-distance reinforces North American ethnocentricity and jingoism. It feeds negative views of foreigners, the inferiority of their culture and the danger they pose to 'our way of life.' The construction of a heightened foreign threat to US citizens at home and abroad allows policy makers to pursue with the full approval of a majority of citizens means and measures that would otherwise be controversial. For example, the battle cry 'We need to hit them before they hit us' allowed the Reagan Administration's false rumors of Libyan 'hit squads' and a Libyan terror network to escape close public and media scrutiny. In 1986, the high-pitched rhetoric paid off. According to Gallop polls, the 14 April US bombing of Libyan cities garnered 77 per cent approval ratings. Eighty percent of North Americans surveyed wanted more strikes on Libya and 64 per cent approved bombing raids on Iran and Syria even though a vast majority doubted strikes would have any effect on curbing terrorism. Likewise, public opinion polls taken in the wake of the 1988 USS *Vincennes'* 'accidental' downing of Flight 655, an Iranian Airbus with 290 civilians on board, displayed little sympathy for the Iranian victims, and their families. Sixty-one percent were against compensating the victims' families. After all, they were citizens of a 'terrorist state'. Seventy-four percent in a *Washington Post*-ABC poll and 86 percent in a *Los Angeles Times* poll blamed Iran for the tragedy.[20]

After the 1993 New York World Trade Center bombing, the major media operated exclusively using the terrorism-at-a-distance thesis. In his *Time* piece 'Tower Terror,' Richard Lacayo wrote that the bombing 'raises the specter of terrorism in America' and that terrorism had 'seemed like something that happened somewhere else – and somewhere else a safe distance over the horizon.'[21] Cover stories in both *Time* and *Newsweek*, acknowledging they had no evidence, immediately fingered an array of foreign enemies. Bosnian combatants and Russian nationalists, along with the usual suspects – Muammar Kaddafi, Saddam Hussein, Ahmed Jabril, Abu Nidal, Hamas and the Palestinians – were charged with ending US innocence and 'raising the specter of terrorism in America – hitting us at home.'[22]

Even after the first Trade Center bombing, US citizens remained convinced terrorism would not recur in the United States. Gallop polling found only 12 percent of those surveyed admitted to a personal sense of danger from terrorist acts in their workplace or their home. This was down from 19 percent at the end of the 1991 Gulf War. In short, despite the foreign bombing on US soil, the terrorism-at-distance theme held a powerful place in the public psyche.

For Clinton Administration policy makers, the 1993 World Trade Center bombing provided ample opportunity for new counter-terrorist measures against foreigners, in particular those obstructing United States foreign policy goals. Acting on the assertion that 'grave acts of violence committed by foreign terrorists are disrupting the Middle East peace process,' President Clinton barred any US citizen from donating anything, including humanitarian aid, to twelve 'terrorist' (ten Palestinian and two Israeli) groups. In April 1996, a year after the Oklahoma City bombing, which terrorism industry experts had immediately projected as the work of Middle East terrorists, President Clinton focused the nation's attention on foreigners. Despite the domestic source of the Oklahoma City tragedy, he signed new counter-terrorism legislation permitting the deportation of aliens 'suspected' of terrorism. The legislation also authorized the President to designate any foreign group and its US branch as 'terrorist' with no court review of the designation allowed.[23] It was a harbinger of things to come in the hysteria that followed 9/11.

Finally, the imagery of distance permits US citizens to dissociate themselves from the atrocities perpetrated on foreign peoples in the name of counter-terrorism. It is not part of their immediate experience. It is happening 'over there' to terrorists and their sympathizers who, like the uncivilized peoples of the colonial past, only understand and respond to force. Thus the 'iron fist' of Israeli 'counter-terrorism' in southern Lebanon or the Occupied Territories, or US-sponsored 'counter-terrorism' violence in East Timor, Central America, Southern Africa and Iraq are justified as appropriate responses. In this highly charged climate, the brutality happens to 'those who deserve it', as Secretary of State Alexander Haig said after the murder of four Maryknoll nuns in El Salvador. A similar sentiment was implied in Secretary of State Madeleine Albright's emphatic 'yes!' when asked if the enormous civilian suffering and death that resulted from US-imposed economic sanctions and bombings of Iraq was worth it.

The silence of North Americans and the Western media – conditioned to equate Palestinians with terrorists – following the Israeli Baruch Goldstein's massacre of Muslims attending a mosque prayer service in 1984, reflects the same view. High public approval recorded in opinion polls after both the USS *Vincennes*–Iranian Airbus case and the brutal 1989 US invasion of Panama in which thousands of civilians were killed, confirms similar attitudes.

The Clinton Administration's missile attacks on Afghanistan and the Sudan in August 1998 were widely applauded though they killed many civilians, belatedly reported as numbering in the thousands.[24] In a pattern to be repeated in the bombing of Afghanistan after 9/11, those polled were divided as to whether the bombings would actually reduce terrorism against the United States. An ABC News poll indicated a bipartisan 80 percent approval of the strikes with 98 percent in support among those who thought the use of force would reduce terrorism. Among citizens who thought the strikes would increase terrorism, 68 percent still approved of the missile attacks. A USA Today/CNN/Gallup poll found a 76 percent approval for further missile attacks on Afghanistan and Sudan.

US public approval is high for US counter-terrorism even when it violates international law. Notable cases include the 1986 violation of Italian airspace to force down an airliner with suspected terrorists on board, the 1989 invasion of Panama, and the 1985 mining of Nicaraguan ports, all violations of other nations' territorial sovereignty. Public acquiescence accompanied the training of anti-Sandinista Contras in Florida and California though it violated US neutrality laws. Popular support is also apparent when counter-terrorism policy violates human decency. For example, in its counter-terrorist effort in Angola, the United States kept selling landmines to rightwing UNITA rebels in a war-ravaged country with the world's highest per capita rate of limb amputations among children. Politically expedient 'counter-terrorism' terrorism goes without public scrutiny let alone opposition. Obvious recent cases include US support for Pol Pot, the architect of Cambodia's 'killing fields,' and for Saddam Hussein's gassing of Iranian troops, and for the anti-Soviet efforts in support of Osama bin Laden and the Mujahadeen in Afghanistan.

Armed with their starkly polarized view of terrorism, for nearly three decades after the Munich Olympics the terrorism industry, in service to both Republican and Democrat administrations, monopolized the discourse on terrorism. As a result, on the eve of 9/11 their view of terrorism held a prominent and virtually unchallenged place in the Western psyche. For US citizens and their leaders, in particular, the construction of the terrorist as an enemy of the West made political and moral sense.[25] Following the triumph over communism, now only the terrorists and their sympathizers stood in the way. Well schooled in a self/other identity, they knew whom this new aggressor was, what they were up to and how to deal with them. For Western expert and layperson alike, the analytic refrains ring true. Terrorism is primarily the result of psychological infirmity. Terrorists are the uncivilized other from foreign lands and morally inferior cultures. Conversely, terrorism is not an instrument of the civilized self. Terrorists, like all historically designated 'others' of Western civilization, be they the 'savage Indian,' African slaves, colonized subjects or in more general terms 'the enemy,' only understand and respond to force. It is useless, indeed morally bankrupt to negotiate with them. Thus, only overwhelming military force works. It offers a quick fix to the disease of terrorism infecting the Western body politic. Similar to cancer in the human body, the prescription for ridding the world of terrorism is total annihilation. Like US Cold War counter-insurgency doctrine before it, if this counter-terrorism medicine kills a few good cells (civilians) as it wipes out the disease, well, that is an unfortunate but necessary part of the cure.

In short, in the decade prior to the 9/11 attacks, a vast majority of the US citizens and their political leadership had come to accept that success against foreign-inspired terrorism required an approach in which 'might makes right' and 'the end justifies the means' and a jingoist context of 'my country right or wrong.'[26] Certain of their moral bearings and well versed in the evils of terrorism as they were, what mattered most to them was that the US – that is, the civilized world's – 'way of life' be protected by keeping terrorism at a distance. During the 1990s, air power became the key instrument employed to do just that.

Strategic Bombing
in the 1990s

For the United States and its Western allies, the pushing of terrorism to the forefront of their political and policy agenda has brought political bounty but also a dilemma. On the one hand, rationalizing their foreign policy as 'counter-terrorism' has allowed them to confront their adversaries with righteous purpose and strong national and at times international backing. Yet they face the prospect that, with heightened awareness of terrorism, any military strategy and deed endangering or victimizing civilian life faces greater scrutiny and criticism than ever before. Launching bombs from on high or from hundreds of miles away, even on designated 'terrorist targets,' runs the risk of its victims and those who observe their fate accusing the bombing nations of terrorism. It also increases the potential that the countercharge of terrorism could gain credibility with millions of people looking to diminish their own vulnerability to terrorism, regardless of its source. Either way, the moral compass allegedly guiding the policies of the 'counter-terrorist' bombers becomes suspect. Potentially, the political usefulness of the 'counter-terrorist' posture could be diminished, if not rendered obsolete. Strategic terror also provokes the sentiment 'what is good for the goose, is good for the gander,' and with it a rise in the 'counter-terrorism' violence of others.

The Western nations' determination to fight modern wars with air power deepens this dilemma. This is especially true of the US civilian and military leadership who, in part due to the Vietnam experience, became cautious about another long and costly ground war. Thus, air power is the preferred offensive weapon. When applied 'appropriately' it allegedly produces a decisive 'clean' victory, meaning few 'friendly' force casualties and minimal or 'acceptable' numbers of enemy civilian victims. Of course, the US desire for few friendly casualties is assured when their bombs fall on Third World adversaries who have meager air defense capabilities. Yet, in spite of improved accuracy, the use of air power – either through traditional bombing or long-range missile strikes – has not produced a level of civilian casualties acceptable to all. Thus the dilemma facing the bombing nations remains.

In this delicate and potentially explosive climate, the old question remains: can air power alone win wars? The political setting in which this question is asked is different from that of the Cold War, yet somewhat the same. Unlike in the past, this question is now solely asked and answered by the self-anointed 'family of nations' who have made counter-terrorism their political *cause célèbre*. For the first time in the age of air power, with the addition of Russia and to some degree China, this family includes all nations with the ability to bomb with nuclear and conventional weapons. Because of their industrial/postindustrial status they have the luxury and means to think about and utilize air power in dramatic fashion and with Shock and Awe effect. But, the question 'can air power alone win wars?' is meaningful not just to those who bomb. Because of advances in the instruments of mass destruction, in a horrible sense it is more meaningful to those nations and peoples who are to be the guinea pigs in the search for an answer.

As in the past, the airpower strategists pondering this question see themselves first and foremost as warriors for their nation and as power brokers in a postwar world order. In the emerging context of a global economy, they seek to use air power to build and/or destroy other nations. Situated against their agenda are Third World citizens and their racial, class and gendered nationalisms, the components of which reflect both new and historical antagonisms.[1]

These new nationalisms pose a threat to the 'family of nations' who remain committed to the Western concept of nation state and its patriarchal, secular and capitalist traditions. In their view, other constructs, notably an 'Islamic' or 'atheist' nation state, or one built on non-liberal notions of gender, class or racial equality, are not just inappropriate but politically and morally bankrupt. In the post-Cold War context, taken together they become another aspect of 'other' and thus the enemy. For the 'family of nations' and their warrior classes, the goal is to sustain their prominent place in the globalization process while destroying or crippling the nations or national aspirations of these new/old enemies. As in centuries past, the point is to build another New World Order set in 'civilized' Western political, economic, social and cultural traditions.

It was for these purposes that the bombing nations used air power during the 1990s in the Persian Gulf War, Chechnya and Kosovo-Serbia. The strategic bombing occurred within a highly charged moral context in which the bombing nations donned the mantle of counter-terrorists. Yet in all of these conflicts, strategic bombing killed thousands of civilians, wounded thousands upon thousands more and made an even larger number homeless, propertyless, familyless or victims in some other way.

In order not to blow their 'counter-terrorism cover', the bombing nations have had to create intellectual distance between themselves and orthodox strategy bombing doctrine. Throughout the twentieth century, directly targeting civilians was generally conceived as the essence of terrorism. This was true even for those, such as the Prophets Douhet and Trenchard, for whom bombing civilians was morally appropriate and superior military strategy. In the current moral and political context in which terrorism is portrayed as the most evil of acts, to propose orthodox strategic bombing is political suicide. Acutely aware of this politically hazardous climate, over the 1990s the bombers recast their strategic bombing doctrine and trumpeted the technology of their new precision weapons. Their initial attempt at this strategy came during the 1990–91 Persian Gulf War.

THE PERSIAN GULF WAR: PLANNING THE AIR ATTACK

On 2 August 1990, Iraqi troops crossed into Kuwait, quickly subdued Kuwaiti military forces and occupied strategic sites throughout the country. The USA immediately took the leading diplomatic and military role in opposing the invasion. Within hours, the George Bush Administration pushed Resolution 660 through the UN Security Council. It condemned the invasion and demanded the withdrawal of Iraqi forces. At the Pentagon, a war plan developed in late 1989 and early 1990 under the direction of General Colin Powell, Chairman of the JCS, came under review. It had two goals, to attack a belligerent Iraq and to ensure the flow of oil to the industrial nations.[2]

From the outset, strategic air power emerged as a central component of the military plan. This was extremely important to the US Air Force. The US Army's operational war concept, AirLand Battle, adopted as official military doctrine in 1982, had limited the role of the air force to interdiction and support of army ground forces.

General Norman Schwarzkopf, the head of US Central Command, wanted to attack what he called 'strategic' targets. On 8 August 1990, he brought to his command Colonel John A. Warden III. Warden was a disciple of Douhet, Hart and LeMay, and his stated goal was 'to bring the Air Force back into prominence. To bring it back into prominence we have got to develop the concepts that will work in the real world, and we want to win wars for our country.'[3] He had previously been head of the Pentagon's Deputy Directorate for Warfighting Concepts and then director of Checkmate, a Pentagon air strategy think tank. Throughout his assignments, Warden pushed his 'centers of gravity' strategic doctrine first articulated in his *The Air Campaign: planning for combat.*[4]

Like Douhet, Warden argues that offensive air power concentrates greater force on an enemy and causes fewer casualties than ground combat. He also subscribes to Hart's Achilles' heel concept, though he doesn't suggest bombing civilian targets directly, at least not initially. ACTS doctrine is at the heart of Warden's theory of concentric circles. In both scenarios, air power is the decisive and offensive instrument for winning wars. Indeed, in Warden's opinion, the Linebacker Two Christmas bombing had been the decisive factor that finally forced the North Vietnamese to seek peace. Both strategic doctrines target the will and capacity of the enemy to prosecute war and both view the enemy as a system. For ACTS, the system has vital links that if destroyed will bring quick victory. Warden views the system as a human body. It consists of a brain (core leaders), a need for 'organic essentials' (fuel, food and ammunition), a skeletal-muscular infrastructure (roads, communication lines, air-sea-rail routes, pipelines and roads), a population of cells (support personnel and civilians), and a self-protection mechanism (military forces). Arranged into five concentric rings, each dependent on the inner ones, Warden argues that the 'brain' controls the entire system. Borrowing from Liddell Hart's close associate the British theorist J. F. C. Fuller, Warden asserts that killing (decapitating) the core leaders directly or cutting off their ability to communicate with the other circles would result in the collapse of the entire system.[5] As with the ACTS industrial web, strategic bombing is used to incapacitate the enemy. In Warden's scheme, the air force's task is either to kill the core leadership directly or to target the system's other rings in order to cut 'the brain' off from the general population and military forces. Allegedly, either bombing scheme will produce a win.

Warden's immediate superior, General Jimmy Adams, thought his 'theorizing was radical.' But with Schwarzkopf's support, Warden offered his concentric circles option under the name Instant Thunder. In early September, Warden's plan was renamed CENTAF Offensive Campaign – Phase One, and his concentric circles terminology was dropped in favor of 'strategic target sets.' The air campaign's strategic goals were announced as: a change in the political regime, hopefully via decapitation of its leaders, elimination of Iraq's strategic military capability, including short- and long-range missiles and nuclear, chemical and biological programs, and the disruption of its economy while leaving the oil sector intact. In addition, air power was to reduce the capacity of Iraqi military forces, particularly the elite Republican Guard, to resist a US-led ground assault or to threaten its neighbors after the war. Specific aerial assault targets were laid out as follows:

- Leadership: the Saddam regime, telecommunications and military and civil command, control and communications;
- Key Production: electricity, oil (internal distribution and storage, not production), nuclear, chemical and biological research facilities, and military research production and storage;
- Infrastructure: railroads;
- Population: psychological operations directed at Iraqis, foreign workers and soldiers in Kuwait;
- Fielded force: strategic air defense and strategic offensive forces (missiles, bombers).[6]

Consistent with ACTS doctrine, the Warden plan for Iraq did not envision directly bombing the civilian population. Rather it intended to utilize psychological operations (Psyops) in order to lower civilian morale and undermine support for Saddam Hussein's government. The planners were well aware that the issue of terrorism held a pre-eminent place in global discourse. They were concerned the strategic bombing would result in enough civilian deaths to provoke accusations of United States aerial terrorism. According to Richard Davis, as the plan developed, great care was taken to 'minimize' civilian casualties and collateral damage as 'its destruction, even on a minor percentage basis, contradicted US policy and would produce worldwide ill will.'[7] It also would undermine the effort to separate the civilians from the government. Like bombers of the past, Warden wanted the Iraqi people to think of the North Americans 'as liberators, not conquerors.'[8] To accomplish this Psyops goal, Phase One bombing would concentrate on Iraqi media facilities. Once destroyed, the desired imagery and political message of the 'liberators' would monopolize Iraqi airwaves.

In classic strategic bombing fashion, the plan also targeted Iraq's economic infrastructure with the expectation that its destruction would lead to public disenchantment with the regime. Also in play was the assumption that, like all Third World leaders, Saddam was protective of his meager industrial base. Indeed, in an effort to counter a Rand report that viewed ground war as necessary for victory, Warden asserted that Saddam Hussein greatly valued his industrial economy. Warden believed the air campaign would force Hussein into the 'rational' choice of capitulation in order to save any remaining industry.

Overall, as conceived in the Fall of 1990, the war plan was to 'shock' the Iraqi nation with an air–land strategic attack on 238 sites in all five concentric circles. New precision weapons, developed since Vietnam, could allegedly hit all strategic target sets while minimizing 'collateral damage.' Warden and the strategic air war planners believed that their bombing strategy, especially the innovation of targeting the 'brain' and its 'organic essentials,' would bring complete victory and the removal of Saddam Hussein. Warden predicted that the Phase One air campaign 'would isolate and incapacitate the regime and create the conditions under which Saddam's departure from power would be more likely.'[9]

THE 'HYPERWAR'

The bombing campaign began in the middle of the night on 17 January 1991 and lasted for almost six weeks. As planned, the initial phase of the eventual 11,160 'surgical strikes' was, according to General Merrill McPeak, a 'very heavy attack, very precisely delivered.'[10] Early hits on Scud and SAM missiles sites and military airfields established air superiority. All strategic target sets reportedly hit their intended targets. Heavy damage or destruction was inflicted on the 'brain,' notably Saddam Hussein's presidential headquarters, government and Baath Party buildings and Iraqi 'communication command and control.' The key economic infrastructure suffered as well. Around-the-clock bombing hit bridges, electric power grids, water supplies, oil distribution and storage facilities and tankers, sanitation centers, railroads, dams, military and civilian airfields, and suspected nuclear, biological and chemical research and production centers.

The Allied military and civilian commands asserted the bombing objectives were reached while taking great care not to injure the civilian populations in the Kuwaiti Theater of Operations, specifically Baghdad and Kuwait City. This 'robo' or 'techno' war, as Western media and

Pentagon officials quickly labeled it, was declared highly effective and moral since it ended quickly and, it was claimed, with minimal destruction to material and human life.[11] Shortly after the Persian Gulf conflict ended, US Air Force commanders coined the term 'hyperwar' to describe their military operations. In May 1991, a triumphant Warden gave specific meaning to the concept, defining hyperwar as 'one that capitalizes on high technology, unprecedented accuracy, operational and strategic surprise through stealth, and the ability to bring all of an enemy's key operational and strategic nodes under near-simultaneous attack.'[12]

HYPERWAR: ASSESSING THE CARNAGE

According to the Geneva Protocol of 1977, specifically under Chapter III, Articles 52, 53, 54 and 55, war is not to be prosecuted against civilians, civilian infrastructure or the environment.[13] In a briefing on 27 January 1991, General Norman Schwarzkopf assured his audience: 'We're being very, very careful in our directions of attacks to avoid damage of any kind to civilian installations.'[14] The Schwarzkopf statement, when compared with the Geneva Protocols, would appear to confirm United States' compliance with the prohibitions against bombing civilian objects. Yet, by their own admission, the architects of the air campaign both planned to attack the civilian economic infrastructure (defining it as a military target) and did so with intent and knowledge of the devastating short- and long-term effects on civilian life. Even General Schwarzkopf, in his effort to demonstrate bombing restraint and the Allied Command's good intentions not to destroy '100 percent of all the Iraqi electrical power ... making sure civilians do not suffer unduly,' inadvertently acknowledged that material damage and civilian suffering was intentional and acute.[15] His military command readily spoke of their desire to conduct bombing that 'resulted in turning out the lights in Baghdad.' But, as Diane T. Putney, a historian working for the Pentagon, notes, such bombing has far-reaching effects on civilian life. She reluctantly concludes: 'Shutting down electric power plants shut down water purification and sewage treatment facilities, causing disease levels to rise, especially among infants and children.'[16] In fact, the Defense Intelligence Agency accurately predicted increased levels of disease due to the bombing of Iraq's economic infrastructure.[17] In short, the US purposefully bombed infrastructure required for water sanitation and purification systems knowing that this would cause massive suffering for years to come. It was, charge critics such as Dr Jack Geiger of Physicians for Human Rights, an intentional 'bomb now, die later' policy.

Francis Boyle, a professor of International Law and a member of the Commission of Inquiry into US war crimes during the Persian Gulf War, asserts that the strategic bombing violated the Geneva Accords Governing Civilian Objects in a wholesale and purposeful manner.

> Most of the targets were civilian facilities. The United States intentionally bombed and destroyed centers of civilian life, commercial and business districts, schools, hospitals, mosques, churches, shelters, residential areas, historical sites, private vehicles and civilian government offices. In aerial attacks, including strafing over cities, towns, the countryside and highways, the United States aircraft bombed and strafed indiscriminately. The purpose of these attacks was to destroy life and property, and generally to terrorize the civilian population of Iraq.[18]

Boyle also claims that the intentional attack on the leadership 'brain,' in this case Saddam Hussein, with 'superbombs' was 'a war crime in its own right.'[19]

UN observers concurred. Reporting in March 1991 on the devastation, they labelled damage to civilian infrastructure as 'near apocalyptic': the bombs destroyed fifty years of development and sent Iraq back into a 'pre-industrial age.'[20] Early UN estimates reported 9,000 homes destroyed and 72,000 Iraqis left homeless. Patrick Cockburn, a journalist who witnessed the initial bombing, says Baghdad's residents were in a 'collective state of shock.' Describing the effects on civilian life after one day of bombing shut down Baghdad's electricity, he says there quickly arose 'a penetrating stench which hung over entire districts' from stockpiles of previously frozen, now rotting meat. Air attacks on Iraq's oil storage and distribution systems created a crippling 'petrol famine' and 'thieves' market' throughout the country.'[21]

According to Nora Boustany of the *Washington Post Foreign Service*, four days of aerial attacks produced refugees fleeing to Jordan with reports of civilian casualties, residential areas in Baghdad and Mosu hit by 'terror' bombs, and cars full of coffins in Basra.[22] By April, the number of war-related refugees in camps on the hostile Iran/Iraq and Turkey/Iraq borders was put at 1.8 million, mostly women and children. Dr Betty Smith of Physicians for Global Survival reported estimates of 1,000 refugees dying each day in the camps.[23]

Other events and accounts contradict the alleged 'surgical' and 'precise' nature of the Persian Gulf hyperwar. Testimony from the initial bombing crews describes Baghdad after one hour of bombing as a city on fire and neighborhoods 'lit up like a Christmas tree.' From his post on the ground, Patrick Cockburn verified this assessment. Among the few journalists who remained in Baghdad during the weeks of bombing, he detailed the 'collapse of civil life' severely affecting the Iraqis who 'being too poor to leave' remained in Baghdad.[24]

The sheer amount of bombs dropped and the high percentage of conventional 'dumb' bombs released from high altitude together severely undercut the precision bombing claim. In turn, they lend credence to those suggesting there was large-scale and indiscriminate destruction of both civilian and military targets. Much of the supporting data actually comes from the US military. For example, General McPeak estimated that 88,500 tons of explosives were dropped over six weeks which, if sustained, averages out to 58,000 tons per month. In comparison, the average monthly total in Vietnam was 34,000 tons and 22,000 tons for Korea, although over a much longer period.

In all, an estimated 250,000 bombs were dropped on Iraq and Kuwait, with over 3,000 bombs targeted on 'metropolitan' Baghdad alone. The Pentagon calculated that conventional 'dumb' bombs, with an estimated 25 percent accuracy rate, made up 93.6 percent of the total amount. The Mk 82 (500 pounds), Mk 83 (1,000 pounds) and Mk 84 (2,000 pounds) were the favorites among the 'dumb' bombs. Paul Walker and Eric Stambler, while noting that precision weapons were used mostly against 'hard' targets, say 'the strikes against ground troops, armored formations, widespread defenses, and other large targets, many located in civilian areas, were undertaken with less discriminating weapons.'[25] According to Aviation Week & Space Technology, thirty-two F-16 jets, loaded with unguided general-purpose bombs, hit a nuclear research facility located on the outskirts of Baghdad.[26] It was Pentagon officials who offered the estimate that 70 percent of the total bombs dropped missed their targets.

In bombing nuclear and chemical facilities, Pentagon officials also readily admitted they expected contamination of the surrounding urban areas. Evidence of contamination, they predicted, would confirm Iraq had nuclear and chemical programs. Some targets designated as military turned out to have only civilian commercial functions. For example, air attacks struck two reactors that produced medically related isotopes and destroyed Iraq's sole baby formula factory. Though the attacks stirred immediate controversy, only after the war did the Pentagon admit to any targeting mistakes.

Massive amounts of firebombs, including Fuel Air Explosives that destroy anything within an area of 50,000 square feet, were used. The arsenal included the BLU-82 'Daisy Cutter' containing the chemical GSX (gelled slurry explosive). Because it does not create a crater, it was used in Vietnam to clear helicopter landing zones. As a concussion bomb, the BLU-82 can destroy human internal organs. Its firestorm incinerates as it sucks the oxygen out of the air, causing human asphyxiation. In Iraq, military officials said it was used more for its 'psychological effect' than its explosive impact. Other anti-personnel weapons such as the by-now infamous napalm and new, more lethal cluster bombs were also dropped. The new cluster bombs, such as the BLU-26, are filled with Sadeye, a cast steel shell with TNT and 600 razor-sharp steel shards imbedded in it. The CBU-75 disperses its deadly Sadeye contents over an area 800 feet in diameter, equal to 157 football fields.

Over the course of the air war, the Pentagon announced its intent to 'kill', 'destroy', 'annihilate' or 'attrit' (attrition) all Iraqi forces. Though prohibited in Article 51 of Geneva Protocol One, in pursuit of the Pentagon's goal 'area' or 'carpet bombing' became routine, particularly in southern Iraq and Kuwait. B-52 bombers sent 'dumb' explosives from altitudes of 40,000 feet on US Air Force-defined 'low-density targets.' In this bombing scheme, everything is designated military. In Kuwait, the practice resulted in the indiscriminate destruction of military and civilian human life and material along the infamous Highway of Death. In the strategic bombing of Basra, Iraq's second-largest city, of 800,000 people, there was no pretense of surgical strikes. According to Brigadier General Richard Neal, 'Basra is a military town in the true sense ... the infrastructure, military infrastructure is closely interwoven within the city of Basra itself.'[27] With General Neal's declaration that there were 'no civilians left in Basra,' the Air Force could treat Basra as a 'free fire zone.' The aerial bombing commenced, resulting in massive loss of life and complete devastation.[28]

TERRORIZING THE ENVIRONMENT

1. Care shall be taken in warfare to protect the natural environment against widespread, long-term and severe damage. This protection includes a prohibition of the use of methods or means of warfare that are intended or may be expected to cause such damage to the natural environment and thereby to prejudice the health or survival of the population.

2. Attacks against the natural environment by way of reprisals are prohibited.[29]

The Geneva Convention 1977
Article 55: Protection of the Natural Environment

As the world's major oil production location, the Middle East, in particular the Persian Gulf area, is extremely vulnerable to short- and long-term environmental damage. In the course of production, oil wells, storage depots, refineries, pipelines and tankers are susceptible to leaks, spills, fires and explosions that can and do adversely affect human, animal and plant life. As the Persian Gulf War approached, the Bush Administration predicted that Saddam Hussein, in violation of Article 55 of the Geneva Protocol, would live up to his threat to create and light a 'sea of oil.' Bush officials warned that an environmental holocaust would ensue if the Iraqi leader set the oilfields of Kuwait ablaze or dumped oil into the Persian Gulf.

Saddam Hussein did follow through on his threats, although not to the extent the Bush Administration had forecast. It is also clear from its planning and actual bombing campaign that the US also purposely attacked and either destroyed or damaged oil refineries, tankers and depots. In Warden's concentric circles air plan, oil distribution and storage facilities were designated as 'key production' sites vital to Iraq's internal economy. They were to be destroyed while leaving the oil production sites (wells) untouched. True to the plan, over the six weeks of strategic air war, 540 aerial strikes were made on oil targets. A week into the air campaign, British authorities announced that Iraq had lost 50 percent of its refining capacity as a result of bombing.

The bombing of oilfields, tankers and installations created huge oil fires. According to Navy Lt. Commander Mark Jensen, the fires 'made the Louisiana oil fire look small.'[30] Oil spills and slicks resulting from the purposeful bombing of oil tankers caught birds and other animal life in their sticky goo. In one case, a British submarine hiding underneath a targeted tanker was damaged. General Schwarzkopf openly admitted that tankers were bombed. He also made clear he was prepared to hit an oil terminal again if necessary to stop the flow of oil that was already creating a huge slick. Napalm was dropped on oil-filled trenches, setting the oilfields ablaze and covering the region with black smoke. Bombing of chemical plants created mushroom clouds spoiling the air with chemicals. Independent eyewitnesses held both Iraq and the US-led forces responsible for the environmental carnage. Yet Western media reports and government statements charged only the Iraqis with being 'environmental terrorists.'[31]

COUNTING THE HYPERWAR DEAD

Article 51 of the Geneva Protocol 1977 lays out the protections due against attacks on civilians during the course of war. In part it says:

1. The civilian population and individual civilians shall enjoy general protection against dangers arising from military operations.
   To give effect to this protection, the following rules, which are additional to other applicable rules of international law, shall be observed in all circumstances.
2. The civilian population as such, as well as individual civilians, shall not be the object of attack. Acts or threats of violence the primary purpose of which is to spread terror among the civilian population are prohibited.
3. Civilians shall enjoy the protection afforded by this Section, unless and for such time as they take a direct part in hostilities.
4. Indiscriminate attacks are prohibited.[32]

The question of civilian casualties goes to the heart of the terrorism issue. In the Persian Gulf War, their number was hotly contested. For its part, the US refused to count civilian casualties. As Defense Secretary Richard Cheney explained, 'we have no way of knowing precisely how many casualties occurred.'[33] When asked to release film of bombs that missed their target, Cheney refused, saying the video would be 'pretty dull, boring stuff.' Meanwhile, his Pentagon officials were busy counting Iraqi military losses. General Schwarzkopf, in a press briefing at the end of the war, estimated Iraq had lost 100,000 military personnel in the fighting. Since then the Pentagon has determined that 25,000–30,000 Iraqi military losses is a more realistic figure. As well, throughout the conflict the Pentagon reported precise figures on Iraqi tank, truck and artillery losses. Though it could not or would not count Iraqi civilian casualties, the Pentagon could tally the civilian dead and wounded in the wake of Iraq's Scud missile attacks on Israel and Saudi Arabia, both US allies.

It can be difficult to get a precise count of civilian casualties. The same is true of enemy military deaths. Yet, the US did not hesitate to announce enemy casualties, especially if the numbers reinforced the desired political image of an effective military campaign. In contrast, to this day the US government has neither produced nor shown any intention of producing a count of Iraqi civilian casualties during the air campaign in the Kuwait Theater.

Various other groups, governments and individuals have offered data on civilian deaths. A brief sampling gives evidence of the wide range and the political stakes involved. Two researchers, John Heidenrich and Dr John Mueller, working independently of each other, concluded that about 1,000 civilians died as a direct result of the air campaign. Higher civilian casualty numbers come from *Human Rights Watch* (2,000–3000), Dr Beth Daponte, an analyst for the US Census Bureau (3,500), *PeaceAware Factsheet* (5,000), Greenpeace (5,000–15,000), the Iraq government (8,000), the International Commission of Inquiry (25,000) and the Jordan Red Crescent Society (113,000). Because of the intentional and direct attacks on Iraq's economic infrastructure, some researchers, most notably Dr Daponte, argue it is appropriate, indeed imperative, to include in the estimates deaths indirectly caused by bombing. By her calculations, 'there were 111,000 "excess deaths" in 1991 – due to disruptions in Iraqi society and economy.'[34] From her data, Daponte estimates that 70,000 children under fifteen years of age were among the air campaign's 'indirect' dead.

Despite its adamant lack of interest in counting civilian casualties, the Pentagon has been keenly aware of the calculations of others. When pushed, Pentagon officials fully embraced the low estimates as evidence of their success in minimizing 'collateral damage.' The Pentagon vigorously dismissed the higher estimates, particularly those including 'indirect casualties' resulting from bombing the economic infrastructure. In Dr Daponte's case, the Pentagon and White House purposely punished her for contradicting their official statements. Her report, authorized by the Census Bureau, came shortly after Cheney's claim that it was impossible to count civilian casualties accurately. Dr Daponte was dismissed from her job days later and charged with 'falsifying data.' She filed a legal suit and won. Meanwhile, Daponte's methodology and findings remain highly credible among demographers and those with no political stake in managing the terrorism issue in their favor. According to David Prochaska, although 'Total Iraqi dead will never be known with any precision, most current estimates range between 100,000 and 200,000, with many commentators leaning toward the higher rather than [the] lower figure.'[35]

PLAYING THE TERRORISM CARD

In the Persian Gulf War, both Saddam Hussein and President George Bush focused attention on the terrorism of the other side to rationalize their policy and provide a moral edge to their cause. Saddam Hussein made clear he would resort to terrorism as a counterweight to the overwhelming military might and terrorism of the US-led forces. With bombs dropping on Iraqi civilians, he pledged to bring the war home to nations attacking his people. As he hit Israeli and Saudi Arabian cities with Scud missiles and poured millions of barrels of oil into Persian Gulf waters, he sought the moral high ground, urging all Muslims to wage a 'holy war' on his terrorist enemies.

The Bush Administration leveled the terrorism charge at Saddam and his forces early and often. Confident they had the full attention of a Western audience well versed in the Western 'ideology of terrorism,' they effectively turned 'Hitler-like' Saddam's threat to use terrorism against him. In doing so, they sustained their own high moral standing and began constructing the post-Cold War face of terrorism.

By the end of August 1990, terrorism industry expert Bruce Hoffman had reported that Baghdad had replaced Moscow as the center of an international terrorist network. The Bush Administration added detail to this claim, asserting the infamous terrorist Abu Nidal had reopened his Baghdad office. Saddam, they claimed, was preparing to reactivate dormant Baathist 'terrorist' cells and 'freelance' terrorists throughout the Middle East to carry out his evil plans. Some Western media reported that the long-vanished Carlos the Jackal was now working as an agent of Saddam's terrorism.[36]

In January 1991, following reports of a huge oil spill, President Bush attempted to counter growing evidence that Allied bombing was in part responsible for the impending 'environmental holocaust' by accusing Saddam of being an environmental terrorist. Bush characterized the oil spill and oil field fires as 'sick' and the 'totally irrational' deeds of the Iraqi leader. On 29 January 1991, with US bombs blasting Iraqi cities, President Bush used his State of the Union speech to remind his Western audience of who the terrorist was. Decrying Saddam's terrorist attacks on Israel and Saudi Arabia and his environmental terrorism, Bush took the high moral ground, asserting: 'our cause is just, our cause is moral, our cause is right.'[37] These accusations made during the course of the war were intended to support the Bush Administration's new portrait of Saddam as an 'international terrorist.' In fact, by March 1991, Iraq was officially back on the State Department's list of states supporting terrorism.[38] In contrast, they asserted, the US was conducting a 'clean' counter-terrorist war. For example, General Colin Powell, who often hailed the precision of the US-led coalition weaponry, saw no such capability in Iraq's Scud missiles. To him they were highly inaccurate 'weapons of terror.'[39]

The major media never questioned Pentagon assurances that it was conducting an accurate bombing campaign with no negative environmental impact, despite their full knowledge that the Pentagon was bombing biological, chemical, oil and nuclear facilities. Instead, they consistently broadcast the Bush Administration's claim that the Allies were at war with an Iraqi terrorist who was prepared to launch a global environmental disaster. Later, when independent sources verified that Allied bombing was the major cause of the oil spills and oil fires, the charge of Iraqi 'environmental terrorism' disappeared from Pentagon briefings – and from media discourse. By the end of the war, fearful satellite images would confirm their bombing's disastrous effect on the region's ecology, the Bush Administration ordered its officials not to disclose any information on the environmental damage. With the exception of news about the benevolent role of private contractors in cleaning up the 'Iraqi-induced' disaster, Western corporate media complied with the government censorship.

In the end, the Bush Administration and its military–media complex effectively used its monopoly on terrorism discourse to mobilize large numbers of people and a compliant 'independent' media in favor of their counter-terrorism war and their sanitized view of it. Particularly powerful was the imagery of Iraq's environmental terrorism, poignantly displaying pictures of dead birds and oil-soaked beaches. Douglas Kellner suggests that these particular images and the terrorism charges accompanying them, mined even greater political gold than usual. He notes, 'the powerful images of environmental terrorism intensified hatred of Saddam Hussein and demoralized the peace movement, many of whose members were strong environmentalists.'[40]

RACE, CLASS AND GENDER IN THE NEW TERRORISM

The new face of terrorism proved critical to leaders of the 'family of nations' as they went about molding the New World Order in their image and in service to their interests. In the Persian Gulf War, race, class and gender biases helped demonize the Iraqi terrorist-at-a-distance, his constituency and his culture, just as they soothed the bombers' consciences.[41] Although an emerging social awareness (denigrated by political conservatives as 'political correctness') challenged their accuracy, all the historical stereotypes of Islam, Arabs and the 'Arab mind' were on display in 'learned' academia, popular culture and media discourse.[42] All Muslims and Arabs were assumed to be either terrorists or associated with terrorists, with the adjectives 'heartless' and 'sneaky' attached to them for good measure. For Islamophobes and Arabophobes, found in all walks of Western society, the regrettable but unavoidable collateral damage of the air war were racially inferior 'rag-heads' 'towel-heads' 'camel jockeys' 'sand-niggers' or 'maggot-infested women' whose lives didn't really matter much.

This general assault on the 'uncivilized' Islamic and Arab world was also reflected in the military culture. For example, General Norman Schwarz-kopf could, with impunity, publicly characterize Iraqis who allegedly had committed atrocities as 'not part of the same human race.' The mentality in which foot soldiers were schooled to conduct war on Iraqi civilians is revealed in military bootcamp training chants such as this one:

> Rape the town and kill the people.
> That's the thing we love to do.
> Throw some napalm on the schoolhouse.
> Watch the kiddies scream and shout.
> Rape the town and kill the people.
> That's the thing we love to do.[43]

Racist and sexual degradation of the Iraqi enemy seemed particularly important to Air Force personnel. Though they rarely saw their victims, pilots drew images of those they were bombing. Racist graffiti such as the 'giant banner of a US "Superman" holding a limp and terrified Arab with a big hooked nose in his arms,' found in an Air Force hanger, and T-shirts depicting planes 'smoking' an Arab on a camel are but two examples among many.[44] To pilots, the Iraqi civilians who scrambled for cover to avoid the 'justice' screaming from the sky were 'cockroaches.' Graffiti on the bombs identified them as 'Mrs Saddam's sex toy,' 'a suppository for Saddam' and a 'Ramadan present.'

The most common idea expressed in US military culture required Iraqis in general and Saddam in particular 'to bend over' when confronted with superior firepower. This sexually explicit theme found its way into Western newspaper cartoons in which praying Muslims were depicted with missiles projecting from their anuses.[45] Conversely, pilots were encouraged to watch pornographic films in case they weren't in the 'proper frame of mind' before their bombing runs over Baghdad. A songbook produced in the late 1980s by the 77th Tactical Fighter Squadron made the rounds, graphically describing the point of bombing the Islamic other:

> Phantom flyers in the sky,
> Persian-pukes prepare to die,
> Rolling in with snake and nape,
> Allah creates but we cremate.[46]

These few verses are only the tip of the racist and sexist iceberg. In his summary of the content of the songbook and the purposes behind the US military's racist and sexual degradation of Islam, Yusuf Progler writes:

> Other lyrics are too disgusting to mention, with verses about raping prostitutes and a host of other violent obscenities. Imagine the brave American servicemen singing such songs, 'just for a few laughs,' perhaps after loading up on burgers and booze at the end of a day's killing. Sex and violence inform the American war effort in many ways. ... This links up the necessity to denigrate the enemy with the necessity to denigrate women, another long-held American tradition.[47]

Thanks to air power, the devastation visited upon the Iraqi society was done with little loss of Western life. Meanwhile, the Bush Administration's domination of Western media coverage and global diplomatic discourse rendered any eyewitness reports contradicting the alleged minimal effect on Iraqi civilian life, virtually invisible. Meanwhile, the gendered, racist and 'terrorist' stereotyping of the enemy played so well in Western popular culture that anti-war critics were promptly dismissed with the customary wartime sentiment that enemy civilians were 'deserving of what they got.'

As a result of the 'nerve and resolve' displayed in the Persian Gulf War, top US civilian and military authorities, cheered on by a militarized media and a 'yellow-ribboned' populace, proclaimed the Vietnam Syndrome over. Now, they looked to future hyperwars in which Western technology, in particular air power, aggressively but 'cleanly' applied against agents of terrorism-at-a-distance, would enforce a moral and political order based on Western principles. Within the US military, no one was more enthusiastic about this prospect than the Air Force. Once again, the question 'can air power alone win wars?' was at the forefront of their strategic agenda. Further counter-terrorism forays against the new face of terrorism promised to keep it there.

BOMBING THE TERRORISTS OF THE NEW WORLD ORDER

The Persian Gulf War ended in 1991, but Western bombing of Iraq continued for over a decade. In the longest bombing campaign since Vietnam, British and US jets pounded 'military targets' on a near-daily basis to enforce their self-imposed no-fly zones in northern and southern Iraq. The Pentagon defended the more than 280,000 'protective retaliation' strikes on 60 percent of Iraq as necessary to prevent Saddam Hussein's regime from massacring Kurdish and Shi'ite minorities. As the 'invisible or for-gotten war' continued, charges that Iraqi civilians were bearing the brunt of the strikes multiplied. According to Iraqi officials, a total of 1,400 civil-ians died in a decade of Allied 'state terrorism' bombing. In five months between December 1998 and May 1999, 41 percent of the victims were reported to be civilians.[48] The UN counted over 300 civilian bombing deaths between 1998 and December 2002. In his 'Air Strike Reports' to the UN Security Council, Hans von Sponeck, Coordinator of the UN Humanitarian Program from 1998 to 2000, recorded in 1999 alone that 132 attacks caused 120 dead and 442 wounded Iraqi civilians.[49] British and US officials countered that the collateral damage or 'unintended' civilian bombing victims resulted from Saddam Hussein moving civilians close to military targets. Yet in the northern Iraq no-fly zone, US officials allowed NATO ally Turkey to carpet-bomb Kurdish towns and villages as part of its campaign against the Kurds. US pilots reported seeing 'burning villages, lots of smoke and fire' after the 'Turkish Special Missions.'[50]

ISRAELI AND RUSSIAN STRATEGIC BOMBING

During the 1990s, Israel and Russia, two upstanding members of the 'family of nations,' purposely bombed civilians and civilian infrastructure in their self-proclaimed counter-terrorist ventures.

Israel used its control of the skies over Lebanon to produce, as Israeli diplomat Abba Eban said, the 'rational prospect' that punishing the civilian population would force the government to concede to Israeli demands.[51] In 1993, under Operation Accountability, Israeli planes and rockets blasted towns and villages in southern Lebanon. Israeli officials said the purposes of the bombing were 'eradicating the threat posed by Hezbollah ... and to disrupt civilian life and force the population to flee north.'[52]

In 1996, in Operation Grapes of Wrath, Israeli jets hit Lebanon again, this time to ravage civilian life in Beirut. The bombing knocked out the electrical grid, plunging the city into darkness. Israeli jets, naval weapons and helicopter gunships struck at more civilian targets, including, water reservoirs, villages, towns and UN's refugee camps in southern Lebanon. Israeli leaders justified the bombing of civilian targets as a response to Hezbollah's rocket bombardment of Israeli civilians across the border and the need to establish a security zone in southern Lebanon. Israeli bombs killed 152 civilians, with 102 dying at the UN refugee camp at Qana alone. According to Reuters news agency, Israel initiated the civilian bombing in clear violation of the 1993 peace agreement requiring both sides to target only military sites. Over 400,000 people became refugees as a result of the effort to force them out of the 'security zone.' Even the conservative *Economist* magazine castigated the Israeli strategy as 'over the top' and 'two eyes for one.'[53]

In the ceasefire agreement, Israel agreed to stop all attacks on civilian targets and electrical power. Yet, on 25 June 1999, Israeli bombers launched a ten-hour aerial assault on Lebanon's civilian infrastructure. Targets included roads, bridges, telephone relay stations and the electrical power network. As in 1996, the attacks did great damage to Beirut's energy power supply and an economy that like Israel's is highly dependent on a flourishing tourist trade. Reportedly, eight Lebanese civilians were killed and 62 wounded in what Israel claimed, and Western leaders accepted, were 'response strikes' to Hezbollah terrorism.

In this long war on the Israel–Lebanon border, both sides used civilians as pawns in violation of international humanitarian law and have drawn universal criticism for doing so. Yet, indicative of the stranglehold Israeli and US officials have over the subject of Middle East terrorism, no Western government official has ever linked Israeli bombing of Lebanon's civilians and civilian infrastructure to terrorism. That charge was left to its victims and those from other nations who attempted to speak for them. Their complaints barely registered in the Western world. Meanwhile, Hezbollah and terrorism were and remain synonymous in the Western psyche.

Russia, the newest member of the 'family of nations,' also targeted civilians and civilian life in their self-described counter-terrorist efforts in the 1990s. In December 1994, the Russian military began bombing Chechnya, hoping to prevent the oil-rich and strategically located republic from leaving the Russian Federation. In its targeting, the Russian air force focused on the enemy's 'centers of gravity.' Targets included the economic infrastructure, principally industrial plants, bridges, utilities and civilian residential areas in Chechnya's major cities, particularly Dudayev and the capitol Grozny. Within five months, the bombing had destroyed Chechnya's economy and played havoc with civilian life.

Like all strategic bombers, the Kremlin claimed it was using precision weapons to bomb military targets. Yet eyewitnesses on the ground and Western military analysts disagreed, claiming early on that the Russians 'eliminated some self-imposed restrictions and unleashed an onslaught of firepower on Grozny, including air assaults.'[54] Benjamin Lambeth of Rand and retired colonel Timothy Thomas of Air University recorded in separate accounts that 'despite the occasional effective use of precision-guided weapons against key targets, quantity prevailed against quality in air force operations in Chechnya.'[55] Thomas describes two Russian tactics that he says severely compromised bombing accuracy. First, pilots attempting to avoid rebel air defense ordnance dropped high-explosive 'dumb' bombs from lofty altitudes. Second, helicopter pilots launched unguided rockets with a 'pitch up' maneuver that, while increasing the rocket's range, reduced their accuracy, causing a greater number of civilian casualties.

By April 1995, the aerial bombardment and ground war had killed an estimated 25,000 civilians and created more than 500,000 refugees. The Russian assault continued until January 1996 when a ceasefire was negotiated. In April, a Russian Su-25 bomber launched a TV-guided bomb and killed Chechen President Dzhokha Dudayevthe. Known as the 'brain' of the rebel forces, Dudayevthe was a former Russian bomber pilot. By the time of his death, the major cities of Chechnya were destroyed and estimates of civilian deaths had risen to over 30,000. Human Rights Watch researchers were told of 'Russian bombs, shell or mortar fire leveling apartment buildings, entire neighborhoods, and single-family homes in Grozny and hitting civilian areas in outlying villages' with no military units close by.[56] Eyewitness accounts during the Russians' December–January winter campaign reported up to 4,000 detonations an hour in Grozny. According to Alexander Lebed, former head of the Russian Security Council, the war resulted in a death rate of eight civilians to every one rebel killed. Colonel Timothy Thomas claims the Kremlin's air campaign against Grozny turned the capitol city 'into another Stalingrad,' a reference to the total destruction of the small but strategically and politically important Russian city in World War Two.

In late September 1999, Russian planes again bombed Chechnya. Russian officials defined the new bombardment as a 'NATO-style' effort to destroy 'terrorists' and 'establish peace' while avoiding civilian targets. Their reference was to the US-led NATO air campaign in Kosovo-Serbia earlier that year and its strategy of 'bomb till victory and win without heavy casualties.' The Kremlin also invoked the rhetoric NATO had used to rationalize its bombing campaign, explaining it was conducting 'limited air operations' and was engaged in a 'fight against internal terrorism.'[57]

Contrary to Kremlin denials, on the ground reports told of thousands of civilian deaths from the Russian aerial attacks. The ordnance included the anti-personnel weapons napalm, cluster, vacuum and fuel–air bombs. Daily accounts, even from friendly Western media circles, described the

Russians 'bombing everywhere' and 'civilians deaths mounting.' Residents were reported as 'terrified to leave their basements.' Medical facilities allegedly were totally destroyed.[58]

The Russians did admit that their 'tragic mistakes' caused civilian deaths and injury. Still, with no objection from his superiors, a three-star Russian general openly admitted: 'yes we are committing war crimes in Chechnya, and so what? War is itself is a crime, and the Geneva Convention is never observed by anyone in real armed conflict.'[59] By the early months of 2000, the civilian death count was a matter of bitter dispute. Russian officials, who barred all foreign journalists from entering Chechnya, offered civilian death estimates in the low hundreds. Chechen officials placed the dead at 5,000 and the internally displaced civilians at 230,000. With both sides blaming the other for introducing chemical weapons, in early January a visible green chemical cloud hung over a devastated Grozny.

In the two Chechen wars between 1994 and 2003 an estimated 100,000 people, most of them civilians, died.[60] Throughout, Russian presidents Boris Yeltsin and Vladimir Putin vigorously portrayed the air and ground campaigns as a war against terrorism. In the first war, Yeltsin's officials routinely dismissed criticism of their bombing campaign, claiming civilian deaths are 'normal' and an 'unavoidable' part of war. As his air force was relentlessly bombing Chechnya in November 1999, President Putin echoed his foreign minister Igor Ivanov's earlier comments about a 'war against terrorists.' For his part Putin urged the international community to help 'fight rebels using "terror" in the North Caucasus.'[61] In contrast, Western leaders and media refused to apply the word 'terrorism' to Russian military actions in the first Chechen war. President Bill Clinton 'urged restraint' but referred to the conflict as an 'internal matter.' European leaders took a stronger stand, condemning Russian policy and threatening economic sanctions. But they too avoided the terrorism label in their condemnation of the aerial destruction of Chechen civil society.

In the second Chechen war, officials of the 'family of nations' again pointedly avoided the issue of Russian terrorism. President Clinton accused Russia of 'uprooting the civilian population' and said the military campaign was a 'self-inflicted wound.' In October 1999, with civilian casualties mounting from Russia's intensified air war, the British Broadcasting Corporation (BBC) quoted Secretary of State Madeleine Albright describing events in Chechnya as 'deplorable and ominous.' In December 1999, leaders from the USA and Europe condemned their Russian counterparts for using tactics that kill civilians. Again they managed to so without uttering the word 'terrorism'.

Placed in historical context, these mild reactions underscore the political nature of the West's fight against New World Order terrorism. Fifteen years earlier, a Russian air force in service to the Soviet 'evil empire' had conducted a similar bombing campaign in Afghanistan. Western leaders, particularly those in lockstep with the Reagan Administration's Cold War counter-terrorism, such as the British prime minister, Margaret Thatcher, had routinely and correctly criticized the Soviet air war as terrorism. From the mid-1990s on, however, Western leaders, led first by President Bill Clinton and later George W. Bush, have steadfastly refused to apply the terrorism label to Russian strategic bombing of Chechen civilians. The refusal to do so, and President Bush's continuing robust praise for Russia's 'counter-terrorism' efforts, stand in marked contrast to their predecessors' critique of Soviet violence in Afghanistan. The fact that the contradiction largely escapes comment, let alone criticism, in major Western political and media institutions, reflects the strength of the US hold on global political discourse and its ability to manipulate terrorism to its political advantage.

NATO'S 'HUMANITARIAN' BOMBING OF KOSOVO-SERBIA

Twice in the first decade of the New World Order, United States and NATO jets bombed the Balkan region to enforce the claims of national and ethnic identity for some over similar claims of others. The first time was in Bosnia. From 29 August to 20 September 1995, as part of Operation Deliberate Force, NATO jets flew 3,315 air sorties against Bosnian Serbs. The stated goal of the air campaign was to stop Serb attacks on 'safe areas' in Bosnia. Serbian officials in Bosnia accused the United States of state terrorism alleging the bombing was producing civilian casualties. In a significant decision, US Air Force Major General Michael Ryan prohibited the use of cluster bombs in Bosnia because of the danger they posed to civilians. According to an Air Force-sponsored study, 'The problem was that the fragmentation pattern was too large to sufficiently limit collateral damage and there was also the further problem of potential unexploded ordnance.'[62]

The Bosnian conflict ended in the Dayton Accords of 1995. The negotiated agreement was reached with the aid of the Serbian President, Slobodan Milosevic, the man NATO officials would soon label the 'Butcher of Belgrade' and accuse of state terrorism.

Three and a half years later, on 24 March 1999, the US-led NATO alliance began bombing the areas of the former Yugoslavia known as Kosovo-Serbia. President Bill Clinton immediately announced that NATO's air war was a 'humanitarian intervention' to stop Milosevic and his policy of 'ethnic cleansing' and genocide against the Albanian residents of Kosovo. Pronounced as the 'most accurate air campaign ever,' the NATO bombing of Kosovo-Serbia lasted 78 days. It ended with Milosevic accepting a US-dictated settlement.

Planning for this military effort had actually begun in April 1998. Even though ground forces were part of the early planning, air and cruise missile strikes were the preferred method of coercing the Serbs into a negotiated settlement. In July 1998, NATO and US officials, fearing a ground war would cause 'unacceptable' losses among NATO troops, ruled out the entry of ground forces. On the day the bombing began, President Bill Clinton declared, 'I do not intend to put our troops in Kosovo to fight a war.'[63] Throughout their year of planning, military officials focused solely on air operations to win, with the expectation that if war came 'President Milosevic would capitulate under threat of air attack or after a few days of bombing.'[64]

From its inception, the announced goal of the strategic air campaign was to end Serbian violence against Kosovar Albanians. Yet there was differing opinion within NATO and within the US command itself as to the scale of the operation and the 'center of gravity' to be targeted. In the planning stages, US commanders envisioned a 'robust' use of air power against Yugoslavia. But in July 1998, the other NATO members rejected air plan Nimble Lion as being 'too large, too threatening.' They urged a less ambitious aerial assault scheme. Part of the European reluctance to support wholesale bombing of Belgrade was because 'most of the alliance's members sustained severe damage during World War Two, and those experiences continue to haunt politicians.'[65] The US command, aware of European 'sensitivity,' agreed to strategic targeting restraints.

Though not intended, this NATO decision offers further proof that 'race matters' in bombing decisions. No such 'sensitivity' was ever recognized or applied to the bombing of Asians in Japan, Korea or Indochina. In addition, unlike the approach the US took in bombing the Third World peoples of Asia and Iraq, 'NATO allies were reluctant to punish Yugoslav citizens for the policies of the Milosevic regime, and they did not want to impoverish or embitter Yugoslavia.'[66]

Within the US command, a highly publicized internecine conflict raged between the Supreme Allied Commander in Europe, General Wesley Clark, and his air commander, Lieutenant General Michael Short. Both generals were committed to targeting the enemy's 'center of gravity.' The Army's Clark wanted to concentrate on the Serbian ground forces in Kosovo. General Short, in the tradition of Air Force ACTS/Warden strategic bombing doctrine, urged the targeting of the Serbian leadership, communications centers and civilian infrastructure throughout Yugoslavia. His primary target was the capital city of Belgrade. In the end, their disagreement proved to be meaningless. To the planners' chagrin, the initial stages of bombing failed to intimidate the Serbs. The air campaign quickly went through Phases One and Two to Phase Three. Starting in late April and lasting to the end of Operation Allied Force, both Serbian armed forces in Kosovo and Yugoslavia's civilian infrastructure were attacked as legitimate military targets.

In a targeting scheme described as 'boilerplate in nature and deriving from Second World War theories,' NATO officials assigned bombers to attack targets that closely paralleled Colonel John Warden's concentric circles approach.[67] Targets were viewed as part of networks in which 'meaningful effects are measures not in terms of physical destruction but according to systemic (or functional) impact.'[68] NATO went after Milosevic's 'Four Pillars of Power,' consisting of the political machine (brain), the media (communications), the economic system (economic infrastructure), and security forces (army).

A total of 38,000 sorties were flown during the 78-day air campaign. Air Force B-52, B-1 and B-2 bombers, flying at altitudes of 15,000 feet and above, delivered 11,000 of the 23,000 air-to-ground munitions. The US Air Force Europe command provided data to prove Operation Allied Force was the most accurate air campaign ever. They claimed 90 percent of the strike aircraft were precision-guided missile (PGM) capable. The US Air Force launched 5,285 PGMs or 78 percent of all the 'smart' weapons NATO used. In addition, 'some 65 percent of the 9,815 aim points altogether were hit by PGMs, for a total hit rate of 58 percent.'[69] NATO planes launched a variety of munitions. Some, such as the Maverick, graphite and laser guided bombs, were 'smart.' Others like the cluster and the traditional general-purpose gravity bombs, were 'dumb.'

Specific targeting followed the parallel prescripts of the vital centers/ concentric circles/four pillars approach. The 'brain' was a primary target. Purposeful attacks on the business and political interests of the Milosevic-led economic elite led to the label 'crony war' being attached to the targeting scheme. In Belgrade, bombs fell on government buildings,

Milosevic's socialist party headquarters and the underground military command center. Media installations were hit, including military communications sites, civilian telephone and computer networks, and state radio and television stations. Transportation targets included military and civilian airfields, railway lines and bridges. Targeted also were factories alleged capable of producing cars and vehicle spare parts for military use.

The political will of the civilian population was of paramount concern to the US military. In classic strategic bombing terms, Air Force General Michael Short revealed that the goal of NATO bombing was to make life for Serbian civilians so miserable they would rise up against President Milosevic and force him out. Directing his wrath at the citizens of Belgrade for their non-violent protests and stubborn resistance to his bombers' aerial assault, Short warned:

> If you wake up in the morning and you have no power to your house and no gas to your stove and the bridge you take to work is down and will be lying in the Danube for the next twenty years, I think you will begin to ask, 'Hey Slobo, what's this all about? How much more of this do we have to withstand?'[70]

In his assessment of NATO bombing motives, David Ramsey Steele agrees that the issue of civilian will was at the very heart of the NATO strategic bombing policy. He adds a further dimension:

> The bombing was not intended to maximize civilian deaths, but neither was it intended to minimize them. The aim of the bombing was to destroy civilian installations on which people's lives and comfort depended, killing a few thousand random civilians for good measure, and thus weakening the will of the population to resist, so that they would submit to NATO occupation.[71]

In late April all remaining bombing restrictions on the civilian economic infrastructure were lifted. Graphite and gravity bombs destroyed the integrated national power grid, putting Belgrade and many of Serbia's cities in the dark. Schools, hospitals, water purification plants, dams, oil refineries, fertilizer factories, a petrochemical plant that produced plastic bags, national parks and marketplaces, were among the sites now bombed as newly declared military targets. Bombs were dropped close to nuclear reactors and nuclear waste facilities.

Whether the destruction of the economic infrastructure caused Milosevic to sue for peace is a matter of debate. Yet the bombing had its expected and desired devastating effect on civilian life. According to Benjamin Lambeth, halfway into the bombing campaign, and with the heaviest bombing yet to come, the 'infrastructure targets had halved Yugoslavia's economic output and deprived more than 100,000 civilians of jobs.'[72] Others, such as International Monetary Fund economist Professor Mladjan Dinkic, asserted that the bombing, in cutting Yugoslavia's economic output in half, had produced an 'economic catastrophe.'[73]

The claim that Operation Allied Force was the most accurate air campaign ever conducted might be true when compared with past 'precision' efforts. For example, in the Persian Gulf 'robo' war, 9 percent of the weapons dropped were 'smart' PGMs compared to 29 percent in Yugoslavia. Yet, in non-comparative terms, 71 percent of the munitions launched on Yugoslavia were inaccurate 'dumb' gravity bombs. Even in the bombing of Belgrade, when PGMs were used exclusively, *Human Rights Watch* reports the capital city 'experienced as many incidents involving civilian deaths as any other city.'[74] As in the past, controversy swirled over the employment of the famously indiscriminate cluster bomb. The US stopped using them in mid-May after it became clear that the cluster weapon was responsible for at least twenty civilian deaths in the city of Nis. In contrast, British planes continued to drop cluster bombs throughout the war.

Other factors contradict the accuracy claim. As in past air wars, cloud cover hindered target visibility. In the 78 days of the Kosovo campaign, only 25 days had sufficiently clear skies for good visibility. Serb tactics, such as setting up dummy tanks, armor and planes, setting bonfires and rigging microwave ovens, seriously compromised missile accuracy or fooled missiles into 'seeing' targets. More important, due to the 'humanitarian' nature of the mission, NATO officials spoke often of the great need to minimize civilian casualties, now officially known as collateral damage. In addition, so as not to undermine already shaky European and North American domestic support for the war, there was a need among the NATO allies to keep military losses low. These dual and potentially contradictory requirements placed the air planners in a political if not moral quandary. They resolved their dilemma in favor of assuring low casualties within the warrior class. Pilots were instructed to fly above 15,000 feet to avoid anti-aircraft fire. As Miron Rezun, a pro-NATO observer, documents, the tactic caused a number of 'accidents' in which civilians were killed and wounded:

> On April 12, NATO attacked a passenger train, killing ten Serb civilians. On April 14, a NATO pilot, thinking a column of vehicles were soldiers who had set fire to surrounding villages, bombed civilian refugees in a convoy. Seventy-five men, women and children were killed. Forty-seven bus passengers were killed when NATO planes bombed a bridge near Luzane on

May 1, and more were killed when the ambulances trying to save the wounded were bombed themselves.[75]

Among critics and supporters of the war, there is universal recognition that targeting and weapons decisions, bad weather, technical malfunction, pilot human error and aircraft maneuver techniques undermined bombing accuracy. Even NATO officials readily admit to 'accidents' and 'mistakes,' including the bombing of the Chinese embassy in Belgrade. But in most cases they blamed President Milosevic for purposely putting civilians in harm's way. Yet it is clear 'rather than risk pilots' lives to shield innocents on the ground, NATO protected its pilots even though this increased the likelihood of additional civilian casualties, through less accurate bombing.'[76] Indeed, Amnesty International goes one step further, charging that in the 12 April 1999 attack on the passenger train at Gurdulica bridge 'NATO's explanation of the bombing – particularly General Clark's account of the pilot's rationale for continuing the attack after he had hit the train – suggests that the (American) pilot had understood that the mission was to destroy the bridge regardless of the cost in terms of civilian casualties. ...'[77]

Eyewitnesses on the ground support Amnesty International's conclusion that bombing civilians was purposeful and consistent with strategic bombing theory, also repetitive. Biijana Marjanovic, who compiled multiple eyewitness accounts, including accounts of the bombing of an apartment building in Novi Pazar, saw the attacks and wondered: 'Dozens and dozens of dead, the old, children, the sick. ... They've been returning after the first hits, to bomb the relief workers and good Samaritans again too. ... How can repeated bombing of the same civilian target with a break of 10 to 15 minutes in between the raids be a mistake?...'[78]

As elsewhere, the number of civilian casualties from the bombing was and remains in dispute. NATO and Pentagon officials put the number of Albanian civilians massacred by Serbs in Kosovo variously at 100,000–500,000. They eventually settled on 11,000. Only 4,000 bodies have been found to date. Yet they excused themselves from counting Serbian bombing victims, concluding an accurate 'calculation is beyond their powers.'[79] However, Pentagon officials, including General Wesley Clark, and Defense Secretary William Cohen were willing and able to count the number of 'incidents of collateral damage.' Both testified to Congress the number was 'between 20 and 30.' Human Rights Watch put the number of incidents in which civilians died at 90 and counted 500 civilians as having died directly from the bombing. NATO officials have unofficially but gladly accepted this number as it is the lowest among several tallies.

Amnesty International analysts say civilian deaths totaled between 500 and 1,500. In their scathing report, they also assert that NATO did little to protect civilians and purposely bombed civilian targets, including a hospital in Surdulica and a Serb television station, killing dozens of civilians. *Time* magazine and Fred Kaplan of the *Boston Globe* put civilian deaths at around 1,200 while Serb government sources say between 1,200 and 5,000 civilians died from NATO bombing.

The air campaign in Kosovo-Serbia continued the pattern begun in World War One in which 'precision bombing' produced more civilian than combatant deaths. Though the actual total of direct civilian deaths was low compared with past wars, in Operation Allied Force close to 100 per cent of the casualties were civilians. In the judgement of Dr Piotr Bein, an independent writer on ecological issues, given the pace of civilian deaths from NATO bombing, had the 'precision war lasted longer, there would have been not thousands, but tens or hundreds of thousands of casualties.'[80] In Bein's view, President Milosevic did the Western alliance a huge favor in capitulating before the horrors of its humanitarian intervention, particularly the sustained bombing of civilians and their infrastructure, could come to light for all to see. For Mitchel Cohen, the direct effects of the bombing on civilians and their lives were apparent early on and, as NATO officials saw it, purposeful:

> The unnerving truth is that urban civilian structures and the farming country-side were purposely targeted by NATO, in violation of all existing war crimes codes. Planes returned to a bridge, hospital, factory, school or dam that they had 'accidentally' bombed just 20 minutes earlier, to bomb the rescue teams arriving at the scene. This was standard procedure. Said Germany's General Klaus Naumann, 'We will see how they feel after a few more weeks or months or what have you of continuously pounding them into pieces.[81]

Analysts at the World Policy Institute agreed with Cohen on the purpose of NATO bombing. They concluded: 'The killing of civilians by NATO bombs is not a 'mistake.' It is a logical and predictable outgrowth of the way NATO has chosen to wage the war.'[82]

BOMBING THE ENVIRONMENT: INDIRECT CIVILIAN DEATHS

As in the Persian Gulf War, the issue of 'indirect' deaths from the bombing is steeped in controversy. US and NATO officials refuse to accept calculations of civilian deaths occurring 'indirectly' as a result of after-effects of the bombing campaign. Unlike the Persian Gulf campaign, there is no precise estimate of civilian deaths or injury resulting indirectly from bombing the environment. Yet health officials and environmental experts conclude that the NATO bombing and the use of depleted uranium did immediate and long-lasting damage to the environment and human life of Yugoslavia and beyond. The scope and extent of the damage is too great to detail here.[83] Two observations will suffice. The first is from Ruth Yarrow, an environmental biologist from the American Friends Service Committee. She documents the immediate effects to human life:

> Nearly three months after NATO's devastating attack on Pancevo – almost a month after it dropped the last bomb of its air war on Yugoslavia – here's a glimpse of the enduring environmental and human nightmare the alliance left behind. Physicians in this city 10 miles northeast of the Yugoslav and Serbian capital, Belgrade, have privately recommended that all women who were in town that night avoid pregnancy for at least the next two years. Women who were less than nine weeks pregnant in mid-April were advised to obtain abortions, and doctors say most have complied. The ground in and around Pancevo is saturated with ammonia, mercury, naphtha, acids, dioxins, and other toxins that leaked and burned out of the factories that night. ... Farm workers, plunging their fingers into the earth, say they come away with rashes that burn and blister. Those who eat the river fish and vegetables or drink the tap water, which trickles out of faucets because of the damage to the purification plant, come down with diarrhea, vomiting, and stomach cramps. There are twice as many miscarriages as there were during the comparable period last year, doctors here [in Pancevo] say. The air strikes unleashed tons of chemicals into the air and water. An estimated 1,500 tons of vinyl chloride, the building block of a type of plastic, 3,000 times higher than permitted levels, burned into the air or poured into the soil and river, said municipal officials in Pancevo, which is controlled by opposition parties hostile to President Slobodan Milosevic.[84]

There are also claims of long-term and broad catastrophic damage to the environment of the Balkans and Europe. A member of the UN task force concludes: 'By burning down enormous quantities of naphtha and its derivatives, more than a hundred highly toxic chemical compounds that pollute water, air and soil are released, endangering the entire Balkan ecosystem.'[85] Mikhail Gorbachev, the former President of the Soviet Union and celebrated friend of the 'family of nations', drew the same conclusion:

The massive destruction of oil refineries, petrochemical plants, chemical and fertilizer factories, pharmaceutical plants and other environmentally hazardous enterprises puts both the population and natural environment in the Balkans under clear threat. ... One of the most dangerous consequences is the pollution of underground waters.[86]

Some of the contamination comes from the use of depleted uranium munitions (DU). Calculations of the number of civilians affected indirectly by the environmental damage have yet to be done or published. Still, the UN Balkan Task Force warned in July 1999 of increased future health problems such as miscarriages, birth defects, deadly nerve and liver diseases and various forms of cancer.

US and NATO officials have denied any responsibility for what others claim is a clear and purposeful violation of the environmental provisions of the Geneva Protocol of 1977. Air campaign planners assert that environmental effects were very much included in their targeting calculations and the level of bombing damage done to the environment was acceptable under international law. Mark Laity, a NATO spokesperson, went one step further. Seeking to blame the bombed Serbs, he asserted that any pollution 'reflects poor environmental standards on [Yugoslavian] industry, and was not caused by us.'[87]

The Operation Allied Force air campaign did produce a negative indirect effect on civilians about which there is no debate. The stated goal of the humanitarian bombing of Kosovo was to end the alleged Serbian ethnic cleansing, defined as the forced removal of non-Serbians from Kosovo, either by flight or death. There is disagreement over whether Serbian ethnic cleansing was happening before the bombing began. NATO argued it was, and said 2,000 civilians had already died from Albanian and Serb fighting before 24 March 1999. Others, including the *Wall Street Journal* and the German Foreign Ministry, in documents withheld from the public until the end of the war, concluded there was 'no ethnic cleansing, no genocide.'[88]

Debate over when Serbian ethnic cleansing began rages on. Yet there is universal agreement that NATO's strategic bombing had the opposite effect on the Albanian civilians in Kosovo from its stated goal. After the war, NATO officials alleged that during the course of the bombing, the Yugoslav army had 'cleansed' close to a million Albanians from Kosovo, including the 100,000 to 500,000 Albanian men who were massacred. Later US and NATO officials lowered the total to 11,000. Others, in particular the International Committee of the Red Cross and the NATO controlled Hague Tribunal, strongly disagreed, reporting casualties from ethnic cleansing ranging from 3,500 to 4,000, with many non-Albanians among the dead and missing.[89] All agree that the NATO bombing caused mass civilian flight from Kosovo. As expected, the Serb response to the bombing was a terror campaign against Albanian residents to force their expulsion from Kosovo. According to the Organization of South Central Europe, Serbian terror was extremely successful, displacing either externally or internally close to 900,000 civilians. But thousands of other civilians of diverse nationality and ethnicity fled to escape the torrent of NATO bombs inflicting terror on Kosovo.[90]

In short, US and NATO officials clearly understood their bombing of Kosovo would result in a massive number of refugees. In fact, the Italian Prime Minister Massimo D'Alema, warned Sandy Berger, President Clinton's National Security Advisor, that the bombing would produce a flood of refugees. Berger responded by saying that in that case 'NATO will keep on bombing.'[91] During the bombing campaign, General Wesley Clark admitted the Serbian response to the bombing was 'entirely predictable' and claimed that NATO had 'fully anticipated' it. He did so while denying the air assault was ever intended to stop the ethnic cleansing.

For US and European strategic bombing enthusiasts, Operation Allied Force was the high point in nearly a century of fighting wars with air power. Milosevic's capitulation to NATO's demands came with few pilot casualties and without having to introduce ground forces into the conflict. In the view of NATO's political and military authorities, the 'precision' bombing met their unstated criteria of minimal or acceptable civilian casualties even though they refused to account for them. Finally, the Western media's enthusiastic coverage of Serbian terrorism in the form of ethnic cleansing had provided a large reservoir of moral outrage toward those being bombed. In this 'humanitarian' context, a few 'tragic mistakes' in which deserving civilians were killed could easily be admitted to, in the knowledge that they would be dismissed as unimportant.

With these attributes assigned to it, Operation Allied Force appeared to be the long-desired 'clean war' fought for a good cause. For the British and US strategic bombers, it provided the desired answer to the longstanding question; could air power alone win wars? Finally, for most of them, the answer was an unqualified Yes![92]

Other members of the 'family of nations' did not miss the military and political significance of Operation Allied Force. For NATO it solidified its 'new strategic concept' according to which 'NATO can bomb any country which is doing bad things domestically, even though it has neither attacked nor threatened any NATO member, and that NATO can decide what to do entirely on its own, without consulting the UN.'[93] A few months later, the Russians were describing their bombing of Chechnya as a 'NATO-style counter-terrorist' effort. In the midst of their battle with Hezbollah in southern Lebanon, Israeli officials referenced Kosovo-Serbia, warning 'that if the attacks move[d] over to sovereign Israeli territory, it [would] do to Lebanon what NATO did to Kosovo.'[94] Indeed, for many Israeli strategists, air superiority had become the single guarantor of their national survival. It was not surprising then, as Noam Chomsky noted, that 'Israeli forces are being restructured for a quick and destructive air war, relying particularly on the Kosovo incident.'[95]

As the architects of Operation Allied Force, the US military command looked to the twenty-first century with utmost confidence. In their view, the Kosovo–Serbia war had clearly demonstrated that the USA had the technology, the political will and the strategic bombing doctrine to win wars the moral way without doing great harm to enemy civilians, unless they deserved it. In essence, they and their predecessors had embraced the Prophets' doctrine of bombing to win war and shaped it to fit the modern economic and social environment. Now, with precision technology, they could bomb at will and still safeguard enough civilians to satisfy the moral and political requirements of the day.

This approach would be particularly valuable in a post-Cold War climate in which murky 'humanitarian interventions', as in Sudan, took precedence over wars against a readily identifiable enemy that aggressively threatened another's national sovereignty. As David Steele writes, a new context had emerged in which:

> The new world religion is the belief-system of politically correct social workers. It is essentially ignorant, irrational, and vindictive. People must behave nicely' or they will be bombed. What constitutes nice behavior changes with the winds of politically correct fashion, and whether people are behaving nicely is not, as a factual matter, determined with any great exactitude. ... It is enough to bomb a country's civilian population if its leader is considered a bad man.[96]

As the New World Order ended its first decade, the Western 'social workers' made it clear that 'bad men' were those who practiced or supported terrorism against the 'family of nations.' Because of the attributes it demonstrated in the Kosovo–Serbia theater, strategic bombing became the best way to battle the designated terrorists of the day while promoting the moral distinction between the civilized 'us' and the uncivilized 'them.'

Bombing to Win:
9/11 and the War on Terrorism

For the United States, the twenty-first century begins with strategic bombing as its signature means of war.[1] True, a commitment to ground and naval forces remains. Yet, because air power can quickly and precisely strike any flashpoint in the global US empire, it has captured the imagination of the civilian and military commands. Should anyone miss the obvious, the US Air Force adopted the motto 'global reach, global power.' The Clinton Administration clearly understood. In addition to the celebrated air war in Yugoslavia and enforcement of the no-fly zones in Iraq, President Bill Clinton launched missile strikes on Sudan and into Afghanistan's mountain caves to punish those he held responsible for the 1998 terrorist attacks on US embassies in Tanzania and Kenya. The bombing of Sudan indirectly caused thousands of Sudanese civilian deaths, a fact still hidden by a US-enforced silence.[2] The strikes also had a demonstration effect on friend and foe, proving that United States had the ability and political will to strike anywhere and anytime with impunity. In sum, strategic bombing has become the instrument of choice for the leader of the 'family of nations' in its quest to orchestrate the post-Cold War world and 'civilize' its peoples. As Edward Herman notes, US elites 'are often eager to bomb lesser peoples of the world ... without fear of retaliation because of the huge military advantage of a superpower and the subservience of the international community.'[3]

Citing the complexities of wartime environments, bombing nations have refused to count their enemy's civilian casualties. US officials have been particularly vigorous in their opposition to doing so. The practice has shifted from Defense Secretary Dick Cheney's claim that civilian body counts are always inaccurate or in General Colin Powell's opinion 'uninteresting,' both made during the Persian Gulf War, to General Tommy Franks's blunt declaration during the 2003 attack on Iraq: 'We don't do body counts'.[4] Further, they have consistently either criticized or embraced the methodology and findings of those who have attempted to provide enemy civilian casualty counts. Their posture has depended on whether the body count matches their political and as yet undefined notion of 'acceptable' or 'minimal.' In contrast, the bombing nations gladly provide estimates or precise tallies of enemy combatant casualties and are especially resolute about reporting civilian casualties they hold the enemy responsible for. The reports of civilian death and injury resulting from Iraq's missile attacks on Israel during the Persian Gulf War and the NATO governments' and media frenzy about Albanian civilian victims of Serb ethnic cleansing are two examples *par excellence.*

All of these body count patterns gained importance as the issue of terrorism came to dominate a political landscape in which, depending on whose civilians are being harmed, body counts can either mobilize or undermine public support for military action. Also evident in this highly charged context has been the bombing nations' consistent and concerted effort to maintain the high moral ground on the terrorism issue. To do so, they have invoked multiple reasons as to why their aerial assaults do not constitute terrorism. The labyrinth of rationalizations is to be explored later. Suffice it to say here that for preemptive political purposes, this practice is common and especially important when there is any likelihood others may deem the civilian carnage to be beyond even the undefined minimal or acceptable levels. The current wars in Iraq, Afghanistan, Chechnya and Israel-Palestine reflect this practice.

THE STRATEGIC BOMBING OF 9/11

The terrorist attacks of 11 September 2001 punctured the political and moral cocoon the 'family of nations' had spun around their strategic bombing. Suddenly it was obvious that aerial bombardment was neither precise nor humane, but rather an instrument of terror. In the name of the victimized, 'jingoist' agents invoked their version of air power to 'precisely' attack targets in the principal bombing nation, the USA. Like the bombing nations, the 9/11 terrorists used modern aviation technology to traverse great distance and strike at the heart and political will of their own demonized other. In doing so, they forced those who claimed civilian casualties could not be counted, to count them down to the very last victim. They also made it clear that the bombing nations are not alone in lifting restrictions on targeting civilians or dismissing international agreements inconvenient to their purposes. In sum, on 9/11 the terrorists-at-a-distance and their jingoist mentors confronted the 'family of nations' with the truth about strategic bombing. In a matter of minutes, it became evident that, while the bombers rationalized, moralized about and manipulated the reality of strategic bombing, the 'other' had been watching with growing disbelief and anger. While waiting to take their revenge, they had developed their own strategic bombing doctrine.

But a reality obvious to millions would require the West and in particular the United States to focus on the why of 9/11; to reflect on the veracity of its long-cultivated image of having a civilized people and benevolent role in the world. Since doing so would run counter to the Bush administration's righteous sense of self and political agenda, it went about enforcing its own perception of what 9/11 was about. Its immediate task was to focus public attention away from the dangerous why of 9/11 (except for the self-serving notion of a jealous adversary) onto who the 9/11 terrorists were and what they were up to. Aided by a citizenry imbued with imperial mentality and well schooled in the tenets of the 'ideology of terrorism,' and with the compliance of the major media, Bush Administration officials effectively silenced or overwhelmed those who suggested that past and present US foreign policy played a role in determining the 'who' and 'why' of 9/11.[5] Like Western imperialists of the past, they used their virtual monopoly on the instruments of persuasion to construct an evil, irrational, subhuman enemy said to be under the hypnotic power of religious zealots bent on conquering the rational West and pushing the world back into the dark ages. Convinced of the USA's moral and technological superiority, the Bush Administration placed the United States and the world once again on a permanent war footing in which strategic bombing was to play the decisive role.[6]

BUSH'S POST-9/11 WAR ON TERRORISM

The 9/11 attacks on the World Trade Center and the Pentagon and the subsequent crash of United Airlines flight 93 resulted in 2,752 deaths.[7] The victims were from a variety of nations. In addition to civilians, the dead included military and Department of Defense civilian personnel. Over the next two weeks, President George W. Bush and his top foreign policy officials invoked familiar imagery and terminology, including the controversial notion of 'crusade,' to mobilize US citizens and the 'family of nations' behind a political agenda actually determined before 9/11.[8] On 20 September, Bush announced that in response to the attacks the United States would lead a 'war on terrorism.' The world, he insisted, was rigidly polarized between good and evil. Thus, 'Every nation in every region now has a decision to make: Either you are with us or you are with the terrorists.'[9]

A week earlier, Secretary of State Colin Powell had previewed the President's stark 'good versus evil' imagery. Invoking the time-tested notion of the civilized self set against the uncivilized other, Powell made a plea for:

> Countries, the OAS, everybody — to join us once and for all in a great coalition to conduct a campaign against terrorists who are conducting war against civilized people. ... The attack that took place in Washington and the attack that took place in New York were directed against America, but they really are directed against civilization.[10]

Leaders of the Prophets' home nations echoed Powell's comments. British Prime Minister Tony Blair said, 'We all agreed that this is an attack not only on America but on the free and democratic world.'[11] In language full of Western imperial imagery, the Italian prime minister Silvio Berlusconi, chimed in, saying:

> Italy joined the US in condemning these monstrous criminals who have demonstrated a vile and brutal affront against humanity. ... We must be aware of the superiority of our civilization, a system that has guaranteed well-being, respect for human rights and — in contrast with Islamic countries — respect for religious and political rights, a system that has as its values understandings of diversity and tolerance.

Berlusconi declared Western civilization to be superior to Islam also because it 'has at its core, as its greatest value, freedom, which is not the heritage of Islamic culture.'[12]

In designating who the enemy was, President Bush relied on the tenet that terrorist 'fish' require a friendly sea to swim in.[13] His nation's war, Bush warned, 'will pursue nations that provide aid or safe haven to terrorism. From this day forward, any nation that continues to harbor or support terrorism will be regarded by the United States as a hostile regime.'[14] The President also invoked the terrorism industry's assertion that the battle against terrorism constituted World War Three, while preparing his audience for a new kind of conflict:

Now this war will not be like the war against Iraq a decade ago, with a decisive liberation of territory and a swift conclusion. It will not look like the air war above Kosovo two years ago, where no ground troops were used and not a single American was lost in combat. Our response involves far more than instant retaliation and isolated strikes. Americans should not expect one battle, but a lengthy campaign unlike any other we have ever seen. It may include dramatic strikes visible on TV and covert operations secret even in success.[15]

With his allusion to a terrorist 'network,' he also drew upon the popular and politically useful imagery of a terrorist web spun by a single-headed monster. He declared, 'We will direct every resource at our command ... to the destruction and to the defeat of the global terror network.'[16]

These pronouncements echoed an earlier press release in which President Bush made clear his War on Terrorism would be a 'no holds barred' effort. During his visit to the ruins of the World Trade Center, rescue workers urged him to do 'whatever it takes.' A day later, Bush publicly adopted their revenge-motivated battle cry, asserting: 'But they have stirred up the might of the American people, and we're going to get them, no matter what it takes.'[17] In the same breath he disclosed who would suffer the wrath of his 'whatever it takes' approach: 'We will not only deal with those who dare attack America, we will deal with those who harbor them and feed them and house them.'[18]

On 25 September 2001 the Bush Administration got the 'legal' authority for its 'no holds barred' war. In a secret memo to White House lawyer Alberto Gonzales, Justice Department attorney John Yoo opined that the President had the constitutional authority to wage preemptive war of 'no limits' against terrorists and nations harboring them, whether they were connected to the 9/11 attacks or not.[19]

Armed with its secret 'legal' opinion and backed by an outraged public and media well tutored in the 'ideology of terrorism' and imperial mentality, the Bush Administration launched its War on Terrorism. As President Bush would say three years later, the strategy was to 'strike terrorists abroad so we don't have to face them at home.'[20]

Since the 'home' of the designated terrorist was 'over there' and their terrorist network was global in scope, it was a foregone conclusion that air power would be the primary instrument to satisfy the thirst for vengeance. The first and immediate targets were those held responsible for the attacks: the Osama bin Laden-led Al Qaeda organization and its protector, the Taliban regime in Afghanistan. The strategic concept was to fight a conventional war, applying 'overwhelming force' with the twin objectives of destroying Al Qaeda and 'regime change,' that is, overthrowing the Taliban government.

THE REVENGE BOMBING OF AFGHANISTAN

The revenge bombing of Afghanistan, labelled Operation Enduring Freedom (OEF), began on 7 October 2001. In preceding weeks, media pundits, in particular Bill O'Reilly of Fox TV News and A. M. Rosenthal, former editor of the *New York Times*, had expressed President Bush's 'whatever it takes' mantra in concrete strategic bombing terms. With revenge in mind, they focused their nation's fury on Afghanistan's civilians. On 17 September 2001 O'Reilly insisted:

> the US should bomb the Afghan infrastructure to rubble—the airport, the power plants, their water facilities, and the roads. ... This is a very primitive country. And taking out their ability to exist day to day will not be hard. ... The Afghans are responsible for the Taliban. We should not target civilians. But if they don't rise up against this criminal government, they starve, period.[21]

Two days later O'Reilly urged the bombing of Afghanistan 'in strategic ways' and hoped the people themselves would rise up and throw the Taliban out. Noting Afghanistan's civilians 'are starving as it is,' he proposed the United States increase their suffering by destroying 'what little infrastructure they have' including 'every truck you see' so there is 'not going to be anything to eat.'[22]

For Rosenthal, the enemy was much broader and included the governments and civilians of Afghanistan, Iraq, Iran, Libya, Syria and Sudan. He wanted an ultimatum that warned that officials could either produce documents and information about weapons of mass destruction and terrorist organizations in three days or their civilians would face horrible consequences: 'the residents of the countries would be urged 24 hours a day by the US to flee the capital and major cities, because they would be bombed to the ground beginning the fourth day.'[23] O'Reilly and Rosenthal clearly understood the nature of strategic bombing and saw it as the suitable wrecking ball of their desired vengeance.

Though furious about the 9/11 attacks, particularly on the Pentagon, the military command reassured the world that the USA would not answer terrorism with terrorism. As in past wars, top military officials, including this time General Tommy Franks, the head of Central Command, labeled the bombing campaign 'the most accurate war ever fought in the nation's history.' Pentagon civilian officials went further, boasting of a 'new kind of low risk precision warfare' resulting in low casualties for all sides.[24] Later, President Bush reiterated the new warfare concept, boasting: 'By a combination of creative strategies, and advanced technologies, we are redefining war on our terms. In this new era of warfare, we can target a regime, not a nation.'[25] Amidst Defense Secretary Donald Rumsfeld's requisite refusal to rule out the use of nuclear weapons, the military stated its intent to 'bomb cleanly,' taking 'great care to minimize collateral damage' with little loss of pilots and aircraft.

The first day of Operation Enduring Freedom consisted of bombers, jets and 50 cruise missiles striking pre-planned 'military' targets throughout Afghanistan. Within a week, the US Air Force introduced 'time-critical' targeting that, true to past practice, greatly expanded bombing options and opportunities. Under this 'flex-targeting,' after bombing pre-planned targets, pilots remain aloft awaiting orders to attack 'emerging targets' defined as 'any moving or moveable target of high importance, especially one that through electronic emissions, communications, or other telltale signs gave only brief indication of its location.'[26] Accordingly, pilots received their targets after takeoff an estimated 80 percent of the time.

By 10 December, 4,700 attack 'sorties' had been flown. High-flying B-52 and B-1 bombers did the bulk of the bombing after the first week. The US Air Force increased its use of 'accurate' Global Positioning System (GPS) weapons over the Kosovo-Serbia War, (30 percent to 60 percent) but employed fewer of the more 'precise' laser-guided bombs. 'Dumb' bombs ranging from 500 pounds to the 15,000-pound BLU-82B Daisy Cutter and fuel–air explosives were dropped from high altitudes. Anti-personnel ordnance was also used. Finally admitting to its 'killing impact on civilians,' the US Air Force had stopped using napalm.[27] Despite its known danger to civilians both at the time of its use and for a long time afterwards, the cluster bomb remained an important weapon in the US arsenal. In the first week, the Air Force B-1s conducted five missions launching fifty CBU-87 anti-personnel cluster bombs. An estimated 1,210 cluster bombs were dropped in the first ten weeks of bombing.

The air campaign provided a glimpse into the future of strategic bombing. It included a 'clandestine air war' conducted with a variety of space-age technology, intelligence techniques and unmanned vehicles.

Echoing past enthusiasm for technological advances and their positive effect on waging air war, Air Force Colonel Phillip Meilinger proposed aerospace power 'should be our weapon of choice because it is the most discriminate, prudent, and risk-free weapon in our arsenal.'[28]

The Air Force also used a new type of carpet-bombing over Afghanistan. It was intended to be more effective against entrenched troops and have greater psychological effect than Vietnam-era box bombing which Air Force studies had discredited as both ineffective and inaccurate.[29] National security analyst Anthony Cordesman is enthusiastic about the new carpet-bombing concept even though he admits 'weapons accuracy has not improved' since the Persian Gulf War. Instead of sending many bombers to repeatedly hit an area, in the carpet-bombing of Afghanistan only one bomber strikes 'with large numbers of 500-pound dumb bombs on the same target area (the size of one to five football fields).'[30]

The targeting scheme matched contemporary strategic bombing theory. Initial bombing focused on traditional 'high-value' command-and-control targets such as alleged Al Qaeda terror training camps and mountain redoubts and Taliban air defense and military infrastructure. These targets were selected despite Secretary of Defense Donald Rumsfeld's declaration that the Afghans 'do not have high-value targets or assets that are the kinds of things that would lend themselves to substantial damage from the air.'[31]

Air superiority was quickly established, leaving the United States free to bomb the entire country with impunity. Rumsfeld's quip 'We aren't running out of targets; Afghanistan is' left little doubt as to the broad range of intended targets.[32] By late October, the Pentagon declared the Al Qaeda infrastructure and training camps destroyed. Targets were then selected to realize the Bush Administration's goal of overthrowing the Taliban government. As in the Persian Gulf and Kosovo–Serbia campaigns, bombing was centered on the enemy's 'brain,' in this case Taliban and Al Qaeda 'leadership' targets and 'dual use' (military–civilian) infrastructure. Throughout Afghanistan, but particularly in populated areas, communications, energy and transport targets, including bridges, roads, vehicles, airports, dams, radio stations, food storage warehouses and hydropower stations, were allegedly bombed with 'precision.' Indeed, from November through December 2001, 'anything rolling on the roads of southern Afghanistan' was fair game.[33]

With 'regime change' as a goal, the political will of Afghan civilians became an immediate primary consideration. On 16 September, five days after the 9/11 attacks and weeks before the bombing started, the Bush

Administration had demanded from Pakistan 'a cutoff of fuel supplies ... and the elimination of truck convoys that provide much of the food and other supplies to Afghanistan's civilian population.'[34] In classic strategic bombing terms, British Chief of Defense Staff Admiral Michael Boyce told reporters: 'the squeeze will carry on until the people of the country themselves recognize that this is going to go on until they get the leadership changed.'[35]

By mid-November, the Taliban government was gone. Air power enthusiasts were ecstatic; crediting loss of civilian support and Special Forces' ground-directed bombing of Taliban positions as decisive in the regime's quick exit. Journalist Stephen Budiansky joyously credited 'The spectacle of B-52s, the quintessential strategic bomber of yore' with the victory.[36] For many others, Operation Enduring Freedom 'offered convincing evidence that airpower is flexible enough to take the lead in many different types of conflicts.'[37] With General Tommy Franks warning that the Taliban would remain an effective force 'until the last individual man puts down his weapon,' aerial bombing, though most intense from October 2001 to January 2002, remained an essential component of so-called 'mop up' operations well into 2005.

THE NEW PRECISION WAR: HOW ACCURATE?

Within the first days of bombing, reports of high civilian casualties raised serious questions about US strategic bombing of Afghanistan. Taliban accusations that on 10 October 2001, a hundred civilians died in a bombing raid on the village of Karam followed earlier reports of 400 hundred civilian deaths near Jalalabad. The reports brought street protests in Pakistan and a curt reminder from Defense Secretary Rumsfeld: 'Everyone in this country knows that the United States of America does not target civilians ... there's no question but that when one is engaged militarily, ... there is going to be unintended loss of life. It has always been the case. It certainly will be the case in this instance.'[38]

Over the next few months of bombing, Pentagon officials spoke of regrettable 'mistakes' but 'only dozens of dead civilians.' Yet, voices at home and around the world raised doubts and produced contrary evidence. For example, three days into the bombing, Amnesty International called for all parties to avoid civilian casualties and for a 'prompt investigation' into non-combatant deaths.[39] In mid-November, Justin Huggler of the *Independent* reported carpet-bombing had killed 150 civilians.[40] International polling found that people around the world thought the US was not trying very hard to avoid civilian casualties.[41] In early December, Professor Marc Herold of the University of New Hampshire issued the first report on total civilian casualties in Afghanistan.[42] He charged that in the first eight weeks the US-led bombing had killed more civilians (3,767) than had died in the 9/11 attacks. The report directly contradicted the Bush Administration's assurances that it was conducting a 'clean' war. The media and Pentagon dismissed Herold's report as yet another case of Taliban propaganda.

Unfortunately, the conduct of Operation Enduring Freedom supports Herold's findings. Contrary to the Pentagon's familiar refrain of a 'new precision warfare,' except for the obvious and exceptional fury accompanying it, the revenge bombing of Afghanistan paralleled past practice and produced similar results. True to strategic bombing theory, the overall objective was to undermine the enemy's military and political capacity to wage war. To affect public support for the Taliban, what little remained of Afghanistan's industrial infrastructure after years of war against the Soviet Union was purposely targeted. This meant bombing urban areas over and over. Adding to the willingness of military planners to do so was the fact most of the Taliban's military assets, like the Soviets' before them, were located in the cities. The Pentagon pledged that bombing densely populated areas could be done with minimal collateral damage. Yet, while an estimated 60 percent of bombs dropped were 'smart,' the remaining 40 percent of the bombs were 'dumb' and launched from high altitudes. Of the 'smart' ordnance, the Pentagon chose to use a lower percentage of the precise laser variety. Once again, the military command remained 'in love' with the deadly cluster bomb.

In response to constant accusations of rising civilian casualties, Pentagon officials stuck to their precision claim while blaming targeting mistakes and 'poorly programmed smart bombs.' A case in point was the mid-October 2001 'mistaken' bombing of six International Red Cross (IRC) warehouses and a residential neighborhood in Kabul. After pilots 'mistakenly' bombed two of the same warehouses again, the Pentagon apologized and explained that the bombing of the residential area was because 'the bomb's guidance system malfunctioned.' After two weeks of public lying, Pentagon officials admitted they had designated the IRC warehouses military targets and had hit them on purpose.[43]

In his assessment of the bombing campaign, Carl Conetta notes the military's claim for the 'precision' of its bombing was a result of controlled non-battlefield tests. He concludes, 'even given perfect intelligence and accuracy, most guided weapons in the 500-to-2000-pound range are sufficiently powerful to routinely cause some degree of collateral damage.'[44] Whether 'some degree of collateral damage' meets the criteria of 'acceptable' damage is of course a political decision the Pentagon jealously and secretly reserves for itself. Yet, even if precisely 'locked on' the target, the immense destructive power within the 'footprint' of the bombs leaves little standing or alive. Reports of purely civilian targets, such as homes, mosques and medical clinics being hit means either they were bombed with precision or they fell within the Circular Error Probable (CEP) measurement (the radius of a circle into which a missile bomb or projectile will land at least half the time) and/or the weapon's destructive footprint. Early in the bombing, the 500-pound bomb with a lethal range of 20 meters was dropped most often. Later, the 2,000-pound ordnance, whose lethal blast range is 34 meters and has a 'safe' distance half-kilometer out from the bombed target, became the weapon of choice. The 10,000-pound bomb provided less accuracy and produced even greater destruction. By mid-December 2001, half of the USA's 10,000-pound bomb inventory had been dropped. Requests for more were quickly placed.

Challenges to the cleanliness of the Pentagon's precision warfare concept came from members of its own 'family.' The most devastating was from military analyst Anthony Cordesman of the Center for Strategic and International Security (CSIS). His critique was issued after only two months of Operation Enduring Freedom and included the following observation:

> The US military has developed a targeting doctrine that ultimately places a very heavy emphasis on strategic and interdiction targets in populated areas. It is far from clear that this doctrine achieves military results proportional to the priorities given to logistic and military industrial targets, sustainability and maintenance targets, leadership targets, and C4I. It also often means bombing buildings and area targets that require repeated restrikes, and even then, an inability to assess the importance of the resulting damage in many cases. The resulting civilian casualties and collateral damage are only part of a broader problem, but they are certainly increased as a result of the fact that much of US targeting and battle damage assessment for bombing in populated area is not an art form, much less a science. In fact, US targeting and battle damage assessment comes closer to being military doctrine practiced as witchcraft.[45]

Despite such critiques, the Bush Administration doggedly supported the Pentagon's claim that it conducted precision warfare in Afghanistan. Even with a cooperative media, they had quite a challenge doing so.[46] From the beginning, the Pentagon strategy of hitting with 'maximum force' on questionable 'emerging' (flex) targets over broad areas (carpet-bombing) produced numerous incidents of 'collateral damage.' Many parallel an attack on an alleged ammunition dump in which the entire village of Niazi Qala was wiped out, leaving 42 people dead.[47] This 'shoot and bomb targets of opportunity first' approach should have renewed questions about civilian casualties – questions including the actual number of civilian dead and wounded, whether they should be counted and whether or not they can be counted accurately.[48] But thanks to the media's self-imposed refusal to show photos of civilian casualties on the front page of newspapers and the public outrage against any newspaper that did, it was nearly impossible for these questions to surface.[49]

COUNTING CIVILIAN CASUALTIES: BUSINESS AS USUAL

Marc Herold's 'A Dossier on Civilian Victims of United States Aerial Bombing of Afghanistan' shattered the glasshouse mythology the Pentagon had created on the subject of civilian casualties. Based on first-hand accounts, major world-wide newspapers, official news agency reports, non-governmental agencies and cross-corroboration, Herold estimates that close to 5,000 civilians died in US bombing from 7 October through the first week of December 2001.[50] Due to some minor over-counting, Herold reduced his original conservative estimate of civilian deaths from 3,767 to 2,650–2,970 for 'an average of 62 innocent civilians a day.'[51] Even so, his count was higher than what the Pentagon derisively called the 'unreliable and propagandistic' Taliban sources. Other reports on civilian casualties followed Herold's. In February 2002, with an obvious sigh of relief the Associated Press found only hundreds (500–600) not thousands of Afghan noncombatants had perished. By August 2002, nine studies attempting to count civilian casualties in the first three months of bombing had been undertaken. Herold offered their findings in his 'Map of Studies Counting Afghan Civilian Casualties.'[52]

Author	Deaths
Marc Herold	3,100–3,600
Francoise Chipaux	over 1,000 during first two months
Reuters	982
Carl Conetta	1,000–1,300

Laura King et al.	500–600
John Donnelly and Anthony Shadid	830
David Zucchino	1,067–1,200
Marla Ruzicka	812
Dexter Filkins	396

Herold says the discrepancies arise from methodological issues such as the sources relied upon and restrictions on the number of incidents sampled. For example, Carl Conetta relied only on Western sources. Donnelly and Shadid and Reuters independently sampled only fourteen incidents, Razicka eleven, and Filkins eleven while Zucchino covered 194. Still, all indicate civilian deaths were in the hundreds or thousands rather than the dozens that Pentagon officials claimed. Other reports indicate that the ratio of civilian deaths to weapons used was higher than in past wars, and in particular Operation Allied Force over Kosovo–Serbia. Carl Conetta concludes that less bombing accuracy is the major reason. Marc Herold's comparative study of United States–British air campaigns finds that Afghanistan had the highest civilian kill ratio per 10,000 tons of bombs (2,643) compared with Cambodia (1,852), Kosovo–Serbia (522) and the Persian Gulf (341). He also concludes that for every 3 Taliban leaders killed, the bombing produced 400 civilian deaths.[53]

The bombing made an already catastrophic refugee problem worse. The *Council on Foreign Relations* estimates that 200,000 bombing refugees joined 4.1 million Afghans who had fled to other countries in the previous years of fighting.[54] The *United States Committee on Refugees* says a million refugees were added in 2001. Numerous relief organizations reported that the bombing was preventing food supplies from getting through to refugee camps. In his analysis of the impact of bombing on refugees, Marc Herold offers more specifics:

> Just during the month of October, US bombing limited the amount of food delivered to Afghanistan to 13,000 tons, or one-fourth the minimum estimated needed to cover those at risk. The US air war has disrupted food and medical supplies, has instilled panic leading to mass exodus, and in some instances has involved the direct bombing of refugee camps—an obvious war crime—as well as vehicles carrying fleeing refugees and also bombing Red Cross warehouses [twice] and World Food Programme trucks and facilities.[55]

Among numerous other accounts, Doug McKinlay of the *Guardian* wrote that 350,000 refugees were located in Maslakh camp alone, with an estimated 100 dying per day from starvation and exposure, a rate of one 9/11 victims' toll per month. Raising the issue of 'indirect' deaths from bombing, Jonathan Steele estimated in May 2002 that 20,000 civilians had died of various bombing-related maladies.[56]

In Operation Enduring Freedom, the greater ratio and number of civilian casualties can be blamed on high-altitude bombing, ordnance with great destructive power, heavy use of cluster bombs, and a penchant for targeting civilian-rich urban areas and civilian facilities. As in past 'clean' air campaigns, the military command also pursued a strategy that valued planes and pilots over civilians.[57] Other factors, such as political and military decisions, were also at work. In his careful analysis of US strategy, Carl Conetta says 'regime change' that required undermining the civilian political will, urban targeting, prioritizing time over accuracy and relying upon intelligence from local sources who had a political axe to grind all combined to produce the high level of civilian suffering.[58]

True to form, the United States military and civilian officials have refused to 'officially' count civilian casualties in Afghanistan. As in all post-Vietnam wars, they feigned no interest in tallying enemy fatalities at all, either combatant or non-combatant. Yet Carl Conetta asserts the Pentagon did indeed count enemy combatants and provided them 'unofficially' to the media. As to civilian casualties, it was top Pentagon officials, particularly Defense Secretary Rumsfeld, who provided the specific rationale for not counting them in Afghanistan. At a 4 December 2001 press briefing, while asserting the 'United States has taken extraordinary measures to avoid civilian casualties in this campaign,' he explained:

> With the disorder that reigns in Afghanistan, it is next to impossible to get factual information about civilian casualties ... we generally do not have access to sites of alleged civilian casualties on the ground ... in cases where someone does have access to a site, it is often impossible to know how many people were killed, how they died, and by whose hand they did die. By comparison — and think of this — consider how difficult it has been to get accurate casualty estimates for the attack on the World Trade Center towers.[59]

Rumsfeld and other Bush Administration officials, aided by a compliant media, derisively dismissed reports of high civilian casualties as products of Taliban propaganda or 'ridiculous.'[60] Reports from the battle of Tora Bora indicating US bombers hit three villages causing dozens of civilian deaths brought instant denials from Pentagon officials. In a strange twist on his Defense Secretary's claim that it was impossible to count civilian casualties, Rear Admiral Craig Quigley explained: 'If we had hit a village causing widespread death that was unintended, we would have said so. We have been meticulous in reporting whenever we have killed a single person.'[61] True to form, the Pentagon embraced civilian death counts fitting their undefined notion of precision warfare and minimal collateral damage. A *Human Rights Watch* study headed by William Arkin, who had gained notoriety for undercounting civilian casualties in NATO's bombing of Kosovo-Serbia, is a case in point. Severely critical of Herold's report, Arkin and his group reportedly estimated civilian deaths in the first three months of bombing at between 100 and 350. Close to a year after 9/11, despite Arkin's later criticism of Rumsfeld's management of civilian casualty counts, the unpublished study's conclusion that only 350 Afghan civilians had died was 'still bandied about as if it has some scientific basis.'[62]

THE PENTAGON MAKES CIVILIAN CASUALTIES DISAPPEAR

If you kill a lot of civilians, the people inside Afghanistan will believe you're not discriminating and that you are against the people of Afghanistan. ... To the extent you behave in a way that suggests that you don't really care about whether or not you're killing soldiers and people that are terrorists or civilians ... it makes life difficult for countries that are supporting us.[63]

By his own admission, Secretary of Defense Donald Rumsfeld was fully aware of the political stakes involved in the issue of civilian casualties. In Operation Enduring Freedom, he sought to monopolize the flow of information about civilian death and injury. To this end, the Pentagon bought the exclusive rights to photographs taken by Space Imaging's Ikonos satellite, the sole commercial satellite imagery available. It also relied on sympathetic journalists. For example, the *Washington Post*, recycling the old idea that people of other cultures don't value life as much as the West does, offered quotes from Afghan officials asserting Afghanistan's civilian population was so delighted to be liberated, they were not dwelling on the deaths of their family and friends.[64] Doing his part, *New York Times* columnist Nicholas Kristof called upon the shopworn, yet enormously effective idea of North American benevolence, arguing that killing Afghan civilians and Taliban forces was a humanitarian adventure. The war, he said, demonstrated that 'troops can advance humanitarian goals just as much as doctors and aid workers.'[65]

In evaluating the Bush Administration's approach to the civilian casualty issue in Afghanistan (and Iraq), Carl Conetta says Rumsfeld's Pentagon purposely used their virtual monopoly on the discourse of war to frame the issue in their favor. When faced with reports of civilian deaths, Pentagon officials relied on the 'fog of war' defense and minimized the deaths as 'unfortunate and regrettable.' Confronted with Taliban accusations that US bombing was targeting civilians, they dismissed them as propaganda or claimed the casualties were the responsibility of the Taliban for purposely putting civilians in harm's way. In other cases, alleged dead enemy 'civilians' were tagged as supporters of the 9/11 terrorists. In obvious political maneuvering, while Bush officials discouraged consideration of 'why' North American civilians become casualties (except for the gratuitous bow to their benevolence, innocence and humanitarianism), they jumped at every chance to explain who (terrorists) was responsible and why (malice).

Even before Operation Enduring Freedom, the Pentagon began its sophisticated managing of the civilian casualty issue. First, they trumpeted the concept of 'new precision warfare.' Second, they engaged in what Conetta coins as 'casualty agnosticism, the attempt to sink the whole issue of war casualties in an impenetrable murk of skepticism.'[66] There are several tactics involved in this strategy. One is to claim the United States does not have resources with the expertise or access to battlefield sites to do a credible count. A second is to plant stories in the media that it is impossible to derive an accurate estimate of casualties. Another is the employment of phrases such as 'completely well-determined,' 'known with certainty' or 'full knowledge of all casualties and all secondary effects.' Finally, Conetta says the Pentagon engaged in exaggerating or exploiting several indisputable facts such as that 'battlefield reporting is difficult' or the statistical reality that 'aggregate casualty estimates are imprecise.' Overall, Conetta charges that the practice of 'casualty agnosticism' insists on an unnecessarily (and impossible) high standard of what passes for 'precision' in aggregate statistical analysis. It also depreciates the value of hundreds of detailed reports from the 'battlefield.'[67]

Conetta and others find the Pentagon claims to be untrue, manipulative or unfounded. For example, the United States is the most technologically advanced and richest nation in the world, sending 'special ops' forces and sophisticated multi-million dollar missiles and planes loaded with thousands of dollars of ordnance across the world. For critics, it stretches credulity to insist that the same nation lacks the resources or expertise to investigate the effects of its bombing. Indeed Conetta claims the number of reporters and advanced technology mean the 'flow of information from the battlefield has never been richer.'[68] His most telling point goes to the contradiction inherent in the Pentagon's approach: that it 'simultaneously maintains that today's wars are low casualty events while denying that we can know even approximately how many people are being killed in those wars.'[69] In short, how does one know these wars are not creating 'killing fields' if one doesn't count? Why does the United States and other bombing nations have the ability to document the enemy's killing fields in Kosovo, Israel and Cambodia, but not their own in Serbia, Palestine and Cambodia? How can the Pentagon report 1,000 Al Qaeda fighters killed in battle while in the same breath denying any ability to verify civilian deaths on the same battlefield? Finally, why can the Pentagon set standards for 'statistical precision' but refuse to do so for bombing precision?

The Pentagon's campaign of obfuscation and denial did not escape notice. Eyewitness reports of civilian targets being bombed, of rescuers being attacked, refugee camps and fleeing families being strafed and of all Afghans being treated as 'the enemy' began to create doubts about the Pentagon's veracity. Even some ardent war-supporters found the civilian death counts credible and recognized there was a concerted effort to hide the facts.[70] By July 2002, as Pentagon officials again dismissed the counting of civilian deaths, American–Afghan organizations, originally supportive of the war, protested in front of the White House at the killing of Afghan civilians.

Other problems undercut the Pentagon's credibility. For example, once the Taliban were overthrown, newly appointed anti-Taliban government officials provided the civilian casualty lists. Journalist David Corn notes that if the Pentagon is to be believed, it means after the Taliban's demise the eyewitnesses to the bombings 'were all participating in an elaborate and sophisticated propaganda campaign that entailed faking craters, persuading anti-Taliban officials who are working with American forces to lie to benefit the Taliban, enlisting dozens of persons with god-awful injuries for the con, and encouraging children to tell false stories about how they came to be harmed.'[71] Professor Ira Chernus called the Pentagon's purposeful campaign to 'disappear' Afghan civilian casualties 'worse than treating civilian suffering as incidental. It is denying that the suffering even exists. It is denying that these millions of people exist. By the miracle of modern television, the Afghan civilian population has been disappeared.'[72]

Finally, evidence the United States military was directly targeting civilians came from within the military itself. Reacting to eyewitness reports of civilians dying in the bombing of Chowkar-Karez, 'unidentified Pentagon officials told CNN that the village was "a fully legitimate target" because it was a nest of Taliban and al-Qaeda sympathizers.'[73] Although targeting civilian sympathizers is a clear violation of the Geneva Convention, an unidentified Pentagon official said: 'The people there are dead because we wanted them dead.'[74]

Revenge for the 9/11 attacks and President Bush's 'whatever it takes' instruction loosened not only the US military bombs but at times their tongues. Army Major Bryan Hilferty, of the Tenth Mountain Division, spoke for many North Americans as he linked the terrorist attacks on New York with the carnage visited on the civilians of eastern Afghanistan. With obvious satisfaction he said: 'It took only 20 terrorists to kill 3,000 of the world's citizens in the World Trade Towers. We've killed hundreds and that means we've saved hundreds of thousands of lives. This is a great success.'[75] Army Private Matt Guckenheimer, also of the Tenth Mountain Division, confirmed the military's policy of treating all civilians as the enemy. He asserted: 'We were told there were no friendly forces. ... If there was anybody there, they were the enemy. We were told specifically that if there were women and children to kill them.'[76]

All the historical patterns associated with strategic bombing are found in the conduct of Operation Enduring Freedom. By mystifying the reality of strategic bombing, they worked to the political advantage of those who ordered the bombing, namely the revenge-bent Bush Administration. Indeed, the added dimension of revenge made it easier to portray all citizens of the Afghan 'other' as an enemy deserving of their fate. As presumed terrorists and terrorist sympathizers responsible for the 9/11 attacks, they were, as a people, on the wrong side of George W. Bush's great divide between 'us and the terrorists.' In a larger historical sense, they were on the wrong side of the self and other distinction carefully cultivated since the sixteenth century under the rubric of the 'West and the Rest.'[77] As such, they became legitimate targets for the military and civilian command of the self-professed leader of the 'family of nations.'

The bombing scheme and the political context in which Operation Enduring Freedom was launched, and continues, is a return to a past when North American bombs were dropped with righteous vengeance and instruction to kill anything that moves. In the most obvious sense, whether intended or not, 9/11 produced 'a new Pearl Harbor.' As in World War

Two, strategic bombers were chosen to conduct war from the skies on an enemy viewed as less than human. Now it was against an Afghan people described in the media as 'Huns, roaming packs of savage, heartless beasts who feed on each other's barbarism. (Expletive) cavemen with AK 47s.'[78] As in the aftermath of the real Pearl Harbor, the bombers were sent with virtuous indignation to right a perceived wrong against a benevolent North American people.

Many military strategists have noted that the chosen bombing strategy of Operation Enduring Freedom was not, in military terms, necessary to accomplish the stated goals of destroying Al Qaeda training camps and strongholds and ridding Afghanistan of the cruel yoke of the Taliban.[79] By late November 2001, these aims were realized and in less time than those of the Persian Gulf or Kosovo–Serbia conflicts. But after 9/11, it was the political message that mattered. Thus the bombing continued and, along with it, large-scale human suffering In comparing the Afghanistan air campaign to the Persian Gulf War, Marc Herold notes the influence of the post-9/11 political fury on bombing decisions when he writes; 'Afghanistan has been an air war characterized by a low bombing-intensity and high civilian casualty-intensity while Iraq was the reverse.'[80]

In their post-9/11 wars on terrorism in both Afghanistan and Iraq, the Bush Administration has employed an 'anything goes' bombing strategy that has killed thousands of civilians, while holding the high moral ground on the subject of terrorism. To the millions of civilians who have been, are now or are about to be bombed, this is troubling. How and why the Bush Administration and previous bombers have been able to escape the label of 'terrorism' is to be explored next. This discussion is relevant to the entire history of and – unless something changes – to the future of strategic bombing. For as renowned author and peace activist Arundhati Roy points out, 'The bombing of Afghanistan is not revenge for New York and Washington. It is yet another act of terror against the people of the world. Each innocent person that is killed must be added to, not set off against, the grisly toll of civilians who died in New York and Washington.'[81]

Dodging the Terrorism Label

THE POLITICS OF DEFINING TERRORISM

Historically, the North American and European nations have generally offered a narrow definition that excludes the actions of nation states from being labeled 'terrorism.' This position is largely based on Max Weber's framework in which states use 'legitimate' violence and condemn the violence of others as 'terrorism' or 'barbarism.'[1] For example, Title 22 of the United States Code defines terrorism as 'premeditated, politically motivated violence' against 'noncombatant targets by subnational groups' usually with the goal to influence an audience.[2] When politically convenient they have labelled out-of-favor nation states, such as the Soviet Union, Iran, Iraq, Libya, Syria, Sudan and Cuba, as states sponsoring, controlling or actually involved in terrorism.[3] Meanwhile, the FBI hunts state and not-state terrorists based on terrorism being 'the unlawful use of force against persons or property to intimidate or coerce a government, the civilian population or any segment thereof, in the furtherance of political or social objectives.'[4] In contrast, the Iranian religious scholar Ayatolla Taskhir defines terrorism more broadly as 'an act carried out to achieve an inhuman and corrupt objective and involving threat to security of any kind, and in violation of the rights acknowledged by religion and mankind.'[5]

Disagreement on a definition has left terrorism a 'politically loaded' concept. Thus, political leaders of all stripes are free to invoke the terrorism issue to push their own political agenda. For example, on the advice of their favorite 'in house' terrorism experts, many have taken a 'we know terrorism when we see it' approach that has resulted in pointing the finger of terrorism solely at the violence of others. The lack of a universal consensus has meant they can apply their own definition in a 'consistently inconsistent' manner to suit their political convenience, in order to avoid the terrorism label being applied to their own violence.[6]

Yet in most definitions and popular discourse there is a core meaning to terrorism that separates it from other forms of violence. In the post-9/11 context, this core can be ascertained by asking: what bothered most people about the attacks of 9/11? Or, why was it an act of terrorism? When asked in informal surveys, participants overwhelming said what disturbed them most about the attacks was the death and injury caused to innocent civilians (noncombatants).[7] Overall, the events of 9/11 were deemed to be 'unfair attacks on innocents' fostering public outrage in the United States and global sympathy for the victims. In essence, the distinction between combatants and noncombatants continues to hold meaning when applying the terrorism label to acts of violence. For this reason, political leaders around the world, in particular those who possess and use instruments of mass destruction, attempt to convince themselves and others that harming innocent civilians is not their purpose, intent, policy or fault.

For over a half-century the United States has used strategic bombing to wreak havoc on millions of civilians and on all aspects of civilian life. Those responsible for this violence against non-combatants have escaped any link to terrorism by constructing an elaborate and ever-evolving rationalization scheme, utilizing multiple aspects of human knowledge and discourse. Some, such as the language of 'collateral damage,' are familiar. Others, like the proposition that liberal democratic governments by definition cannot be terrorists, are likely known only to the academy of terrorism experts.

Historically, the rationalization scheme has been invoked to dodge any link between every aspect of United States military action and terrorism. The focus below pertains only to efforts to disconnect strategic bombing from terrorism.

THE INSTRUMENT OF POLITICAL SOCIALIZATION

In the broadest terms, the rationalization scheme begins with political socialization, a process that occurs in every society by which individuals acquire, and in most cases sustain, their 'worldview.' Political socialization involves multiple institutions of idea storage, access and transmission, principally the family, government, schools, media, social organizations, and formal religion. Agents such as events, race, class, gender, region and age are also important shapers of a political orientation focused principally on the question: what does our society stand for and against? For example, the people in the Middle East who are again being 'liberated' by yet another imperial power and choose to resist appear to many North Americans as ungrateful malcontents. Yet their contemporary resistance is in part a product of their historical experience with Western colonialism, during which they learned to stand for self-reliance and self-preservation and against tyranny. For the same principles, 'ungrateful' North Americans threw off the yoke of 'benevolent' British colonial occupation in 1776.

In the extremely parochial culture of the United States, the politically socialized answers to the question 'what do we stand for and against?' reflect a very positive view of self and a largely negative view of societies organized differently. North Americans are encouraged to believe in liberal democracy based on the notions of freedom, equality, individualism and competition. Other forms of democracy, authoritarianism and totalitarianism are projected as wrongheaded or evil and not to be tolerated or even encouraged. Capitalism is seen as fair and just, any alternative socio-economic system as unworthy, indeed unnatural. As a religious society, though celebrating God differently, US citizens think of themselves as highly moral. Relative to their role in the world, North Americans are taught that when elements and agents of United States power go to foreign lands, it is purely reactive in nature and done for benevolent or humanitarian reasons, generally to protect or spread the blessings of Western freedom, liberty and democracy. As a result, it is no exaggeration to say that when most North Americans peer into the national mirror the characters reflected back are Snow White and Prince Valiant engaged in 'God's work.' Lurking in the dark and threatening background is the evil witch of the 'other.'[8]

No one, including those counted upon for their 'objective' perspective such as educators, journalists and religious leaders, is immune to these learned biases, however subtle. For example, rampant within Western media is a bias that insists upon 'credible Western sources only, please.' Sources reporting events that do not square with the imagery of the moral lens, especially foreign sources, are either not welcome or, if used, tagged as suspect. At times, corrections verifying the reporting of 'other' sources may be necessary. These consistently end up buried in the back pages of the 'credible' Western print media, where they remain eclipsed by the front-page denials.[9] As in the past, Western media coverage of self/other differences and conflicts presents simplistic, exaggerated caricatures of presumed distinctions. True to the historic 'West and the rest' divide, Western culture is represented as natural, rational, calm and dignified while all others are grouped as chaotic, alien, frenzied and arbitrary.[10]

It is through this highly 'moral lens' that North Americans learn to view themselves and the world. Because of it, they permit others to censor information for them as well as engaging in constant self-censorship. Throughout the history of strategic bombing, US administrations past and present and regardless of political bearing have been able to count on this politically constructed prism when the charge of terrorism has been leveled at US violence, including strategic bombing.

After 9/11, Bush Administration officials purposefully plucked the public heartstrings to the tune of 'North America, the benevolent and innocent victim of evil.' In the context of the War on Terrorism, any allegation that a US 'Top Gun' bombed noncombatants is the antithesis of what the nation and its warrior class in particular stand for. For the vast majority of citizens, it is to be dismissed out of hand. When evidence surfaces suggesting civilian casualties go beyond the acceptable or minimal range, the process of political socialization soothes the Western conscience. Victims of bombing can be easily disappeared or 'sanitized' as unimportant since, as the 'other,' they don't value life anyway or are deserving of their fate. Meanwhile, the yellow ribbon culture requiring unquestioned support for the troops and sympathy for 'our' fallen and their families dominates the home front. The few who refuse or question are excoriated as un-American, unpatriotic or subversive. Those who persist are deemed to be 'friends of the enemy.'

In both broad and particular terms, the process of political socialization has proven resilient in sustaining the core elements of the US outlook and voice. Yet it is a dynamic process, constantly subject to the nuances and influence of events, social movements and technological advancement. Since the end of World War Two, air power's sheer destructive capability, the politically socialized abhorrence for terrorism and the revolution in communication technology that can now bring war's horrors into the living room have required other instruments of rationalization and mystification.

IMAGING TERRORISM

Since the early 1970s, the subject of terrorism has been an object of intense, indeed urgent, political socialization. As discussed, on behalf of their political sponsors, the Western-based terrorism industry has utilized a politicized framework to monopolize the terrorism discourse. As a result, most Westerners 'know' terrorism is something 'they' do and 'we' don't. In this 'only-if-they-do-it-is–it–to–be-called-terrorism' context, labeling US actions as terrorism is the most politically incorrect act one can do.[11] Like past administrations, Bush II officials understood this and coded the events of 9/11 in the familiar terms of the 'ideology of terrorism.' Their declaration of a 'war on terrorism' is only the latest and so far highly successful effort to structure terrorism discourse to the advantage of the 'family of nations.' The aim is and has always been to provide cover for their own war of terrorism and rally millions of people against the terrorist 'other.'

Mostly absent from public discourse on terrorism, but well known and accepted within the terrorism industry, is the theoretical basis for excluding 'us,' that is Western liberal democratic states, from the problem of terrorism. British terrorism industry expert Paul Wilkinson deserves credit for this argument. In his *Terrorism and the Liberal State*, he offers a distinction between *force* – the legitimate and legally authorized coercive power of the state – and *violence* – the unauthorized and thus illegal use of coercion by the state or non-state agents.[12] Terrorism is a form of violence. Thus as long as the liberal state uses coercion with the majority consent of the governed (determined exclusively in the election process), that coercion is force, not violence. Since legal, its coercive acts, no matter how violent or whom they are applied against, cannot be terrorism. Thus President Richard Nixon's wholesale bombing of Cambodian and Laotian civilians was not terrorism: even though much of it was kept secret from the public and their congressional representatives: a majority of voters had chosen Nixon in a fair democratic election.

As successful as they have been in imaging terrorism to serve their political interests, there are perils for the human condition if Western power brokers are allowed to pursue their 'jingoistic enterprise.' As Dr Jeremy Henzell-Thomas says, in playing to the 'crippling conditioned beliefs and prejudices that Francis Bacon called the "Idols of the Mind," they place at risk the hallowed principles of objectivity which supposedly underpin Western civilization.'[13] That is, for the sake of political expediency they are undermining the very civilization they profess to be saving from the so-called 'irrationalities of terrorism.' So far, thanks to the success of their rationalization system, they have been able to mask or dismiss this danger. Yet, it is a danger past empire builders ignored to their eventual peril.

THE POLITICS AND ETHICS OF LINGUICIDE

In his *Essay on Liberation*, Herbert Marcuse called for a 'linguistic therapy' based on his recognition that language is a powerful weapon in the 'verbal arsenal of the Establishment.'[14] His point has not been lost on Western architects of war who have long understood the advantage to controlling discourse. They know language can clarify, confuse and conceal reality. US officials in particular have been adept at using terms, concepts and imagery expressing their desired message. For example, to emphasize the non-aggressive nature of US foreign policy and conversely the offensive character of its Cold War communist enemy, in 1949 the War Department was renamed the Department of Defense. The Pentagon, often called the 'fortress of the forties,' is symbolic both of North American military might and, due to its fortress-like architecture, of its alleged defensive posture. Conversely, US officials are constantly imaging potential threats to their nation's benign benevolence as products of 'an aggressor' out to disrupt their 'just peace.'

When war comes, the United States is portrayed as a 'neutral peace-keeper' determined to right the wrongs committed by a violent enemy involved in 'crimes against humanity' such as terrorism, ethnic cleansing or other assorted atrocities. Beginning with the Korean War, code labeling of military operations has been an important public relations tool for the United States and its allies. A dual-purposed instrument, the point is to send the right and often righteous message about the purposes of US violence (freedom and democracy) in contrast with the enemy's evil intent.

The list is long, but a few examples, most relating to air campaigns, will suffice. In Korea, most of the emphasis was on military goals. Offtackle, the football metaphoric joint strategic war plan that included atomic strikes, emphasized the offensive character required to counter communist aggression.[15] Plan Strike, the dropping of leaflets warning of the impending bombing of cities was intended to show the humanitarian side of US violence and lower North Korean civilian morale. Strangle was expected to 'isolate the battlefield' and force Chinese withdrawal. Important counter-offensives were labelled Thunderbolt, Roundup, Killer, Ripper, Courageous, Audacious, and Dauntless. In Vietnam, the first air strikes on North Vietnam, coded FLaming Dart One and Two, sent the message of precision while Rolling Thunder conveyed the idea of a gradually escalating storm-like air campaign. The Christmas 1972 air offensive was labelled Linebacker One and Two. Utilizing the favorite football metaphor again, the code sent the message of 'aggressive defense.'

In order to influence media coverage, political messages have dominated the coding since Vietnam. Operation Urgent Fury, the invasion of Grenada, was meant to signify the immediate and 'angry' United States reaction to alleged subversive Marxist aggression in its Caribbean backyard. The name of the 1989 invasion of Panama was changed from Blue Spoon to Just Cause to differentiate Bush Administration motives from the 'crimes' of the Noriega regime which allegedly included harassment of US citizens and the murder of a marine. In the Gulf War of 1990–91, Desert Shield utilized the metaphor of the natural world to project United States war power as a politically benign 'force of nature.'[16] The concept 'shield' was carefully chosen to contrast the USA's allegedly defensive purposes with Iraqi aggression in Kuwait and possibly against Saudi Arabia. The name given to the offensive phase, called Desert Storm, purposely linked it with the previous defensive stage of the 'operation.' Both were so effective in garnering domestic and international support, that subsequent phases were named Desert Saber (ground offensive), Desert Farewell (the redeployment) and Desert Share (the distribution of leftover food from the military inventory to North American poor people).

In Kosovo–Serbia, the name Operation Allied Force stressed the collective nature of the violence used 'for humanitarian purposes' against the alleged ethnic cleansing of Slobodan Milosevic, the 'Butcher of Belgrade,' and his Serbian 'rogue state.' The same political sensitivity was apparent in naming the strategic bombing campaign. Colonel John Warden's Instant Thunder code name was changed to CENTAF Offensive Campaign – Phase I to disassociate it from the controversial Rolling Thunder bombing of Vietnam. Finally, both post-9/11 military campaigns, Enduring Freedom in Afghanistan and Operation Iraqi Freedom in Iraq, impart exactly what political 'good' justifies the killing. This is not surprising given President George W. Bush's penchant for invoking the 'F' (freedom) word at every turn.

The Pentagon and its military services are notorious for their Orwellian use of language (doublespeak) to place a positive spin on the negative. For example, the MX missile, as tall as the Washington Monument, with intercontinental range and loaded with multiple warheads, each many times more powerful than the atomic bombs dropped on Japan, is advertised as 'the Peacekeeper.' The neutron bomb becomes the 'landlord bomb,' favored because it silently kills people without destroying the buildings they rent. Meanwhile, President George W. Bush reminds wounded soldiers 'the war in Iraq is really about peace.'[17] The point of this 'linguicide,' as media analyst Norman Soloman calls the habitual destruction of common meaning, is to frame the issues of war in terms and imagery assumed acceptable to the public.[18] More and more, it is done with the complicity of mainstream media who so far refuse to enter into 'linguistic therapy.'

As the technology of destruction has advanced, it has also become equally important to soothe the conscience of the warrior class. To minimize or prevent any anguish among its 'air technicians,' the Pentagon converses in what is called 'Warspeak.' This is terminology sanitizing the death and destruction from bombing as it objectifies and devalues anyone and anything below. Thus, 'strike packages,' 'platforms,' 'weapons systems' (aircraft) do not shoot weapons or drop bombs; they fly 'sorties,' provide 'air support,' 'visit a site,' do 'kinetic targeting,' and drop 'force packages,' 'ordnance' or 'vertically deployed anti-personnel devices,' often in a 'routine limited-duration protective reaction' (air raid) causing an 'airburst' (a warhead or shell set to explode above the ground to maximize effect). The phrase 'incontinent ordnance delivery' means that a bomb missed its target and may have caused 'collateral damage' or 'regrettable by-products' (death and destruction). Targets are 'hard' and 'soft' 'assets' that are not destroyed but 'visited,' 'acquired,' 'taken out,' 'serviced,' or 'suppressed.' Weapons do not kill, they 'eliminate,' 'neutralize,' 'degrade,' 'hurt,' 'smoke,' 'blow away,' 'suppress,' 'impact,' 'cleanse,' 'atrit' or 'terminate with extreme prejudice.'[19] Over time, national security officials and media pundits have enthusiastically embraced, if not come to love, the terminology used to objectify modern 'robo' or 'hyper' war.[20]

The realities of air war are also coded in medical terms (surgical strikes), mechanics (tools in the tool box) and as nature's might. In Desert Storm 'the war 'erupted' with 'waves' of attacks the first night. Bombs continued to 'rain' on their targets; planes 'thundered' through the night. Scuds 'showered' their debris below. Baghdad was 'awash' in sounds and lights as the bombs exploded, and the 'fog' of war made it difficult to ascertain if US troops were killed by 'friendly fire.'[21]

True to military tradition, explicit sexual terms 'lighten' the reality of war as they simultaneously masculinize 'our boys and their weapons' while feminizing the enemy.[22] Bombs 'penetrate' radar and targets. Saturation bombing 'softens' the enemy. Ground troops 'thrust deeply' into enemy territory to 'cut off' (castrate) the enemy army. In Desert Storm, weapons systems 'engaged' Iraqi forces that had 'raped' Kuwait and refused to 'pull out.' Saddam had 'married' chemical weapons. The invention of 'candy Saddam balls' led to British soldiers being depicted in the popular press prepared to bite Saddam's testicles off.[23]

According to researchers for the Danish newspaper *Politiken*, the English-speaking press presented the 1991 Gulf War in the following self/other terms.[24]

The Allies have:	**The Iraqis have:**
An army, navy, and air force	A war machine
Guidelines for journalists	Censorship
Briefings to the press	Propaganda

The Allies:	**The Iraqis:**
Eliminate	Kill
Neutralize	Kill
Hold on	Bury themselves in holes
Conduct precision bombing	Fire wildly at anything

The Allied soldiers are:	**The Iraqi soldiers are:**
Professional	Brainwashed
Cautious	Cowardly
Full of courage	Cannon fodder
Loyal	Blindly obeying
Brave	Fanatic

The Allied missiles:	**The Iraqi missiles:**
Do extensive damage	Cause civilian casualties

George Bush is:	**Saddam Hussein is:**
Resolute	Intractable
Balanced	Mad

The above is the tip of a constantly evolving and expanding conceptual iceberg invoked to militarize the home front, sanitize the war effort and demonize the enemy. All of the terms and concepts applied to the 'forces for good' disassociate them from the plague of terrorism. Conversely, the language describing the enemy links them with terrorist acts either directly or as being willing to and capable of doing them. It helps sustain the constructed divide between the moral 'us' and immoral 'them' and mask the controversial and destructive nature of war itself.

The concept 'collateral damage' requires special attention. Used throughout bombing campaigns since Vietnam, North American officials now invoke it without hesitation, explanation or apology to address the issue of enemy civilian casualties. It is a clear example of techno-speak, terminology intended to place a value-free face on this aspect of war. Its use has effectively made the victims of strategic bombing disappear, massaged the public psychic and numbed the conscience of the warrior class. It is now widely accepted, even insisted upon, that collateral damage is not just unavoidable, but a necessary by-product of war in general and aerial attack in particular. This is especially true when collateral damage is combined, as it often is, with minimal, unintended or expected damage. Yet the speciousness of its claim to be value-free is exposed once it is known with certainty that to refer to the 9/11 victims, or Israeli victims of Palestinian 'suicide bombings,' or casualties among occupation forces in Iraq, or victims of the Madrid and London bombings as collateral damage would provoke government, media and public outrage in the 'family of nations'.[25] The same would happen if they were ever described as 'attrited regrettable by-products' of the War on Terrorism.

HOW TO AVOID THE TERRORISM LABEL WHEN BOMBING

The bombing nations have used a variety of methods to avoid the terrorism label being linked to their strategic bombing. Most effective is the assertion that unlike terrorists, they are not directly or 'willfully' targeting noncombatants in their bombing campaigns. As my inquiry into the origins of strategic bombing theory noted, this was not always the case. Yet, even during Britain's admittedly indiscriminate bombing of Germany, Winston Churchill was adamant there was a difference between indiscriminate and wanton (terrorist) bombing. After World War Two, a similar distinction was at the center of the debate between 'horizontal' (the Curtis LeMay–SAC school) and 'vertical' (ACTS) bombing. In the modern era of air power (and terrorism), the bombing nations have insisted there is a meaningful distinction between saturation bombing (indiscriminate or wanton bombing of civilians and cities) and strategic bombing (trying to minimize civilian casualties when targeting military and military-related (civilian) infrastructure. In short, they have insisted there is a moral difference between terrorism, seen as bombing to kill civilians, and war, meaning dropping bombs knowing they will kill civilians.

This distinction is intended to give the 'family of nations' the moral and intellectual space to bomb freely. It has worked. Today they invoke air power not as an anomaly or as Hugo Grotius wrote in 'cases of extreme urgency or utility,' but simply as something done in the normal course of modern warfare.[26] Armed with this distinction and the assertion that strategic bombing saves both friendly and enemy lives, air power enthusiasts have convinced Western audiences that slamming warheads into the earth from great heights is standard moral procedure. As Michael

Neumann notes, support for strategic bombing is so strong in the West that its status as a 'general strategy which is known to mutilate civilians isn't even up for discussion.'[27]

Airpower strategists adamantly insist they bomb only military targets. Historically, when distinguishing between combatants and noncombatants, military targets allegedly were restricted to uniformed forces engaged in battle, their weapons and direct support services. But as strategic bombing doctrine has developed, the definition of a military target has become more inclusive and open to constant reinterpretation. As noted, all of the strategic bombing Prophets accepted Douhet's point that the distinction between the home front and the battlefield no longer held meaning. In essence, their argument has been codified in the Hague and Geneva Conventions. As a result, any target can be hit without legal consequence if the military command determines its destruction to be a 'military requirement' or 'military necessity' to winning the war. Thus, from World War One through to the 'Shock and Awe' bombing of Iraq, terrorizing the civilian population, making them suffer by destroying the civilian infrastructure in order to weaken their political resolve to resist, have been justified as a 'military necessity' to winning. In all the post-1945 bombing campaigns, a central component of US Air Force doctrine has been 'dual-use' targeting, directly and willfully attacking civilian targets such as electrical grids, roads, bridges, dams and communication centers, all determined to be part of the enemy's war effort. Application of the dual-use doctrine has meant erring on the side of inclusion, expanding the meaning of 'military necessity' as the prosecution of war continues to the point of targeting every element of society if that is what it takes to win.

The bombing nations have held to this position even when, as in the case of the Persian Gulf War, they knew the 'indirect effects' of the bombing on Iraq's civilian infrastructure placed the lives and health of thousands of non-combatants, mainly children and the aged, in certain jeopardy. Armed with the dual-use concept, NATO spokesman Jamie Shea could easily dismiss criticism of NATO bombing of Serb radio and television facilities during Operation Allied Force with the comment 'we have nothing against the media, but RTS is not media. It's full of government employees who are paid to produce propaganda and lies ... therefore, we see that as a military target.'[28]

Very often alleged 'facts on the ground' are used to expand the military target category. They include designating a village, town or area as 'enemy-occupied' or claiming that military targets are 'close by.' US officials have used both to rationalize the continued use of anti-personnel ordnance. For example, during Operation Enduring Freedom, the US faced heavy criticism from a variety of sources, including the UN and Afghan civilians, for the use of cluster bombs. Senior Pentagon officials acknowledged the immediate and long-term danger to civilian life but justified bombs intended to shred and dismember human bodies as a 'weapon necessary to win the war.'[29] As US Air Force bombers hit heavily populated sites, an unapologetic Donald Rumsfeld snarled that cluster bombs were 'being used on frontline Al Qaeda and Taliban troops to try to kill them is why we're using them, to be perfectly blunt.'[30] The Defense Secretary and his Pentagon's assurances that everything possible was being done to minimize civilian casualties went unchallenged. The 'patriotic' journalists were again reminded of the difference between weapons that intentionally kill civilians, such as the commercial jets of 9/11, and cluster bombs killing civilians as an unintentional yet predictable side effect of war.

The Pentagon routinely boasts it is able to prosecute air war with 'great success' and still minimize civilian casualties. This claim regularly goes unscrutinized. For example, during the Persian Gulf War, General Norman Schwarzkopf announced on two television shows a bombing mission 'success rate of 80 percent.' Unquestioned as to the definition of 'success,' he left the impression that 'success rate' meant targets were hit 80 percent of the time. In fact, the United States military defines 'success rate' as the percentage of flights able to drop their bombs, not the percentage of targets hit. Likewise, the questions what is minimal or acceptable civilian casualties remain unasked or, if asked, go unanswered. Military officials do take great pains to explain why it is possible to minimize them and how it is done. First, they assert military training and experience allow them to determine what weapons and what circumstances best serve military goals and minimize effects on civilians. In this way, General Richard Myers defended Allied cluster bomb use in Afghanistan while reconfirming the difference between the West and the terrorists:

> We are trying to be very careful in the way we plan this particular conflict. Probably only the US and its allies could do it in such a way that we minimize civilian casualties. If we match up a specific weapon to a specific target and we make the judgment that it's in accordance with the law of armed conflict, and we've worked this very, very carefully, then we'll use that weapon.[31]

More important, the claim to be minimizing civilian casualties rests on the longstanding assertion that advances in technology have resulted in precision bombing. It is true, in a comparative sense, that with new technology, aerial targeting has become more accurate and precise. While political and media officials use these terms interchangeably, the US military defines them differently. Putting the Air Force's 'scientific' jargon in somewhat understandable terms, 'Precision measures the scatter of shots aimed at an identical point, while accuracy measures the deviation of the center of a scatter pattern from the true location of the supposed target.'[32] Regardless of the slight technical difference, the essence of both 'precision' and 'accurate' is the ability to hit the intended target.

The experience of air power confirms that the meaning of 'accurate' or 'precision' bombing has been wonderfully elastic, a circumstance very much to the political benefit of the bombing nations. Originally it meant discriminate as opposed to indiscriminate bombing, a distinction central to Trenchard's proposal to hit 'precisely' Berlin's industrial areas rather than the entire urban setting. In this context, even with rudimentary bombing technology, it wasn't difficult to be 'precise.' With advances in technology, precision bombing has come to mean hitting targets on or near center (how much is elastic as well) in a 'scatter shot ' pattern. Still, as the political liability associated with terrorism increases, the constant talk about 'precision' bombing, 'pinpoint' accuracy or 'robo war' is done not for technical clarity but to silence critics of strategic bombing. It also helps mask the reality that air power technology is more destructive than ever. In the end, Western audiences are assured and accept as true that wars from the sky are increasingly 'clean' for friend and foe alike. Given the bombers' tight control of the discourse of war, this 'truth' is likely to go unchallenged until or unless Western audiences are unfortunate enough to endure someone else's notion of 'precision' bombing.

The claim of precision bombing, particularly in the comparative sense, reveals the prominent place the technological fix has in the Western psyche (and its ability to quieten dissenting opinion). It is especially evident among US elites, notably Defense Secretaries Robert McNamara and Donald Rumsfeld who vigorously pursue their vision of war in which technology always trumps human will.[33] This overriding commitment to weapons of destruction is justified as 'keeping ahead of the enemy' and 'reducing friendly casualties.' It is also offered as the guarantor of national security and the Western way of life. The showcase for the 'technological imperative,' weapons development is rarely questioned. Indeed, throughout the modern era of terrorism, the Western terrorism industry experts have pushed 'outinventing the terrorists' as the centerpiece of their counter-terrorism strategy.

Also assuaging the public conscience is the claim that 'high tech' weaponry has made contemporary war more moral than past wars. Such a comparison makes the very idea of war more palatable and future wars more likely, as 'the US public always believe that in the next war, new military technologies will avoid civilian casualties on the other side.'[34] Thus, for moral, national security and practical reasons, the 'technological imperative' can be counted on to influence the public mindset to the political advantage of those in power who seek to maintain power through violence. As a result, the 'technological fix' is constantly on display.

Yet, the technological fix is not without problems. In technological terms, the destructive capacity of the new weapons far outweighs any 'precision' capabilities. The Pentagon's failure to engage in 'critical self-scrutiny' and the shifting terrain of urban warfare also undermine the advantages of new technology. Thus the assumption the next war will have fewer civilian deaths becomes suspect.[35] Finally, new technology is always used by humans. The Iraqi village of Amiriyah was bombed because satellite photos showed activities in it matched the profile of a 'military command center.' This 'regrettable mistake' and many others demonstrate that technology still requires human interpretation and intervention. As Edward Herman sees it, 'The tradeoff in the shift to high-tech to reduce US casualties is greater civilian casualties in the target states.'[36]

For the bombing nations seeking to escape the terrorism label, the revolution in transportation and communication is a new complication. In the past, military officials could easily monopolize reports from the battlefield, telling whatever tale suited their military and political agenda. Now they must compete with independent agents who gain access to, investigate and report on battlefield events. This, together with rising sensitivity to the terrorism issue and the dramatic increase in the destructive power of modern weaponry, has made the task of dominating the flow of battlefield information more urgent, greater in scope and requiring more ingenuity than ever before.

For the US military, one of the most important lessons of the Vietnam debacle was the need to reassert its monopoly over battlefield reporting. Though it did everything possible to discourage, punish and discredit independent journalism, the Pentagon's version of the Vietnam War was forced to compete for the hearts and minds of the North American people with others shedding a different and often critical light on US military strategy and prospects. Beginning with the invasion of Grenada, the Pentagon, with the active support of its political mentors and a compliant corporate media, has attempted to reconstitute its control over the combat zone. In addition to traditional measures such as press passes, controlling TV and radio access and refusing interviews, a plethora of new techniques, too many to discuss at length, have been in place.[37] Notable among them are the Persian Gulf 'military press pools,' Operation Iraqi Freedom's 'embedded' journalists and the Pentagon's Iraq Media Project. Journalists not 'in the pool' or unembedded are characterized as 'lacking credibility' or 'unpatriotic,' even subversive. Less known are the Pentagon's intimidation efforts, including vetting reporters before the invasion of Iraq, controlling their communication gear during the war and warning 'unauthorized' reporters that they and their gear would be deemed enemy targets.[38]

In a context in which ideological pressures and 'professional biases' produce institutional media censorship and the self-censorship of 'patriotic' journalists, these tactics have once again given US political and military elites the power to shape the discussion of civilian casualties as they see fit.[39] As in the past, their techniques of persuasion begin with the art of denial. Indeed, as Norman Soloman notes, 'Denial is key to the success of public-relations campaigns that always accompany war.'[40] Denial that specific battlefield events ever occurred or that civilian casualties went beyond the 'expected' level have been especially effective when coming from military personnel 'on the ground' and endorsed by the corporate media mantra 'the reports cannot be independently verified.'

Events that even a complicit media cannot ignore have generated other explanations. General William Sherman's famous 'War is hell' comment, now updated to 'This is war, and war is hell' or 'stuff happens,' is offered, often with a resigned shrug of the shoulders, to explain 'unfortunate' civilian deaths.[41] For example, after the 'Shock and Awe' bombing of Iraq, Fox News pundits responded to news of Iraqi civilian casualties with a cavalier 'The fact is they accompany wars' and 'The fact that people are dying, is that really news?'[42]

The more sophisticated 'fog of war' concept is invoked to dismiss battlefield traumas as events of nature and to suggest there are 'unknowns' to war. When it comes to counting civilian casualties, Pentagon officials routinely insist that in the 'fog of war' there are not only the unknown, 'but also the 'unknowable.' As Donald Rumsfeld quipped, 'With the disorder that reigns in Afghanistan, it is next to impossible to get factual information about civilian casualties.'[43]

War is 'hell' and with its complexities there is the unknown. But it is a specious intellectual and convenient political leap to assume the unknown are 'unknowable.' Western citizens depend on their military experts to 'unpack' the fog of war, not package it to fit their professional and political needs or those of their civilian mentors. Yet, time and again on the issues of strategic bombing, this is exactly what occurs.

Though strategic bombing is said to be 'very precise, very accurate,' the caveat 'technology is not perfect ... yet' often accompanies it. Smart bombs are pitched as 'very precise,' but have 'unfortunately gone astray' in all air campaigns. This includes Operation Iraqi Freedom in which the Pentagon calculates they went astray 7–10 percent of the time. Any 'confirmed' civilian casualties are said to be 'unintentional,' 'unfortunate' or 'regrettable' by-products of 'rare or random errors' and 'mistakes' resulting from 'technological failures,' bombs 'going astray' and missiles that are 'loose,' 'off course' or 'improperly targeted.' There are also 'rogue' missiles, like the one launched in 'self-defense' that hit a suburb of Sofia, Bulgaria, during Operation Allied Force. Even in hindsight, the word 'terrorism' is systematically avoided. For example, the British and US decision to bomb civilian centers in World War Two is now couched as a 'regrettable excess.'

Strategic bombing resulting in civilian casualties invariably brings up the 'intentions matter' argument. A frequent lament is: 'our ordnance may have caused collateral damage but unlike terrorists, it was not our intent to do so.' Before the 2003 invasion of Iraq, Pentagon officials warned, 'civilians are going to die ... hopefully not in large numbers ... war is not antiseptic ... our intent is to ensure that we keep those bad effects to the minimum.'[44] Intentions also mattered in public discussion of the Johns Hopkins report that tallied 100,000 Iraqi civilian deaths. 'We didn't go outright and intend to kill any civilians. You make it sound like we are an evil empire bent on destroying the lives of others.'[45]

In language that would make the Prophets proud, a United States foreign affairs specialist tells CNN's Aaron Brown that the ultimate good intention is to pursue the 'humane' goal of ending the war quickly even if 'the United States might have to accept slightly more civilian casualties.'[46] In this case of linguicide, substituting 'inflict' for 'accept' clarifies his true meaning. It is not North Americans who will have to 'accept' casualties among their family members. Colonel Phillip Meilinger is able to rationalize civilian deaths from air power with his argument that compared to 'other coercive mechanisms such as sanctions, modern air warfare stands out as an increasingly efficient, effective and humane tool of foreign policy.'[47] Again, the Prophets would be delighted.

Western elites continue to depend heavily on the 'intentions matter' rationale even though, as Michael Neumann notes, 'the tendency today, as the laws on murder demonstrate, is not to count good intentions as excuses, because the child ends up just as dead.'[48] Such legal tendencies (precedents) must be ignored if the high moral ground is to be held by the strategic bombers. Highlighting the assumed evil intentions of those designated as terrorists, helps the cause. Of course, as bombing keeps killing civilians, claims of good intentions cease to matter or ring empty to those being bombed. This is especially true if, as noted above, the intent to win quickly makes civilian casualties an integral element of strategic bombing. Often, those alive at the end of the war, even if it ended quickly, don't understand or accept the 'humaneness' of the intent. Too often they have sought revenge using their instruments of violence with their own 'best of intentions' for humane purposes.

A number of ways are used to assign the responsibility for civilian bombing victims to others. Usually the enemy gets the blame. In the presumed high moral climate of the West, this tactic is extremely effective in both the arena of public opinion and with 'patriotic' media. Word of bombing casualties is deemed enemy propaganda, often without question, since 'we don't do those things.' Conversely, it is believed with certainty that the enemy routinely invents or overstates civilian casualties as part of its propaganda campaign to undermine the moral edge of the West. It is said the callous enemy is playing a 'game of numbers.'[49] Meanwhile, rumors of enemy 'genocide' and 'ethnic cleansing' go unquestioned and are pursued with cheery investigative vengeance.[50] Other techniques include assuming that, once civilians have been warned to leave a town or area, only enemy combatants and their civilian sympathizers remain. Many cities and towns, such as Fallujah, Iraq, have been razed to the ground under this cynical assumption. In many cases, most recently in the revenge bombing of Afghanistan, the total population is alleged to be supportive of the government. Thus, in the Douhet tradition, all citizens become combatants. In cases of 'industrial web' bombing, as in the Persian Gulf War, the unfortunate dead were blamed for being 'in an area too close' to a military target or were said to be scavengers. In other instances, civilian casualties are said to result from 'our missiles being seduced' (thrown off course) by enemy radar. Again the familiar sexual connotation is evident.

Increasingly, blame is placed on enemy anti-aircraft fire: urban dwellers are victims of the law of gravity in which 'what goes up must come down.' Though military experts argue this is unlikely, the contention plays well in popular opinion and thus is repeated in public venues.[51] Callous and sly enemy leaders, most recently Saddam Hussein and Slobodan Milosevic, the Butchers of Baghdad and Belgrade respectively, are accused of moving civilians close to military targets, trusting the moral West won't attack civilians. They are also indicted for hiding military equipment and personnel among fleeing refugees. If so, enemies of the West will be sorely disappointed. Deemed tactics of war, to the Western military mind any military installation or convoy with a 'human shield' is fair game for the bombers. As US military officials in Afghanistan said, 'In a war to the bone like this one, where the enemy's immorality is publicly proven, if they involve their non-combatants then they become legitimate targets, no matter how regrettably.'[52] Even before 9/11, the US military operated on the premise that when battling terrorism, it is necessary to 'fight fire with fire' in order to win. Thus countering 'terrorism with terrorism' is militarily effective and morally appropriate since allegedly it ends war more quickly.[53]

Here again the enemy is blamed, this time for introducing immorality into the conduct of war. Thus, in 'responding' there is no need for 'moral niceties.' This position has taken on new meaning in the post-9/11 War on Terrorism. It is common for media and military officials now to insist that any discussion or image of enemy civilian victims be presented, as CNN chairman Walter Isaacson said, 'in the context of a terrorist attack that caused enormous suffering in the United States.'[54] Likewise, George W. Bush, responding to the question of why 'suspected' terrorists were being 'renditioned' (sent to other countries for interrogation allegedly involving torture), simply said '9/11.'[55]

No doubt some of the allegations concerning enemy responsibility for civilian suffering have a ring of truth to them. Yet, unlike enemy assertions, no 'independent verification' is required for them to be deemed credible 'facts on the ground.' For a 'patriotic' and militarized audience, they stand as truth statements since they verify what is already 'known' about the terrorist enemy. If the allegations are found to be false, any correction ends as 'back page' truth, still suspect and awaiting 'further independent confirmation.'

Curious as it may sound, when civilian casualties occur in conflicts in which the US shares command with indigenous allies it is attempting to 'save' or 'liberate' from oppression, bombing 'mistakes' are often – without investigation – laid at the feet of the ally's command structure. In Vietnam, Cambodia, Afghanistan and now Iraq, well-meaning yet unsophisticated allies have been said to be responsible for providing US pilots with 'on the ground' intelligence and selecting targets. When bombing, the aircrews are alleged to be only carrying out their orders and thus captive to the personal desires and political priorities of the ally. If civilians are hit, it is the responsibility of those selecting the targets not the US 'Top Guns.'[56]

Recent strategic bombing cases demonstrate that when the United States and its ally controlled the 'facts on the ground' as in South Vietnam, 'the most vicious and civilian-damaging operations by the US war machine were carried out....'[57] The Pentagon's tight control of the flow of information in Afghanistan and Iraq has meant the finger of blame has been pointed first at the enemy and then, when necessary, at the erstwhile allies, the warlords of the Afghan Northern Alliance and the 'poorly trained' security forces of the Iraqi interim government.

In escaping culpability for the scourge of terrorism themselves, North American elites have a long and consistent posture of excluding allies, in particular the other bombing nations, from the terrorism label. In addition to their 'mistakes' 'tragic errors' and 'stray bombs,' allies may at times 'use inappropriate force' 'violate human rights' or 'circumvent, undermine or break the law.' But they never commit acts of terrorism. For example, Israeli bombings of Palestinian and Lebanese civilians are reported as 'a predictable strong response' intended to 'hold the terrorists accountable.' At times, Israeli force is regrettably 'excessive,' 'heavy-handed' or 'disproportionate.' Russian bombing of Chechnya is an 'internal matter,' 'deplorable,' even 'ominous,' in which the civilian population is being 'uprooted.' The slaughter of Cambodian villagers was not in consequence of indiscriminate bombing (terrorism), but because of a mistake in 'box' (area) bombing.

Finally, as the post-Vietnam bombing experiences show, the ultimate US response to civilian casualties is summed up in General Tommy Franks' blunt statement, 'We don't do body counts.' Other comments such as 'we have no way of knowing precisely how many casualties occurred,' or 'accounting for collateral damage is 'uninteresting' or not 'mission essential,' or impossible due to the 'complexities of wartime environments' convey in different ways and tone the same message. Other agencies are in concert with the military's position. After Operation Enduring Freedom, USAID, citing 'security risks,' did not disperse promised funds to independent groups investigating civilian casualties in Afghanistan.

When confronted with studies assessing civilian casualties, the Pentagon responds differently depending on whether the numbers are 'acceptable' to them or not. If they are, they are hailed as proof of the effectiveness of precision bombing. If not, with the active cooperation of the media, if mentioned at all, they are heavily criticized for poor methodology or alleged to be using enemy data. Such was the case with the 'unacceptable' numbers reported in the Daponte study (Persian Gulf) and Herold study (Afghanistan). More recently, the Johns Hopkins Bloomberg School of Health peer-reviewed study claiming over 100,000 Iraqi civilians died, mainly women and children, and 79 percent of them from strategic bombing, was greeted with the same mix of silence, skepticism and scathing criticism as those of past wars.[58] Typical were the responses of David Aaronovitch of the *Guardian*: 'I have a feeling (and I could be wrong) that the report may be a dud,' from Paul Waugh of *The Times*, 'the 100,000 death toll figure could not be trusted because it was based on an extrapolation,' and of Channel 4 News science reporter Tom Clarke: 'Without bodies, can we trust the body count?'[59] The purpose of the government and media campaigns of silence and skepticism on civilian body counts is to befuddle the issue, confirm the Pentagon's assertion that counting civilian casualties is an impossible task and eventually render assessment of even 'expected collateral damage' obsolete.

Largely out of sight of popular venues, but very important for keeping intellectual opinion in line, are scholarly discussions and works focused on why US strategic bombing doesn't violate the Hague and Geneva statutes on protecting civilian life. For example, in his examination of the bombing of dual-use targets, Kenneth Rizer notes the huge loopholes in the Hague Conventions (1899 and 1907), Geneva Conventions (1949) and Protocols I and II to the Geneva Conventions (1977) that permit the bombing of dual-use targets. Claims of 'military necessity' or even Protocol I's requirement to prove 'concrete and direct military advantage' are said to render inapplicable prohibited actions against civilians such as 'wilful killing', 'grave breaches,' and 'extensive destruction.' Concepts such as 'wanton' and 'indiscriminate' go undefined and thus 'subject to interpretation' whose enforcement is in the control of the most powerful, in this case the bombing nations.[60] What becomes clear is that like all statutes standing as current international law, they are products of Western Great Power deliberation and coded in Western legal tradition. Most important, their enforcement is totally dependent on the political will of the powerful nations. Since the end of World War One, the power brokers happen to be the bombing nations who have demonstrated dogged determination to dodge the terrorism label. In the most recent case of manipulating the articles of the Geneva Convention, the Bush Administration decided that the statutes on the treatment of prisoners of war did not apply to members of Al Qaeda since they were not combatants of any single nation state. They ruled that Taliban prisoners, as citizens of the 'failed state' of Afghanistan, were also outside the protections of the Geneva Conventions. Experts on international law disagree on both counts but lack the political clout to overrule the Bush Administration lawyers.[61]

In total, the US efforts to escape the terrorism label have resulted in the construction of an ever-evolving labyrinth of rationalizations, truths, half-truths, double standards, assertions of expertise and manipulation of language, law, science, ethics and professional journalism, and factors of political and economic intimidation. What makes all of this possible and profoundly effective is a politically socialized intellectual climate long structured on race-, gender- and class-based notions of self and other. Western identity is and has been historically constructed in Anglo-Saxon, plutocratic and masculine militaristic terms. Anything or anyone different is projected as less moral, less civilized and deserving of a lesser fate. This is especially true if they are deemed in the way of or resistant to the power brokers' designs – whether it be a post-World War Two Free World, post-Cold War New World Order or, now, the neo-conservative design of a New American Century. The ascendancy of the US to the pinnacle of military power has made the scheme of rationalizations more potent then ever. It is North Americans, backed by their military power, who define the issues, dominate the discourse, set the agenda and dole out reward and punishment.

The terrorist attacks of 9/11 added the element of righteous revenge to the existing rationalization scheme. Indeed, the public callousness toward the bombing of Afghanistan and the Shock and Awe aerial assault on Iraq, too often on display through attempts at boorish humor, is a measure of the success to which the contemporary civilians of the 'other' have been objectified in race, class and gender terms, their lives and plight dismissed as irrelevant. The objectified other and the socialized identity of a benevolent self combine to be the most important and potent factors exempting the United States and its 'family of nations' from any responsibility for the scourge of terrorism, particularly in the jingoistic post-9/11 climate. But millions of people around the world disagree.

10

Terror from the Skies

'You can bomb the world to pieces, but you can't bomb it into peace.'[1]

Perception and deception are two constants in the human endeavor. Everyone engages in both, it is to be hoped more in the former than the latter. While the former can be constructive, deception too often leads to disaster for oneself and others. In the political world, purposeful deception is done for self-aggrandizement and advantage, also often to the detriment of others. Indeed, when powerful people in possession of deadly weapons act on policies based on deception, they dramatically and dishonestly affect the lives and aspirations of millions of people.

In the politicized world of terrorism, deception is rampant and to some degree accepted as part of the terrain. If the average citizen 'knows' anything about terrorism it is that 'one man's terrorist is another man's freedom fighter.' In this apparently innocuous statement, often said in a matter-of-fact and resigned manner, there is an explicit expectation of deceit. Yet, in political practice there is only hysteria and indignation when our 'freedom fighters' are called terrorists or when others deem our designated 'terrorists' to be 'freedom fighters.' Both scenarios illustrate the 'politically loaded' essence of terrorism and the stake all have in somehow convincing themselves and others that they are on the 'right' or 'righteous' side of a terrorism/counter-terrorism divide.

Because of its manipulative qualities and pejorative connotations, everyone has the opportunity to play politics with terrorism. But greater advantage goes to the ruling classes in powerful nations who have a virtual monopoly on the instruments of coercion and political discourse. For example, Western terrorism industry experts have long asserted that terrorism is the instrument of the weak, be they individuals, groups or nations. Unlike the powerful nations who have multiple ways and resources with which to protect or enhance their situation, for the less powerful, terrorism often becomes a last and necessary option.[2] Thus, for these experts it is axiomatic that the 'weak' are the terrorist 'other.' The strong, they argue, need not resort to the dastardly deed of terrorism. Nor is it a tactic to which the moral self would ever stoop. In March, 2005, the Bush Administration inscribed this perception in its new National Defense Strategy: 'Our strength as a nation state will continue to be challenged by those who employ a strategy of the weak focusing on international fora, judicial processes and terrorism.'[3]

The notion that terrorism is a tool solely of the weak is a case study in deception. As we have seen, the history of strategic bombing offers abundant evidence of the most powerful nations on earth willfully and enthusiastically 'stooping' to terrorism. Nowhere is this more apparent than in the US employment of strategic bombing.

In the 1970s, the United States remained committed to strategic bombing, yet sought to construct its identity as the 'champion of counter-terrorism.' As self-appointed head of the 'family of nations,' it employed and continues to exploit an elaborate system of rationalization to escape the terrorism label and silence its critics.

It is within this politicized terrorism/counter-terrorism context that the question is again asked: in their strategic bombing in which thousands of civilians end up as casualties, are the bombing nations agents of terrorism? Of course, the easy (and manipulative) way to answer the question is to define terrorism so that strategic bombing either falls in or outside the definitional criteria. For example, if terrorism is defined exclusively as sub-national violence, as the terrorism industry experts would have it, then as a doctrine of state policy, strategic bombing is excluded.[4] On the other hand, terrorism can be defined so that strategic bombing would fall within its purview. For instance, Charles Webel offers a definition of terrorism that would seemingly (though this is not his intention) be nothing more than a restatement of strategic bombing. For Webel, terrorism is 'a premeditated, usually politically motivated, use, or threatened use, of violence, in order to induce a state of terror in its immediate victims, usually for the purpose of influencing another, less reachable audience, such as a government.'[5]

In essence Webel's definition leads to the conclusion 'war is terrorism.' This equation may be a more useful or more correct reflection of reality. But it is not acceptable to the 'family of nations', who routinely prosecute war and therefore have a vital stake in separating their wars from other forms of violence, particularly terrorism. Moreover, they are in a position to make their definition and its political and moral meaning 'stick.'

This reality requires that if the question 'is strategic bombing terrorism?' is to be answered persuasively, the analysis must start with the Western bombing nations' definition(s) of terrorism, how they use it in their discourse and the criteria they invoke to dodge the terrorism label. In short, since the bombing nations possess an asymmetrical ability to employ violence and the power to characterize (legitimize) it in ways that obviously serve their interests, it is necessary to demonstrate the problematic nature of their own discourse. This may be yielding too much intellectual ground to the powerful.[6] Yet, it is by their definitional criteria that strategic bombing has been, is and in the foreseeable future will be judged. Thus, the core question must be answered within the obviously politicized but prevailing paradigm.

IS STRATEGIC BOMBING TERRORISM?

Throughout the history of strategic bombing, the bombing nations have separated their violence from terrorism on two counts. First, they assert that unlike terrorists, their strategic bombing does not directly target non-combatants. Second, they assert that if or when strategic bombing results in civilian casualties, unlike that of the terrorists, it is not intentional.

Yet, the experience of strategic bombing, even as briefly detailed in these pages, underscores the specious nature of both contentions. First, the Prophets did propose directly targeting civilians, although, except for Douhet, not indiscriminately or 'wantonly.' Still the original theory was proposed and accepted as a strategy of terrorism. The amendments to the Prophets' original doctrine – whether ACTS vital centers, Warden's concentric circles or Horner and Ullman's 'Rapid Dominance' (Shock and Awe) – all reject, at least at the outset, the indiscriminate bombing of civilians. They do, however, propose direct targeting of the civilian will to resist. To be effective, they must bomb the infrastructure civilians need to sustain productive and healthy lives, principally in the immediate but also in the long term. To that end, whether it be pre- or post-World War Two wars, considerable planning for and purposeful targeting of civilian infrastructure was undertaken. Even the elasticity of the concept 'military target' cannot hide the fact that civilian infrastructure was and is being targeted. Otherwise, the bombing of only military targets, traditionally understood to be battlefield military units, has no strategic meaning.

Theoretically, for strategic bombers of whatever stripe, the distinction between civilian and military targets does not 'strategically' exist since the Geneva Accords permit tactics deemed militarily necessary to win. Thus when the distinction is trumpeted it usually is at the start of a war and obviously done for political convenience and advantage. Yet, the longer a conflict persists, the pressure increases on the military command to produce a victory. The result has been a pattern in which over the course of any war, any pretense of a distinction between military and civilian targets is dropped. Direct bombing of civilians in their neighborhoods, villages, homes, schools, hospitals, shopping malls and religious sites occurs to the point where indiscriminate or wanton carpet bombing in 'free fire zones' 'boxes' or 'areas' containing entire villages has become the norm. The US military reportedly continued this tradition in Operation Matador, the bombing of Iraqi villages into rubble on the Iraq–Syria border in mid-May 2005. [7]

Perpetrators of violence that the 'family of nations' judge to be terrorists often do not directly target civilians; nor is their violence always indiscriminate or wanton. Regardless, the charge of terrorism is consistently applied. This ritual, coupled with strategic bombing's routine planning and ordering of the direct targeting of civilians and their way of life, exposes the asserted distinction between strategic bombers and terrorists as political at its core. In sum, if direct targeting of civilians is a defining criterion of terrorism, then in theory and practice, strategic bombing meets the criterion.

The second premise pertains to the issue of intent. Throughout the history of strategic bombing the mantra has been 'Civilians become casualties because terrorists intend them to' or 'Conversely, civilians die from our bombs but it is not our intention.' They are all 'targeting mistakes' or, as Ted Koppel likes to say, 'the unfortunate accidents of war.' [8] Yet, by the very strategy and weaponry they choose to prosecute war, the strategic bombers know they will kill and injure many civilians. For example, purposely targeting military targets in urban or congested areas is standard practice in contemporary bombing campaigns. Even doing so as precisely as possible, the imprecision of precision bombing, together with the level of dispersion and lethality of modern ordnance, guarantees that civilian casualties will occur. Electing to bomb with anti-personnel ordnance such as cluster bombs, phosphorus and napalm, that both critics and defenders agree is horribly destructive to civilian life, makes the bombers' intention crystal clear. [9]

In the same breath with which they utter their 'no intent' disclaimer, bombing planners announce their intention to minimize civilian casualties. They repeatedly and proudly do so under the presumption that in war minimizing civilian deaths is the 'best one can expect.' Purportedly, this 'truth' sets them apart from terrorists, and is therefore a laudable goal. Yet, implicit in the intent to minimize civilian casualties is the intent to cause civilian casualties. If this were not so, announcing the intent to try and minimize civilian casualties would make no sense. It does become logical if the real intent behind the strategic bombers' declaration is to seek political and moral advantage, particularly over those assumed to be intending to 'maximize' civilian casualties. It may be the distinction between those who say they intend to minimize civilian casualties and those who don't say it that helps to separate terrorism from other forms of violence. But this is not a delineation the strategic bombers make. Moreover, in addition to refusing to count bodies, they refuse to define or quantify what is meant by minimal. In Operation Iraqi Freedom, is IraqBodyCount's 10,000 civilian deaths evidence of intent to minimize or maximize? Are the 100,000 civilian deaths documented in the Johns Hopkins University study, a large proportion from bombing, indicative of the Pentagon planners' effort to minimize deaths and thus politically and morally acceptable? Are they evidence of the 'best that can be done' in war? Or do they reflect efforts to maximize civilian deaths? Since US officials refuse to comment on either, it is impossible to know which may have been their real intent. Regardless, in both instances, minimum or maximum casualties, there is intent to inflict some level of death and destruction on noncombatants, thus matching the core meaning of terrorism.

When all is said and done, it could be that the debate over intent is really about a difference in degree of intent. Acts of terrorism would be defined as cases of 'first degree' intent. Other forms of violence, including strategic bombing, would then be, as Marc Herold suggests, cases of 'second degree intentionality.'[10] But this also is not a distinction the bombing nations make. Plus, in terms of accepting or assigning responsibility, this is a distinction without meaning. Regardless of whether it is first or second degree, there is still intent and thus responsibility. Vijay Prashad addresses this point directly. Noting that the early laws on warfare always recognized the arguments about 'intention' as clever but flawed, he asserts:

> To say that the civilian deaths from aerial bombardment are unintentional is sophistry, because if there is a probability that the bombs will hit civilian targets, then ipso facto the civilian deaths are not unintentional. This is

tantamount to saying that a drunk driver who did not intend to kill someone in an 'accident' should be set free for lacking of such intention ... aerial bombardment always already intends to kill civilians, despite the best intentions of military planners.[11]

Taken individually, each scenario noted above undercuts the bombers' intentions argument. Combined, they render it highly suspect, if not legally indefensible. Yet, it continues to have a powerful and persuasive standing in the Western court of public opinion. This is true even as officials from the bombing nations regularly admit their intent to harm civilians. The litany is long and includes the bombing of an Afghan village after which the Pentagon bluntly admitted: 'The people there are dead because we wanted them dead.' Likewise, Israeli Chief of Staff Mordechai Gur publicly acknowledged: 'In South Lebanon we struck the civilian population consciously, because they deserved it.'[12] More recently, on 23 June 2005 the Israeli government announced it would launch air strikes on Gaza 'with the risk of civilian casualties' to protect its pullout from the Gaza Strip. Then, on 17 July, President Sharon echoed President Bush's 'whatever it takes' mantra, giving his military permission to use force 'without limitation' to quell the violence in the Gaza Strip.[13] After 9/11, President George W. Bush's intentions were clear when he boasted: 'When I take action, I'm not going to fire a $2 million missile at a $10 empty tent and hit a camel in the butt. It's going to be decisive.'[14]

In fact, the history of strategic bombing is full of belated confessions that civilian targets were purposely attacked. Menachem Begin's 'partial list' (30 episodes) of military attacks on Arab civilians under Israel's Labor governments or the Pentagon's admission that it purposely hit Afghan civilians are representative of a historical record that Western citizens are encouraged to ignore or excuse. Yet the intentions of the bombers are so apparent in Western militarized popular culture that they now dominate so-called war 'humor.' For example, a list of Afghanistan and Iraqi 'war jokes, ' in addition to being full of the usual racism and sexism, provide crass insinuation of the intended effects of bombing. Among them are:

> Weather forecast for Kabul, Karachi, Baghdad and Damascus for the week of 09/24/01: Very brief period of extremely bright sunlight followed by variable winds of 2000 knots and temperatures in the mid to upper 6000 degree range with no measurable moisture. SPF 12000 sunblock highly recommended if standing near an outside, reinforced structural wall less than 3 meters thick.

Or:

What do Bin Laden and Hiroshima have in common?
Nothing yet.[15]

In addition, the bombing nations' continual assertions that they know the intent of the 'terrorist' compound the sophistry of their premise. As with the strategic bombers, the intentions of enemy 'terrorists' often go unstated, or if stated are postured as the 'best of intentions.' For example, no one truly knows the intentions of the 9/11 attackers. Did they intend to kill about 3,000 or more civilians? Or, in targeting their designated 'military targets' (CIA offices in the World Trade Center and the Pentagon), was it their intent to minimize collateral damage? Is the number 3,000 minimal to them? No one knows the answer, especially since no one has taken responsibility for the 9/11 attacks, nor have the perpetrators ever announced their intentions. Yet, as always, in the 9/11 case, Western officials presumed to know the intentions of the designated enemy and ascribed to the terrorists wicked intentions that matched their politicized image of the 'other' and, not incidentally, their political agenda.

In the end, despite its largely indefensible nature, the intentions argument remains an important tool in the arsenal of deception of the powerful nations because they are able to construct a sophistic analytic framework in which they determine and articulate both their intentions and everyone else's as well. The overriding goal of this endeavor is to make sure the political and moral edge goes to the bombing nations.

Announced or not, the patterns evident in the history of strategic bombing expose the bombing nations' true intentions. First, undermining noncombatant political will has always been the core intent of strategic bombing doctrine and practice. Intent is also evident in the pattern of demonizing the enemy. The architects of strategic bombing, both before and during the air campaigns, always planned on lifting restrictions on bombing targets depending on the length and course of war. Among the most explicit statements of intent in this regard is that of Shock and Awe proponents. Well in advance of the March 2003 attack on Iraq, they warned that if after the initial bombing and a short pause to allow Saddam Hussein to capitulate '... no white flag is seen, the assault on Baghdad will begin. ... At this stage, the political imperative to keep civilian casualties to a minimum will have to be put to one side.'[16] Likewise, the Israeli military's intent to use terrorism is clear when General (Reserves) Eival Giladi, the head of the Coordination and Strategy team of the Prime Minister's Office, announced on television and in print that in the Gaza disengagement, 'If pinpoint response proves insufficient, we may have to use weaponry that causes major collateral damage, including helicopters and planes, with mounting danger to surrounding people.'[17] After every war, the winners' intentions and actions have been directed at excusing the bombing community, both friend and foe alike, from criminal prosecution.[18] Obviously, avoiding legal scrutiny is only necessary when there is fear or evidence of culpability. Since Vietnam, the bombing nations and the United States in particular have also been intent on obfuscating the numbers of enemy civilian casualties, as in 'it is our intention not to do body counts.' Invoking a multi-faceted system of rationales indicates a determined intent to escape the terrorism label. Finally, the strategic bombers have always intended to conduct 'precision' bombing, an intention not yet realized. Still, the intent remains and in the continuing experiment to determine if air power alone can win wars, it is intended and expected civilians will continue to die.

STRATEGIC BOMBING AS TERRORISM

A few days before the January 2005 Iraqi election of a new government, journalist Seymour Hersh summarized the situation in occupied Iraq commencing with the 'handover' of power to Prime Minister Iyad Allawi six months earlier.

.... since we have installed him on June 28, July, August, September, October, November, every month, one thing happened: the number of sorties, bombing raids by one plane, and the number of tonnage dropped has grown exponentially each month. We are systematically bombing that country. There are no embedded journalists at Doha, the Air Force base I think we're operating out of. No embedded journalists at the aircraft carrier *Harry Truman*. That's the aircraft carrier that I think is doing many of the operational flights. There's no air defense, It's simply a turkey shoot. They come and hit what they want. We know nothing. We don't ask. We're not told. We know nothing about the extent of bombing. So if they're going to carry out an election and if they're going to succeed, bombing is going to be key to it, which means that what happened in Fallujah, essentially Iraq — some of you remember Vietnam — Iraq is being turned into a 'free-fire zone' right in front of us. Hit everything, kill everything. I have a friend in the Air Force, a Colonel, who had the awful task of being an urban bombing planner, planning urban bombing, to make urban bombing be as unobtrusive as possible. I think it was three weeks ago today, three weeks ago Sunday after Fallujah I called him at home. I'm one of the people — I don't call people at work. I call them at home, and he has one of those caller ID's, and he picked up the phone and he said, 'Welcome to Stalingrad.' We know what we're doing. This is deliberate. It's being done. They're not telling us. They're not talking about it.[19]

Hersh describes occupied Iraq, but he could easily be writing about bombing campaigns in Chechnya, southern Lebanon, Serbia, Indochina, North Korea, Germany, Japan, Ethiopia or Somaliland, to name only a few. In the end, the events of these campaigns strip away any remaining debris of deception, denial, double standard and self-aggrandizement. Left exposed is the reality that by any 'objective' measure, the bombing nations are engaged in aerial state terrorism. Moreover, as the foremost advocate and active practitioner of strategic bombing since the end of World War Two, the United States has become the major perpetrator of terror from the sky. The historical record of strategic bombing confirms that, since Franklin Roosevelt, all US presidents have fought their wars, even those designated as a 'war on terrorism', by waging a war *of* terrorism.

For many citizens of the self-appointed 'civilized world,' and of the 'benevolent' USA in particular, this conclusion is difficult to comprehend, let alone accept. Because it so pointedly contradicts the politically socialized view about ourselves and others to which individually and collectively there is a huge intellectual commitment, this assertion fosters a myriad reactions among people: from bewilderment, disbelief, righteous indignation and frustration to open hostility and rejection. Yet, it is evident to all but the most jingoistic or delusional person, that in simply too many of the bombers' arguments political convenience is obvious, double standards are applied, eyewitnesses are discounted or credulity is stretched beyond belief. As Jerry Kroth concludes: 'there simply are too many bombing "mistakes" to ignore' in the West's bombing fields.[20] Within the ranks of strategic bombers, this means that the historical debate between Curtis LeMay's 'horizontal' bombing strategy and ACTS vital centers vertical bombing is not, as it has been postured, between advocates of terrorism and those who oppose it. Rather it was and is between advocates of 'indiscriminate' (horizontal) terrorism and 'discriminating' (vertical) terrorism. From the Korean War on there is simply too much evidence of purposeful attacks on certified civilian targets – resulting in thousands of immediate civilian casualties – to ignore, deny or explain away with any veracity. Particularly bogus is the constant refrain about minimizing civilian casualties while refusing to count bodies or define whether minimal means 5, 10, 10,000, 100,000 or many hundreds of thousands. Moreover, the mounting level of 'indirect' civilian carnage attributed to bombing's destructive effect on Planet Earth's environment is neither controversial nor accountable for with the simple pretext 'war is deadly.' Indeed, with strong evidence that the bombing planners know and understand the effects of bombing on environmental and human life and choose to go ahead, it is impossible for them to escape responsibility. As law professor Michael Tonry says, 'In the criminal law, purpose and knowledge are equally culpable states of mind.'[21]

In a climate in which terrorism is such a 'politically loaded' concept, so vulnerable to manipulation, and with great potential to separate self and other on moral terms, it make sense for those who dominate the discourse to seek advantage. Indeed, the great lengths to which the strategic bombers go to escape the terrorism label underscores the political nature of their mission. In this regard, the Bush Administration's War on Terrorism is the latest example of a bombing nation seeking to monopolize the terrorism discourse in order to give political cover to its own terrorism. Other national leaders from across the political spectrum understand this and have raced to be on the 'right' side of President Bush's constructed political divide between 'us' and the 'terrorists.' As always, in this 'war' being on the 'right' side means colluding with the powerful, seeking political shelter from their wrath until a shift in the power dynamics provides room for independent or oppositional positioning. Like the USA, the other members of the current 'family of nations' and their often troublesome 'second cousins' such as Pakistan, China, India and Indonesia also have a policy of state terror, one increasingly implemented through strategic bombing. They are the same nations who then cry 'foul' or 'terrorism' when others follow their example.

THE REAL TERRORISM DIVIDE

There is a great divide, but it is not the one constructed in the political imagination of the bombing nations between the West and the Rest, self and other, Islam and Christianity, civilized/uncivilized or terrorist and counter-terrorist. It is between those interested in dealing with the scourge of terrorism no matter the source or reason and those who are only inter-ested in the 'other's' terrorism. This great divide is between those who see and reject double standards and those who invoke national, class, gender and race consciousness to rationalize their double standards. It is between those who reject the replacement of 'individualistic rationality' with 'technological rationality' and those who embrace it.[22] On one side are those who, in the words of Caleb Carr, 'see that tactics of terror, while they might gratify the angry, vengeful imperative of their rulers, their soldiers and many wronged citizens, were detrimental to the own nations' causes.'[23] They are pitted against those for whom rage, revenge and 'might makes right' matter most.

Finally, there is a great intellectual divide. On one side are those with a sociological imagination, that is 'the capacity to range from the most impersonal and remote transformations to the most intimate features of the human self – and to see the relations between the two.'[24] Those with this capacity are more likely to empathize; to see and feel the pain of the 'other,' to put themselves in the other's place, identify with their 'collateral damage' and own up to their responsibility for it as they expect others to do. If members of the 'warrior class,' they are more likely to believe in the attributes of 'progressive limited war.'[25] Facing them across this divide are those who don't possess an understanding of 'the larger historical scene in terms of its meaning for the inner life and the external career of a variety of individuals.'[26] They are more likely to be without empathy for others, indeed more likely to see those on the other side of their constructed divide as things, to be treated without having to consider their circumstance or feelings or any responsibility for either. In this regard, as 'technicians' of war, the Western warrior class in general and the 'air aces' or 'Top Guns' of strategic bombing in particular have been purposely trained to objectify all those on the ground below as the enemy and to do so in race, class, gender, religious and national terms. Sadly, thanks to the controlled terrorism discourse, a significant part of the Western populace has learned to objectify 'them' as well.

WHAT MUST BE DONE?

For the scourge of contemporary terrorism to be diminished, Westerners, and North American citizens in particular, must comprehend the dangerous nature of the politically constructed divides and whose interests they serve. Then they must comprehend the real terrorism divide and ask themselves: Am I interested in combating terrorism in general, no matter by whom or why it is perpetrated? Or am I only interested in anti-Western, specifically anti-US terrorism? For terrorism to be combated effectively, the answer has to be yes to the former, and no to the latter. In short, the Western political imagination has to be constructed through the process of sociological imagination. In essence this means connecting the personal role in terrorism to the whole plight of humanity. To do so gives insight into Noam Chomsky's observation: 'We certainly want to reduce the level of terror, certainly not escalate it. There is one easy way to do that and therefore it is never discussed. Namely stop participating in it.'[27]

Taking this approach is particularly useful when considering aspects of strategic bombing. First, it means understanding that anyone can dismiss civilian bombing deaths as 'unintended loss of life,' 'accidents' and 'mistakes.' It means knowing that anyone can claim the other side is terrorist while the bombing self is not. Most important, it means comprehending that the validity of both above claims does not necessarily depend on any factual basis. Nor does it depend on whether the results of the West's 'precision' bombing are any different from the other side's terrorism. In the end, what passes as 'truth' depends upon who can enforce their political agenda, their denials and claims in public discourse and public policy. Throughout the course of their strategic bombing, the Western 'family of nations' has been doggedly successful at doing just that.

Second, it must be decided if the distinction between terrorism and strategic bombing that rests on direct versus indirect targeting is meaningful and to whom? If it is not meaningful to the thousands of bombing victims and millions more who are potential victims, then what is the point of insisting on a distinction that is fraudulent to a majority of fellow human beings just for short-term political advantage? This is especially true as there are dire consequences to doing so. For example, it is often said other peoples don't hate the people of the USA, but do hate their government's policies. For many citizens of the bombing nations, especially for those reluctant to engage in political activism, this is a comforting thought. But how long can that distinction hold if the North American public continues to abrogate its democratic and patriotic responsibility to investigate, question and turn a skeptical or critical eye to what its government is doing to other people in their name? How sustainable is it if North Americans who find the application of the concept 'collateral damage' ridiculous or inhumane when applied to their dead, cannot or refuse to recognize that in conveying their distress they have traveled to the other side of President Bush's terrorism divide and constructed the other's view of them?

Finally, the issue is not whether war causes civilian casualties. It does and with the lethality and dispersion effects of air power and the changing nature of war itself, civilian casualties are likely to increase rather than diminish.[28] Indeed, it may be that 'war is terrorism' and any distinction between the two should be abandoned. This is unlikely to happen so long as the powerful, particularly the bombing nations, profit politically, morally and militarily from the distinction. Maybe the best that is possible at this time is to do what this book attempts, to chip away at the Western monopoly on the terrorism discourse, hoping to expose the dangerous deceptions upon which it is based. Regardless, the future cannot be left to the current crop of bombers and their political allies. So far, as self-proclaimed winners of the twentieth-century wars, they have only had to consider the upside of strategic bombing. This has meant an ever greater dependence on and enthusiasm for air power and the continual search for their version of the 'clean' war. But if Caleb Carr's recounting of the history of warfare is correct, those who are victims of the West's 'clean' wars will find that notion absurd and eventually make the experience of wars dirtier than ever for everyone.[29]

Thus it is imperative that the bombers and their supporters be forced to deal intellectually with strategic bombing's 'other' or down side: the one their victims experience. The first step is to challenge the racist, sexist, class- and culture-based stereotypes sustaining the self/other identity, which historically have allowed the bombing nations to conduct war in a context of hate and righteousness. It also requires asking proponents of strategic bombing specific questions and demanding meaningful answers. For example, how prepared are you to accept your civilians suffering in war? How many civilian casualties would you deem 'acceptable' and under what circumstances? What is your understanding of 'minimal' and 'precision' in those circumstances? How meaningful would the 'other' bombers' apologies be (if they came) if they refused to count your civilian bodies, to define 'minimal' or to explain it wasn't their intent that 100,000 North Americans died in their precision bombing? Would you find the concept of 'collateral damage' ridiculous, callous or degrading when applied to your own dead? To the enthusiasts of Shock and Awe: would you deem a Hiroshima-type attack on your cities a moral way to conduct war? Finally, a rhetorical question dripping with obvious sarcasm: should a Shock and Awe bombing of your civilians be treated as an incomprehensible tragedy or the butt of callous racist and sexist humor?

Only with these questions and others is it possible to make clear to the bombers and their apologists what is obvious to millions across the globe: that when President George W. Bush said 'you are either with us or for the terrorists' he really meant 'You are either with our terrorists or for theirs.' Unfortunately, four years after 9/11, with civilians around the world caught in the crossfire of the jingoists' 'war of terrorisms,' the form of violence deemed to be terrorism remains a highly politicized issue in the North American psyche. Too many citizens and powerful elites are wedded to the imperial and privileged mantra that 'might makes right' and view the world through the lens of the 'good versus evil' or 'self/other' divide. Unless their worldview is challenged with purpose and effect, the destiny of the human condition will remain firmly in the hands of strategic bombers who are under strict instruction from their political mentors to do 'whatever it takes.' For certain, that means a future in which more strategic terror will rain from the sky. According to reports in the *New Yorker* (17 April 2006), as this book goes to press the Bush Administration has Iran in its strategic bombsites.

PROLOGUE

1   New research attempts to discredit this claim. See F. Taylor (2004) *Dresden: Tuesday February 13, 1945,* New York: HarperCollins.
2   R. Grant (2004) 'The Dresden legend,' *Air Force Magazine*, October, Vol. 87, No. 10, and Taylor 2004.
3   Grant, R. (2004) 'The Dresden legend.'
4   Stone, I. F. (1951) 'MacArthur ravaged Korea with methodological destruction,' *Compass*, 14 February.

1 SHOCK AND AWE!! SHOCK AND AWE!!

1   'Shock and Awe' was a favorite slogan of the German Nazi magazine *Signal*.
2   *New York Times*, 5 March 2003.
3   *Ibid.*
4   *Sunday Times*, 16 March 2003.
5   'BLITZ-COUP, Latest Confirmation That This Is A War For Regime Stabilization And Leadership Change,' WAR PLAN IRAQ Update Number 16, *Justice Not Vengeance*, 18 March 2003, www.j-n-v.org/AW_briefings.
6   *Sunday Times*, 16 March 2003.
7   West, A. (2003) '800 missiles to hit Iraq in first 48 hours,' *Sun-Herald*, 26 January 2003.
8   'Iraq faces massive US missile barrage,' CBS *Evening News*, 24 January 2003.
9   'Pentagon reveals plans for massive civilian casualties in Iraq,' International Action Center press release, 5 March 2003, www.iacenter.org.
10 *Guardian*, 23 March 2003.
11 Horner, C. and H. Ullman (1996) *Shock and Awe: achieving rapid dominance*, Washington DC: NDU Press, p. 2.
12 *Ibid.*
13 Spannaus, E. (2003) 'Shock and awe: terror bombing from Wells and Russell to Cheney,' *Executive Intelligence Review*, 31 October.
14 http://politics.7gen.com/commentators/chomsky.html.

15   www.nathannewman.org/ 20 March 2003.

16   *Salon*, 21 March 2003.

17   'Baghdad Wakes Up to Explosions,' FoxNews.com, 22 March 2003.

18   Van Wagenen, W. (2005) 'Iraq diaries, Shock and Awe: aerial bombardment, American style,' *ElectronicIraq*, 6 July.

19   'Shock and Awe,' PBS Online News Hour, 21 March 2003.

20   Mall, J. (2004) 'Blood on our hands,' *Impactpress.com*, February/March.

21   Scales, Jr, R. H. and W. Murray (2004), 'Battle plans under fire,' *PBS Nova*, 5 May 2004.

22   'Wolfowitz tells BBC Iraqi civilians not a target,' *BBC World Service*, 25 March 2003.

23   Dine, P. (2003) 'Practical politics guide effort to reduce Iraqi civilian casualties,' *St Louis Post Dispatch*, 16 March.

24   Conachy, J. (2004) 'US killed hundreds of Iraqi civilians in "precision" strikes,' World Socialist Web Site, 18 June, www.wsws.org.

25   Dao, J. (2005) 'A trail of pain from a botched attack in Iraq in 2003,' *New York Times*, 15 April.

26   Jehl, D. and E. Schmidt (2004) 'US 0-for-50 in air strikes on Iraq leaders at war's start,' *New York Times*, 13 June.

27   Jackson, D. (2003) 'US clouds Iraqi civilian deaths,' *Boston Globe*, 13 June.

28   Jackson, D. (2005) 'The tsunami victims that we don't count,' *Boston Globe*, 7 January.

29   Jehl and Schmidt (2004).

30   'Civilian casualties in Iraq,' *Canadian Press*, 4 April 2003.

31   Murphy, M. and C. Conetta (2003) 'Civilian casualties in the 2003 Iraq War: a compendium of accounts and reports,' Project on Defense Alternatives report, 21 May.

32   Ford, P. (2003) 'Surveys pointing to high civilian death toll in Iraq,' *Christian Science Monitor*, 22 May.

33   'Adding indifference to injury,' *IraqBodyCount*, 7 August 2003.

34   Roberts, L., R. Lafta, R. Garfield, J. Khudhairi, and G. Burnham (2004) 'Mortality before and after the 2003 invasion of Iraq; cluster sample survey,' *Lancet*, 29 October.

35   *Australian*, 30 October 2004.

36   *Ibid*.

37   Guterman, L. (2005) 'Researchers who rushed into print a study of Iraqi civilian deaths now wonder why it was ignored,' *Chronicle of Higher Education*, 25 January 2005.

38   Soyer, M. (2004) 'Missing information, US media mishandle the story on 100,000 dead Iraqi civilians,' *Baltimore Chronicle*, 30 October.

39   /blog.infinitemonkeysblog.com/, 28 October 2004.

40   'US and allies "kill most Iraqis",' *BBC News*, 29 January 2005, http//news/bbc.co.uk.

41   E&P Staff (2004) 'Knight Ridder scoop: Iraqi civilian casualties,' *Editor & Publisher*, 25 September.

42   Mall, J. (2004) 'Blood on our hands,' *Impactpress.com*, February/March

43   Georgy, M. and K. Sengupta (2004) 'A city lies in ruins, along with the lives of the wretched survivors,' *Independent* (UK), 15 November.

44   Jamail, D. (2004) 'Unusual weapons used in Fallujah,' *Inter Press Service*, 26

November.

45 '"Wedding cake" of aircraft stacked over Fallujah,' *Australian*, 12 November 2004.

46 *Ibid.*

47 Jamail, D. (2005) 'Stories from Fallujah,' *Truthout*, 8 February.

48 Fisk, R. 'The crisis of information in Baghdad, '*Independent* (UK), 19 July 2004.

49 'President Bush outlines Iraqi threat,' *The White House Office of the Press Secretary*, 7 October 2002, www.whitehouse.gov/news/release.

50 Clark, N. (2003) 'The return of Arabophobia,' *Guardian*, 20 October.

51 Scales and Murray (2004).

52 Horner and Ullman, 1996: 2.

53 'The "shock and awe" experiment: compilation, analysis and discussion of available information on the Pentagon's "shock and awe" battle plan for Iraq, especially as it affects civilian infrastructure and the civilian population,' 19 January 2005, www.notinourname.net/war/shock_awe.htm.

54 'Iraq attack likely to turn into humanitarian disaster: UN,' *Boston Globe*, 21 October 2002.

55 Mitchell, S. (2003) 'Reporting Iraq: the battle for objectivity,' *Sunday Business Post*, 30 March.

56 'Attacking Iraq,' www. globalsecurity.org/military/ops/iraqi_freedom.

57 Scales and Murray (2004).

2 THE ORIGINS OF STRATEGIC BOMBING

1 For the contributions of other British strategists see Higham, R. (1966) *The Military Intellectuals in Britain, 1918–1939*, New Brunswick: Rutgers University Press.

2 Howard, M., 'Men Against Fire: The Doctrine of the Offensive in 1914,' in Peret, P. (ed.) (1986) *Makers of Modern Strategy*, Princeton: Princeton University Press, p. 522.

3 For a history of weapons technology see among others, Peret (1986), and Wintringham, T. (1943) *The Story of Weapons and Tactics: from Troy to Stalingrad*, Freeport: Books for Libraries Press.

4 Callwell, C. E. (1996) *Small Wars: their principles and practice,* Lincoln: University of Nebraska Press.

5 Churchill, W. (1931) *The World Crisis, 1916–18*, Part I, London: T. Butterworth, Limited, p. 19.

6 Wintringham, 1943: 167.

7 Douhet, G. (1998) *The Command of the Air*, Washington, DC: Office of the Air Force History and Museums Program, p. 14.

8 Douhet, 1998: 6–7.

9 Douhet, 1998: 9.

10 Douhet, 1998: 10.

11 Douhet, 1998: 31.

12 Douhet, 1998: 20.

13 *Ibid.*

14 *Ibid.*

15 Higham, 1966: 253.

16 'Bombing Germany; General Trenchard's report of operations of British airmen against German cities,' *The New York Times Current History*, April 1919, p. 152.

17 Trenchard, H. (1928) 'The employment of the Home Defence Air Force,' in Meilinger P. S. (ed.) (1997) *Paths of Heaven*, Maxwell Air Force Base, Alabama: Air University Press, pp. 52-53.

18 Clodfelter, M. (1997) 'Molding Airpower Convictions: Development and Legacy of William Mitchell's Strategic Thought,' in Meilinger, 1997: 84.

19 Meilinger, 1997: 95.

20 *Ibid.*

21 Meilinger, 1997: 96.

22 *Ibid.*

23 *Ibid.*

24 Meilinger, 1997: 97.

25 Meilinger, 1997: 90

26 *Ibid.*

27 *Ibid.*

28 Mearsheimer, J. J. (1988) *Liddell Hart and the Weight of History*, Ithaca: Cornell University Press, p. 88.

29 Liddell Hart, B. H. (1925) *Paris,* New York: Dutton, pp. 40–41.

30 Hart, 1925: 45.

31 Douhet, 1998: 23.

32 Clausewitz, K. von (1873), *On War*, London: Trubner, Vol. I, p. 4.

33 Sherman, W. T. (1957) *Memoirs of General William Sherman, by Himself*, Bloomington: Indiana University Press, Vol. II, p. 111.

34 Douhet, 1998: 5.

35 '*Article XXII Draft Rules of Aerial Warfare*,' The Hague, February 1923, www.dannen.com/decision/int-law.htm

36 Trenchard, H. (1923) 'Buxton speech, 13 April,' *Trenchard Papers*, RAF Hendon, England, file 11/5/1-57, quoted in Meilinger, 1997: 51.

37 For a discussion of the demise of the League of Nations see Elmer Bendiner, *A Time for Angels*, New York: Knopf, 1975.

3 WHO IS TO BE BOMBED?
THE SELF AND OTHER IN IMPERIAL CULTURE

1 Wadham, B. (2002). 'What does the White man want? White masculinities and Aboriginal reconciliation,' in Pearce, S. and V. Muller, (eds.) (2002). *Manning the Next Millennium: studies in masculinities,* Evanston, IL: Black Swan Press.

2 The history of empire building is well documented in numerous accounts. Among them see Kiernan, V. G. (1982) *From Conquest to Collapse: European empires from 1815 to 1960*, New York: Pantheon Books; Landau, S. (1988) *Dangerous Doctrine: national security and US foreign policy*, Boulder: Westview Press, Williams, W. A. (1976) *America Confronts a Revolutionary World, 1776–1976*, New York: Morrow, Kiernan; V. G. (1978) *America, The New Imperialism: from white settlement to world hegemony*, London: Zed Books; Fanon, F. (2004) *The Wretched of the Earth*, New York: Grove Press; and Rodney, W. (1981) *How Europe Underdeveloped Africa*, Washington, DC: Howard University Press.

3 Reade, W. W. (1874) *The Martyrdom of Man*, New York: A. K. Butts & Co.
4 Kiernan, 1978: 88.
5 Zinn, H. (1995) *A People's History of the United States,* New York: HarperPerennial.
6 Kiernan, 1978: 87.
7 Zinn, 1995: 306.
8 Hirst, F. W., G. Murray and J. L. Hammond (eds.) (1998) *Liberalism and the Empire*, London: Routledge/Thoemmes Press.
9 See Zinn, 1995.
10 Baddeley, J. F. (1908) *The Russian Conquest of the Caucasus*, London: Longmans, Green and Co., pp. 96-97.
11 Kiernan, 1982: 158.
12 Grogan, E. S. and A. H. Sharp (eds.) (1900) *From the Cape to the Congo*, London: Nelson Edition, p. 361.
13 See Zinn, 1995: 295–97.
14 Osborn, S., (1860) *The Past and Future of British Relations in China*, London: W. Blackwood and Sons, p. 2.
15 Kiernan, V. G. (1969) *The Lords of Human Kind*, Boston: Little, Brown and Co., p. 27.
16 Archer, W. J. (1885) 'Accounts and Papers, 1884–5,' Vol. 81, June, cited in Kiernan, 1969: 174.
17 Routledge, R. (1879) *Discoveries and Inventions of the Nineteenth Century*, London: Routledge, p. 118.
18 'Colonialism and gender violence in the lives of American Indian women,' www.incite-national.org/involve/colonialism.html.
19 Stoler, A. L. (2002) *Carnal Knowledge and Imperial Power*, Berkeley: University of California Press, p. 1.
20 Kiernan, 1982: 20, 21.
21 *Ibid.*
22 Kiernan, 1978: 85.
23 For a discussion of class, race, religious and gendered aspects of Victorian life. see www. victoriaweb.org.
24 See, for example, Spencer, H. (1865) *Education: intellectual, moral, and physical*, New York: D. Appleton and Co.
25 For a discussion of working-class whites in North America see xroads.virginia.edu/~MA97/price/open.htm.
26 Newsome, D. (1997) *The Victorian World Picture*, New Brunswick, Rutgers University Press.
27 Newsome, 1997: 93.
28 Kiernan, 1969: 28.
29 Beveridge, A. J. quoted in Kiernan, 1978: 100.
30 For a discussion of phrenology and race in nineteenth century Britain see www.victorianweb.org/science/phrenology/rc3.html.
31 Frankenburg, R. (1970) *Displacing Whiteness*, London: Duke University Press, p. 6.
32 Wadham, B. (2002).
33 Kiernan, 1969: 225.
34 Kiernan, 1982: 181.
35 Mitchell, C. 'Biological Review of Our Foreign Policy,' *Saturday Review,*

February, 1896.

36 For a discussion of the black experience in North America see Gutman, H. (1925) *The Black Family in Slavery and Freedom (1750–1925)*, New York: Pantheon; DuBois, W. E. B. (1995) *Black Reconstruction in America, 1860–1880*, New York: Touchstone; and Logan, R. (1965) *The Betrayal of the Negro: From Rutherford B. Hayes to Woodrow Wilson*, New York: Macmillan.

37 For a discussion of gender and the Victorian age see Smith-Rosenberg, C. (1985) *Disorderly Conduct*, New York: Alfred A. Knopf and Baxandall, R., L. Gordon and S. Reverby (eds.) (1976), *America's Working Women*, New York: Random House.

38 Geddes, P. and J. A. Thompson (1901) *The Evolution of Sex*, London: W. Scott, cited in Conway, J. (1972) 'Stereotypes of femininity in a theory of evolution,' in Vicinus, M. (ed.) (1972) *Suffer and Be Still: women in the Victorian age*, Bloomington, IN: Indiana University Press.

39 Wolseley, G. J. (1897) 'War and civilization,' *United States Magazine*, May.

40 Bederman, G. (1995) *Manliness and Civilization*, Chicago: University of Chicago Press, p. 214.

41 Bederman, 1995: 31.

42 For a discussion of militarization see Enloe, C. (2000) *Maneuvers*, Berkeley: University of California Press.

43 Quoted in Gooch, J. (1981) *The Prospect of War*, London and Totowa, NJ: Frank Cass, p. 43.

44 Hobson, J. A. (1901) *The Psychology of Jingoism,* London: G. Richards, p. 1.

45 Kiernan, 1978.

46 Gooch, 1981.

47 For a discussion of the rise of fascism in Italy see Lyttelton, A. (ed.) (2002) *Liberal and Fascist Italy*, Oxford: Oxford University Press; Smith, D. M. (1976) *Mussolini's Roman Empire*, New York: Viking Press; and Berezin, M. (1997) *Making of the Fascist Self*, Ithaca: Cornell University Press.

48 Cook, C. (2003) 'The myth of the aviator and the flight to fascism,' *History Today*, December, Vol. 53 Issue 12, p. 7.

49 *Ibid.*, pp. 2, 3.

50 *Ibid.*, p. 7.

51 Cooke, M. (1996) W*omen and the War Story*, Berkeley: University of California Press, p. 116.

52 For a discussion of the origins of the image of the 'flying ace' see Robertson, L. D. (2003) *The Dream of Civilized Warfare*, Minneapolis: University of Minnesota Press.

53 Robinson, D. H. (1962) *The Zeppelin In Combat*, London: G. T. Foulis, p. 50.

54 Quoted in Wise, S. (1982) 'The Royal Air Force and the origins of strategic bombing,' in Travers, T. and C. Archer (eds.) (1982) *Men at War: politics, technology, and innovation in the twentieth century,* Chicago: Precedent, p. 167.

55 Barnes, J. K. (1921) 'The vindication of Squier and Deeds: what really happened to the billion dollar aircraft appropriation,' *World's Work,* July.

56 On the life of Trenchard see Boyle, A. (1962) *Trenchard*, New York: Norton; and Allen, H. R. (1972) *The Legacy of Lord Trenchard*, London: Cassell.

57 Mearsheimer, J. J. (1988) *Liddell Hart and the Weight of History*, Ithaca: Cornell University Press. See also Danchev, A. (1998) *Alchemist of War: the life of Basil Liddell Hart,* London: Weidenfeld and Nicholson.

58 Hart, L. (1934), 'Woman wanders – the "world wavers" or Woman and the world-quake,' *English Review* 59, September.

59 Quoted in Hurley, A. (1964) *Billy Mitchell*, New York: Franklin Watts, Inc., p. 115.

60 See Mitchell, W. (1924) 'Strategical aspect of the Pacific problem,' *Mitchell Papers*, Library of Congress, Washington, DC; Gauvreau, E. (1942) *Billy Mitchell: founder of our air force and prophet without honor*, New York: E. P. Dutton; Burlingame, R. (1952) *General Billy Mitchell: champion of air defense*, New York: McGraw-Hill; Cooke, J. (2002) *Billy Mitchell*, Boulder, CO: L. Rienner; and Sigaud, L. A. (1941) *Douhet and Aerial Warfare*, New York: G. P. Putnam's Sons.

Bomber Harris

4 STRATEGIC BOMBING COMES OF AGE

1 For a history of colonial bombing see Omissi, D. E. (1990) *Air Power and Colonial Control: the Royal Air Force, 1919–1939*, New York: Manchester University Press; Jones, N. (1973) *The Origins of Strategic Bombing*, London: William Kimber; Lindqvist, S. (2001) *A History of Bombing*, New York: New Press; and Dodge, T. (2003) *Inventing Iraq: the failure of nation-building and a history denied*, New York: Columbia University Press.

2 Dodge, 2003: 13.

3 Dodge, 2003: 133.

4 Dodge, 2003: 153.

5 Glancey, J. (2003) 'Gas, chemicals, bombs: Britain has used them all before in Iraq,' *Guardian*, 19 April.

6 Omissi, 1990: 37.

7 Clayton, A. (1986) The *British Empire as Super Power 1919–1939*, London: Macmillan, p. 80.

8 Smith, D. M. 1976 *Mussolini's Roman Empire*, New York: Viking Press, Chapter 5.

9 Lindqvist, 2001: 56.

10 For a discussion of this event see Lindqvist, 2001: 71; and Tohmatsu, H. and H. P. Willmott (2004) *A Gathering Darkness: the coming of war to the Far East and the Pacific, 1921–1942*, Lanham, MD: SR Books.

11 Lindqvist, 2001: 51.

12 Wavell, Lord, (1960) *New Cambridge Modern History*, vol. 12, Cambridge: Cambridge University Press, pp. 267–8.

13 Smith, 1976: 75.

14 Khalidi, R. (2004) 'Resurrecting empire,' *Globalist*, 10 August, p. 2.

15 Townsend, C. (1986) 'Civilization and "frightfulness:" air control in the Middle East between the wars," in Wrigley, C. (ed.) (1986) *Warfare, Diplomacy and Politics: Essays in Honour of A. J. P. Taylor*, London: Hamish Hamilton.

16 Baldwin, S. (1932) 'House of Commons speech,' 10 November, www.skygod.com/quotes/airpower.htm.

17 For a discussion of German and British collaboration see Buckley, H. (1940) *Life and Death of the Spanish Republic,* London: Hamish Hamilton.

18 Sherry, M. (1987) *The Rise of American Airpower*, New Haven: Yale University Press, p. 72.

19 For this history see Condon, J. P. and J. M. Elliott (eds.) (2000) *Marine Corps Aviation*, Washington, DC: Deputy Chief of Naval Operations (Air Warfare) Naval Air Systems Command and Sherrod, R. (1987) *History of Marine Corps Aviation in WWII*, Baltimore, MD: Nautical & Aviation Pub. Co.

20 MacMullen, J. K. (2001) 'The United States Strategic Bombing Survey and Air Force Doctrine,' thesis presented to the faculty of the School of Advanced Airpower Studies, p. 18.

21 Hansell, H. S. Jr. (1986) *The Strategic Air War Against Germany and Japan*, Washington DC: Office of Air Force History, p. 7.

22 Jones, 1973: 13.

23 Davis, M. (2002) *Dead Cities*, New York: New Press, p. 69.

24 Sherry, 1987: 72.

25 See de Seversky, A. P. (1943) *Victory through Air Power*, Garden City, NY: Garden City Publishing Co., Inc. For an assessment of de Seversky's influence see Sherry, 1987: 127–31.

26 See among others, Arnold, H. H. (1944–45) *Report of the Commanding General of the Army Air Forces to the Secretary of War*, Washington: Headquarters, Army Air Forces; Frankland, N. (1970) *The Bomber Offensive: the devastation of Europe*, New York: Ballantine Books; Jackson, R. (1974) *Storm from the Skies: the strategic bombing offensive, 1943–1945*, London: A. Barker; MacIsaac, D. (1976) *Strategic Bombing in World War Two: the story of the United States Strategic Bombing Survey*, New York: Garland; Morrison, W. H. (1982) *Fortress without a Roof: the Allied bombing of the Third Reich*, New York: St Martin's; Overy, R. J. (1980) *The Air War, 1939–1945*, New York: Stein and Day, Pape, R. A. (1996) *Bombing To Win: air power and coercion in war*, Ithaca: Cornell University Press; and Schaffer, R. (1985) *Wings of Judgement: American bombing in World War II*, New York: Oxford University Press.

27 Zacharias, U. (2003) 'Legitimizing empire: racial and gender politics of the war on terrorism,' *Social Justice*, Summer, Vol. 30, Abstract.

28 For this imagery see Charlton, L. E. O. (1936) *War Over England*, London & New York: Longmans, Green and co.

29 Kennett, L. (1982) *A History of Strategic Bombing*, New York: Scribner, p. 129.

30 For a discussion of this decision see Bidinian, L. (1976) *The Combined Allied Bombing Offensive against the German Civilian 1942–1945*, Lawrence, KS: Coronado Press.

31 'Strategic bombing in World War II,' *American Airpower Heritage Museum*, www.airpowermuseum.org

32 Terriane, J. (1965) *The Right of the Line: The Royal Air Force in the European War, 1939–1945*, London: Hodder and Stoughton, cited in Davis, 2002: 70.

33 Bidinian, 1976: 16–19.

34 Kohn, R. H. and J.P. Harahan (eds.) (1988) *Strategic Air Warfare*, Office of Air Force History, United States Air Force, Washington DC.

35 Davis, 2002: 68.

36 For a full discussion of this racial profile see Sherry, 1987: Chapter 8 and Navarro, A. V. 'Critical comparison between Japanese and American propaganda during World War II,' www.msu.edu.

37 Sherry, 1987: 245.

38 Sherry, 1987: 285.

39 Kohn and Harahan, 1988: 66.
40 Sherry, 1987: 289.
41 Schaffer, 1985: 148.
42 Kohn and Harahan, 1988: 57.
43 Sherry, 1987: 250–55.
44 Kennett, 1982 and Douhet, G. (1942) *The Command of the Air*, New York, Coward-McCann, Inc.
45 Sherry, 1987: 146.

5 COLD WAR STRATEGIC BOMBING: FROM KOREA TO VIETNAM

1 Office of the Chairman (1986) *United States Strategic Bombing Survey: the strategic air-war against Germany and Japan*, Washington DC: Office of Air Force History.
2 Taylor, T. (1945) *Final Report*, cited in Lindqvist, 2001: 113.
3 Waxman, M. C. (2000) *International Law and the Politics of Air Operations*, Santa Monica, CA: Rand, p. 22.
4 Sherry, 1987: 201.
5 Sherry, 1987: 210.
6 Lindqvist, 2001: 70. For a discussion of this attitude see Russell, B. (1938) *Power: a new social analysis*, New York: W. W. Norton & Company.
7 Hoover, J. E. (1947) HUAC Testimony (excerpts) 26 March, www.cnn.com/SPECIALS/coldwar/episodes/06/documents/hoover
8 For this imagery see Kennan, G. (1947) 'The sources of Soviet conduct,' *Foreign Affairs*, July.
9 Lacayo, R. (1998) 'William Levitt,' *Time*, 7 December.
10 Berlin, I. (1949) 'Mr Churchill,' *Atlantic Monthly*, September.
11 www.public.iastate.edu/~hist/1950s.html.
12 *Look*, 10 April 1951.
13 Mandel, A. (1999) 'The Postwar Era at Radcliffe', Senior thesis, Chapter 3, www.radcliffe.edu/print/ ?pid=201&print_parameters.
14 Kennan, G. (1947) 'The sources of Soviet conduct,' *Foreign Affairs*, July.
15 Eisenstein, Z. (1996) *Hatreds*, New York: Routledge.
16 Kaku, M. and D. Axelrod (1987) *To Win a Nuclear War: the Pentagon's secret war plans*, Boston: South End Press.
17 *Syracuse Herald-American*, 12 November 1950 and *Buffalo Evening News*, 20 July 1956.
18 Kaku and Axelrod, 1987.
19 Office of the Chairman, 1986: 7–10.
20 MacMullen, 2001: 68.
21 Sherry, 1987: 145, 146.
22 Crane, C. (2000) *American Airpower Strategy in Korea: 1950–1953*, Lawrence, KS: University Press of Kansas, p. 24.
23 Crane, 2000: p. 37.
24 Crane, 2000: p. 32.
25 Cumings, B. (1997) *Korea's Place in the Sun*, New York: W. W. Norton, p. 293.
26 Stone, I. F. (1952) *Hidden History of the Korean War*, New York: Monthly

Review Press, p. 258.

27 *Ibid.*

28 Macdonald, C. A. (1986) *Korea*, New York: Free Press, p. 239.

29 Clodfelter, M. (1989) *The Limits of Airpower*, New York: Free Press, p. 17.

30 Quoted in Futrell, R. F. (1961) *The United States Air Force in Korea 1950–1953*, New York: Duell, Sloan & Pearce, p. 481.

31 Sherry, M. (1995), *Shadow of War*, New Haven: Yale University Press, p. 181.

32 Quoted in Veale, F. J. P. (1968) *Advance to Barbarism: how the reverse to barbarism in warfare and war-trials menaces our future*, London: Mitre Press, Foreword.

33 'The attack on the irrigation dams in North Korea,' *Air University Quarterly*, 6, no. 4, Winter 1953–54; pp. 40–51.

34 Kohn and Harahan, *1988*: 88.

35 *Ibid.*

36 *Air Force Manual 1–8*, 1 May 1954, p. 6, quoted in Clodfelter, 1989: 29.

37 Tomlin, G. (2001) 'The efficacy of strategic bombing: World War II to the Kosovo Campaign,' p. 2, www.wm.edu/so/monitor/Spring 2001/paper5.htm.

38 Clodfelter, 1989: 36.

39 Clodfelter, 1989: 126.

40 Quoted in Ellsberg, D. (1972) *Papers on the War*, New York: Simon and Schuster, p. 234.

41 Quoted in Clodfelter, 1989: 145.

42 Kohn and Harahan, 1988: 127.

43 Clodfelter, 1989: 184.

44 Clodfelter, 1989: 191.

45 Van Staavern, J. (2003) review of *Gradual Failure: The air war over North Vietnam*, in *Air and Space Power Journal*, Winter.

46 See Clodfelter, 1989 for a good discussion of these anomalies.

47 For references on Agent Orange see www.lewispublishing.com/sources.htm. See Griffith, W. and J. Marciano (1979) *Lessons of the Vietnam War*, Totowa NJ: Rowman and Allanheld, for media coverage of war issues.

48 'Agent orange, operation ranch hand: Vietnam War herbicides,' www.land-scaper.net/agent. htm and 'Executive Summary, The Herbicidal Warfare Program in Vietnam, 1961-1971,http://members.cox.net/linarson/orange.html.

49 Pearson, P. (2003) 'Is the military above negative portrayals?' *USA Today*, 6 August.

50 Interviewed in the Oscar-winning documentary film produced by B. Schneider and P. Davis, *Hearts and Minds* (1974).

51 Ellsberg, 1972: 237.

52 'Chemical warfare, Education on the Internet & Teaching History Online,' www.spartacus.schoolnet.co.uk/Vnchemical.htm

53 Silberman, J. (Director) (2001) *Bombies*, Bullfrog Films, Lumiere Productions Inc.

54 Gibson, J. W. (2000) *The Perfect War: technowar in Vietnam*, New York: Atlantic Monthly Press, p. 157.

55 Shawcross, W. (1979) *Sideshow*, New York: Pocket Books, p. 215.

56 Behar, A. (1967) 'Summary report on the bombing of the civil population of the North,' Vietnam War > International War Crimes Tribunal, www.vietnamese-american.org/a15.html

57 Sherry, 1995: 271–72.
58 *Agence France-Press*, April 1995.
59 'War is increasingly about civilian dead,' *PeaceAware Factsheet*, p. 1, www.peaceaware.com/boje/peace/documents/.
60 Schneider and Davis, 1974.
61 Clodfelter, 1989: 140.
62 Sherry, 1995: 250–251.
63 For this imagery see the films *The Green Berets, Brushfire* and *Gates to Hell*.
64 FitzGerald, F. (1972) *Fire in the Lake*, Boston: Little, Brown, and Company, pp. 367–68.
65 Schneider and Davis, 1974.
66 'Yellow myths on the silver screen, wartime movies,' http://web.mit.edu.
67 Shawcross, 1979: 236.
68 Schneider and Davis, 1974.
69 Tal, K. (1989) 'The mind of war: images of women in Vietnam War by combat veterans,' *Contemporary Literature*, Fall, p.1.
70 Ellsberg, 1972: 241.

6 TERRORISTS IN THE BOMBSIGHTS

1 Discussion of the terrorism industry is in Herman, E. S. and G. O'Sullivan (1989) *The Terrorism Industry*, New York: Pantheon Books.
2 For a fuller discussion of the 'ideology of terrorism' see Grosscup, B. (2002) *The Newest Explosions of Terrorism*, Far Hills NJ: New Horizon Press.
3 Sterling, C. (1981) *The Terror Network*, New York: Reader's Digest Press.
4 Sterling, 1981: 3.
5 These themes are best represented in Laqueur, W. (1987) *Age of Terrorism*, Boston: Little, Brown; Francis, S. (1985) *Soviet Strategy of Terror*, Washington DC: The Heritage Foundation; Sederberg, P. (1989) *Terrorist Myths: illusion, rhetoric, and reality*, Englewood Cliffs, NJ: Prentice Hall; and United States Department of State (1987) *Patterns of Global Terrorism*, Washington DC: Department of State.
6 Cline, R. S. and Y. Alexander (1984) *Terrorism: the Soviet connection*, London: Crane Russak and Company, Inc. and Francis, S. (1985).
7 Shaoul, J. (2002) 'Sharon's war crimes in Lebanon: the record [Part 2],' 25 February, www.boycottisrael.org/Is_crimes_sharon2.htm and www.rundavid.net/deadchildren1.htm, p. 1.
8 Fisk, R. (1982), *Independent*, 7 June.
9 See Chomsky, N. and E. S. Herman (1979) *The Washington Connection to Third World Fascism*, Boston: South End Press; and Herman, E. S. (1982) *The Real Terror Network*, Boston: South End Press.
10 For this discussion see Grosscup, 2002 and Chomsky, N. (1988) *The Culture of Terrorism*, London: Pluto Press.
11 Hoffman, B. (1990) 'Saddam Hussein's ultimate fifth column-terrorists,' *Los Angeles Times*, 26 August.
12 Herman and O'Sullivan, 1989: 9. I use the term 'jingoist,' rather than 'patriotic model' as Herman and O'Sullivan do, to reflect a 'my country right or wrong' position. 'Patriotic' implies an attempt to sort through for oneself what is in the

country's best interest.

13 A more complete discussion of this concept appears in Grosscup, B. (2000) 'Terrorism-at-a-distance: the imagery that serves US power,' *Global Dialogue*, Vol. 2, No. 4, Autumn.

14 For details of this analysis see Kupperman, R. and D. Trent (1979) *Terrorism: threat, reality, response*, Stanford, CA: Hoover Institution Press.

15 Falk, R. (1991) 'Terrorist foundations of US foreign policy,' in George, A. (ed.) (1991) *Western State Terrorism*, New York: Routledge, p. 116.

16 Said, E. W. (1981) *Covering Islam: how the media and the experts determine how we see the rest of the world*, New York: Pantheon Books, p. xxiii.

17 This imagery can be seen on the covers of major Western news magazines such as *Newsweek, Time, Macleans* and *US News and World Report* from 1979 through the 1980s.

18 Ehrenfeld, R. (1990) *Narcoterrorism*, New York: Basic Books, p. xix.

19 'Counter-terrorist experts meet in Chicago,' *Emergencynet News Service*, 3 August 1995, p. 1, www.emergency.com/terrtrnd.htm.

20 For a fuller discussion of the Libyan and USS *Vincennes* attacks see Grosscup, 2002.

21 Lacayo, R. (1993) 'Tower terror,' *Time*, 8 March.

22 'A new era of terrorism?' *Time*, 8 March 1993 and 'Terror hits home,' *Newsweek*, 8 March 1993.

23 For a discussion of this legislation see Grosscup, B. (2000) 'Terrorism-at-a-distance: the imagery that serves US power,' *Global Dialogue*, Vol. 2, No. 4, Autumn.

24 Chomsky, N. (2003) *Hegemony or Survival*, New York: Metropolitan Books, pp. 206–207.

25 A frequent guest on media after anti-Western terrorist events during the 1990s, as a dissident voice on terrorism, I experienced both professionally and personally the powerful grip this analysis has on the North American mindset.

26 Parenti, M. (2004) *Superpatriotism*, San Francisco: City Lights Books.

7 STRATEGIC BOMBING IN THE 1990s

1 For a discussion of these new nationalisms see Eisenstein, Z. (1996) *Hatreds: racialized and sexualized conflicts in the 21st century*, New York: Routledge.

2 For a discussion of pre-war planning see Putney, D. T. (2004) *Airpower Advantage: planning the Gulf War air campaign, 1989–1991*,Washington, DC: Air Force History and Museums Program, United States Air Force.

3 Warden, J. A. (1991) 'Transcript of interview' with Gehri, S. B., R. Reynolds and D. Putney, Washington DC, 30 May, quoted in Putney, 2004: 39.

4 Warden III, J. A. (1988) *The Air Campaign: planning for combat*, Washington, DC: National Defense University Press.

5 See Fuller, J. F. C. (1958) *The Generalship of Alexander the Great*, London: Eyre & Spottiswoode.

6 Davis, R. G. (2002) *On Target: organizing and executing the strategic air campaign against Iraq*, Washington, DC: Air Force History and Museums Program, United States Air Force, pp. 75–6.

7 Davis, 2002: 64.

8   Warden, J. A., 22 October 1991, cited in Putney, 2004: 51.

9   Harvey, B. E. (1992) 'Review comments,' December, cited in Davis, 2002: 78.

10 McPeak, M. (1991) quoted in Jamieson, P. D. (2001) *Lucrative Targets: the US Air Force in the Kuwaiti Theater of Operations*, Washington, DC: Air Force History and Museums Program, US Air Force, p. 42.

11 For a discussion of the media and Pentagon presentation of the 'robo' war concept see Kellner, D. (1992) *The Persian Gulf TV War*, Boulder: Westview Press. Chapter 6.

12 Warden, J. A., quoted in Putney, 2004: 357.

13 For specific provisions see Protocol Additional to the Geneva Conventions of 12 August 1949, and Protection of Victims of International Armed Conflicts (Protocol I), 8 June 1977. www.icrc.org/IHL.nsf/0/f6c8b9fee14a77fdc1256 41e0052b079?Open Document.

14 Schwarskopf, N. (1991) 'Briefing' 27 January, quoted in Lopez, G. (1991) 'The Gulf War: not so clean,' *Bulletin of Atomic Scientists*, September, Vol. 47, No. 7, p. 2.

15 *Ibid.*

16 Putney, 2004: 353.

17 Defense Intelligence Agency, (1991) 'Effects of bombing on disease occurrence in Baghdad,' January, www.gulflink.osd.mil/declassdocs/dia/19950901/ 950901_0504rept_91.html.

18 Boyle, F. (1992) 'US war crimes during the Gulf War,' paper delivered at the symposium: International War Crimes: the Search for Justice, University of Illinois at Urbana-Champaign, 27 February, www.counterpunch.org/ boyle0902.html.

19 Boyle, F. (1992), p. 9.

20 Walker, P. and E. Stambler (1991) '... and the dirty little weapons,' *Bulletin of the Atomic Scientists*, May, Vol. 47, No. 4, p. 2.

21 Cockburn, P. (2001) 'A room with a view: bombing Baghdad,' *Independent*, 16 January.

22 Boustany, N. (1991) 'Refugees describe air raid horrors: Iraqi residential areas feel impact," *Washington Post Foreign Service*, 21 January.

23 Smith, B. (1991) 'The human cost of the Gulf War,' presented to a Hands Across the Border Peace Gathering, 27 July, www.geocities.com/iraqinfo/index.html? page=/iraqinfo/gulfwar/gulfdocs/humancost.html.

24 Cockburn, P. (2001).

25 Walker, P. and E. Stambler (1991), p. 2.

26 *Aviation Week and Space Technology*, 22 April 1991, p. 97.

27 *Washington Post,* 2 February 1991.

28 Finemen, M. (1991) 'Smoke blocks out sun in bomb-blasted Basra,' *Los Angeles Times*, 5 February 1991.

29 eoxy.org/wc/wc-proto.htm.

30 Kellner, 1992: Chapter 5.

31 *Ibid.*

32 Article 51: Protection of the civilian population, www.icrc.org/ihl.nsf/0/4bebd 9920ae0aeaec12563cd0051dc9e?OpenDoc.

33 'Toting the casualties of war,' *Business Week*, 7 February 2003.

34 Daponte, B. (2003) 'Changing the rules of war, *La Monde diplomatique,* March.

35 Prochaska, D. "Disappearing" Iraqis,' www.acdis.uiuc.edu/Research/S&Ps/1991-

Sp/S&P_V-3/disappearing_iraqis.html

36 For a longer discussion of these charges see Grosscup 2002.

37 Bush, G. H. W. (1991) 'State of the union address,' 29 January 1991.

38 This was a new posture for the United States government. Because he was fighting Iran, a US-designated terrorist nation during the 1980s, Saddam's Iraq had been excused from the State Department's list beginning in 1982.

39 For a full discussion of the Bush Administration's imagery see Kellner, 1992.

40 Kellner, 1992: Chapter 5.

41 For a longer account see Qumsiyeh, M. B. (1998) '100 years of anti-Arab and anti-Muslim stereotyping,' January, www.ibiblio.org/prism/jan98/anti_arab.html.

42 See Prochaska, D. '"Disappearing" Iraqis,' and Henzell-Thomas, J. (2002) 'The language of Islamophobia,' *New Humanist*, Summer.

43 Kellner, 1992: Chapter 6.

44 *Ibid.*

45 For a longer discussion of this sexualized imagery see Stannard, D. E. (1992) *American Holocaust: Columbus and the conquest of the New World*, New York: Oxford University Press.

46 Hitchens, C. (1989) 'Minority report,' *The Nation*, 19 February, p. 187.

47 Progler, Y. (1999) *Muslimedia*, 16–31 January, p. 2. www.muslimedia.com/archives/special99/graffiti.htm.

48 Shah, A. 2002) 'Iraq was being bombed during 12 years of sanctions,' www.globalissues.com/.

49 Scahill, J. (2000) "No-fly zones over Iraq,' 10 December, www. IraqJournal.org.

50 Ricks, T. E. (2000) 'Containing Iraq: a forgotten war,' *Washington Post*, 25 October.

51 Chomsky, N. (1996) 'Israel, Lebanon, and the "Peace Process"' *ZMagazine*, 23 April.

52 Lebanon, www.globalsecurity.org/military/world/war/lebanon.htm.

53 Cited in Saad, F. P. (1996) 'Israel's bombing of civilians promotes only violence,' *The Tech*, 26 April.

54 Cushing, D. E. and D. B. Fincher, 'Paved With Good Intentions: Boris Yeltsin's Strategic Road to Chechnya, 1995–1996', unpublished paper delivered in Seminar D, F, *National Defense University, National War College*, p. 11.

55 Thomas, T. (1997) 'Air operations in low intensity conflict: the case of Chechnya,' *Air Chronicles*, April and Lambeth, B. (1995) 'Russia's air war in Chechnya,' Rand draft, December.

56 'Russia's war in Chechnya: victims speak out,' *Human Rights Watch*, January 1995.

57 'Little reaction in West to Chechnya bombing,' *SovietskiStar Collection*, www.sovietski.com/Star/holiday99/chechnya.html.

58 'Russian forces continue pounding Chechen targets,' *Human Rights Watch*, 4 November 1999, p. 1.

59 Felgenhauer, P. (2002) 'Civilized approach is best,' *Moscow Times*, 4 April.

60 Felgenhauer, P. (2003) 'The Russian army in Chechyna,' *Crimes of War Project*, 18 April, p. 3.

61 'Russia snubs Clinton over Chechnya,' *BBC News*, 2 November 1999, p. 1.

62 Quoted in 'Cluster bombs in Afghanistan,' *Human Rights Watch Backgrounder*, October 2001.

63 Nardulli, B. R. (2002) *Disjointed War: Military Operations in Kosovo, 1999,*

Santa Monica, CA: Rand, pp. 22–23,

64 Nardulli: 2002: 19.

65 Tomlin, G. (2001) 'The efficacy of strategic bombing: World War II to the Kosovo campaign,' pp. 5–6, www.wm.edu/SO/monitor/spring2001/paper5.htm.

66 Nardulli, 2002: 45.

67 Graham, P. (2000) 'Report critical of NATO air strikes on Yugoslovia,' *National Post*, 7 February.

68 Arkin, W. (2000) 'Smart bombs dumb targeting?' *Bulletin of Atomic Scientists*, May/June, p. 47.

69 Lambeth, B. S. (2001) *NATO's Air War for Kosovo*, Santa Monica CA: Rand, p. 87.

70 Quoted in Gowans, S. (2001) 'Our terrorists,' *Swans*, 12 November, p. 2.

71 Steele, D. R. (1999) 'Why Clinton bombed Yugoslavia,' *Liberty*, August.

72 Lambeth, 2001: 41–42.

73 Erlanger, S. (1999) "Economist finds bombing cuts Yugoslavia's production in half,' *New York Times*, 30 April.

74 'Civilian deaths in the NATO air campaign-summary,' *Human Rights Watch*, p. 1, www.hrw.org/reports/2000/nato/Natbm200.htm.

75 Rezun, M. (2001) *Europe's Nightmare: the Struggle for Kosovo*, Westport, Conn.: Praeger, p. 59.

76 Nardulli, 2002: 45–46.

77 Quoted in Fisk, R. (2000), 'NATO deliberately attacked civilians in Serbia,' *Independent*, 7 June.

78 Marjanovic, B. (1999) 'Against NATO's war in Yugoslavia,' *Voices From Below*, p. 3, www.thing.net/~oliveworks/marjanovic.html.

79 Scheiber, N. (2000) 'Counting the civilian dead in Yugoslavia,' *SLATE*, 9 February.

80 Bein, P. (2000) 'William Arkin's dumb apology for NATO's smart bombs,' 3 May, p. 2, www. emperors-clothes.com.

81 Cohen, M. (1999) 'Bombing the bridge to the 21st century: behind NATO's bombardment of Yugoslavia,' *Voices From Below*, p. 2, www.thing.net/~olive-works/marjanovic.html.

82 'Current updates,' *World Policy Institute*, 4 June 1999.

83 Many government and private organizations, including a task force from the United Nations Environmental Program (UNEP), the Serbian Regional Environmental Center (RRC), European Green parties, the World Wildlife Fund, the North American Institute for Energy Environmental Research (EER) and the International Action Center (IAC), have investigated and documented the extent of environmental degradation and danger resulting from the bombing.

84 Yarrow, R. (1999) 'The continuing war in Yugoslavia: environmental effects,' *Peaceworks*, September, p. 2.

85 Quoted in Cohen, M. (1999) 'Ecological catastrophe hits Yugoslavia,' 28 April, www.thing.net/~oliveworks/marjanovic.html.

86 Yarrow, R. (1999), p. 3.

87 Quoted in Morgan, C. V. Z. (2000) 'Collateral damage of the environmental kind,' *Mother Jones*, 6 September, p. 2.

88 Cohen, M. (1999) 'Against NATO's war in Yugoslavia,' www.thing.net/~olive-works/marjanovic.html and *Wall Street Journal*, 31 December 1999.

89 Herman, E. S. (2002) 'Body counts in imperial service,' *ZMagazine,* February.
90 Chomsky, N. (2000) 'In retrospect: a review of NATO's war over Kosovo, Part I,' *ZMagazine,* April.
91 *Ibid.,* p. 5.
92 For a discussion of this assessment see Biddle, S. (2002) 'The new way of war,' *Foreign Affairs,* May/June.
93 Steele, D. R. (1999) 'Why Clinton bombed Yugoslavia,' *Liberty,* August.
94 Schiff, Z. (2000) 'The Lebanese madness,' *Ha'aretz,* 4 May.
95 Chomsky, N. (2000), *A New Generation Draws the Line: Kosovo, East Timor and the standards of the West,* London: Verso, p. 5.
96 Steele (1999).

8 BOMBING TO WIN: 9/11 AND THE WAR ON TERRORISM

1   Engelhardt, T. (2004) 'Tomgram: icarus (armed with vipers) over Iraq,' 7 December, www.tomdispatch.com/index.mhtml.
2   Chomsky, N. (2001) *9-11,* New York: Seven Stories Press, pp. 45–54.
3   Herman, E. S. (1998) 'Bombing à la mode,' *ZMagazine,* December.
4   Quoted in Herman, E. S. (2004) 'We had to destroy Fallujah in order to save it,' *Znet Commentary,* 8 November.
5   Four years later they and their right-wing pundits were still at it, as the witch-hunt against Professor Ward Churchill of the University of Colorado demonstrates. See Street, P. (2005) 'National narcissism and the racist, neo-McCarthyite assault on Ward Churchill,' *Znet,* 6 March.
6   For a discussion of this new permanent war concept see Kellner, D. 'Postmodern military and permanent war,' in Boggs, C. (ed.) (2003) *Masters of War,* New York: Routledge.
7   The death toll reported as of 29 October 2003.
8   'Project for the new American century,' www.newamericancentury.org.
9   Bush, G. W. (2001) 'War on Terrorism Speech,' *UPI,* 20 September.
10 Powell, C. (2001) 'Interview with Jim Lehrer,' *PBS,* 13 September.
11 Blair, T. (2001) 'World mourns attack victims' *CNN,* 12 September.
12 Berlusconi, S. (2001) 'Berlusconi comments cause stir,' *New York Times,* 26 September.
13 Laqueur, W. (1987) *Age of Terrorism,* Boston: Little, Brown.
14 Bush, G. W. (2001) 'Transcript of President Bush's speech,' *CNN,* 21 September.
15 *Ibid.*
16 *Ibid.*
17 Bush, G. W. (2001) 'President Urges Readiness and Patience,' *White House, Office of the Press Secretary,* 15 September.
18 *Ibid.* Three years later in his 2004 Presidential acceptance speech at the Republican convention, Bush proudly confirmed that 'whatever it takes' was the mantra he repeated daily when thinking about terrorism. The slogan also found its way into the 2004 're-elect Bush' campaign literature.
19 Isakof, M. (2004) 'The president's constitutional authority to conduct military preparations against terrorists and nations supporting them,' *Newsweek,* 18 December.
20 Bush, G. W. (2004) 'President Bush's acceptance speech to the Republican

National Convention,' *Washington Post*, 2 September.

21   O'Reilly, B. (2001) 'The O'Reilly factor,' *Fox News*, 17 September.

22   O'Reilly, B. (2001) 'The O'Reilly factor,' *Fox News*, 19 September.

23   Rosenthal, A. M. (2001), *New York Daily News*, 14 September.

24   Conetta, C. (2004) 'Disappearing the dead, Iraq, Afghanistan, and the idea of a "new warfare,"' *Project on Defense Alternatives*, 18 February.

25   Bush, G. W. (2003) 'Remarks by President Bush at Boeing, St. Louis, Missouri,' *Voice of America News*, 16 April.

26   Grant, R. (2002) 'An air war like no other,' *Airforce*, November, Vol. 85, No. 11, p. 4.

27   Cordesman, A. (2001) 'Defining "carpet bombing" in the Afghan war,' *CSIS*, 2 November.

28   Meilinger, P. (2001) 'Precision aerospace power, discrimination, and the future of war,' *Aerospace Power Journal*, Fall, Vol. 15, p. 12.

29   Cordesman, A. (2001) 'Defining "carpet bombing" in the Afghan war,' *CSIS*, 2 November.

30   *Ibid.*

31   Grant, R. (2002) 'An air war like no other,' p. 2.

32   Rumsfeld, D. (2001) News briefing, *United States Department of Defense*, 9 October.

33   Herold, M. W. (2002) 'Dead Afghan civilians: disrobing the non-counters,' *Cursor*, 20 August, www.cursor.org/stories/noncounters.htm.

34   Burns, J. F. (2001) *New York Times*, 16 September.

35   Quoted in Gowans, S. (2002) 'Our terrorists,' *Swans*, 17 January, p. 2.

36   Budiansky, S. (2001) 'Sky has its limits: Why bombs defeat armies more effectively than cities,' *Washington Post*, 16 December.

37   Grant, R. (2002) 'An air war like no other,' *Airforce*, November, Vol. 85, No. 11, p. 9.

38   Rumsfeld, D. (2001) News transcript, *United States Department of Defense*, 11 October.

39   'Afghanistan: Amnesty International call for prompt investigation into civilian deaths,' *Amnesty International*, 10 October 2001.

40   Huggler, J. (2001) 'Carpet bombing "kills 150 civilians" in frontline town,' *Independent*, 19 November.

41   For an analysis of these and later polls see Conetta, C. (2004) 'Disappearing the dead.'

42   Herold, M. W. (2001) 'A dossier on civilian victims of United States' aerial bombing of Afghanistan,' *Cursor*, 10 December, www.cursor.org/stories/non-counters.htm.

43   Smith, J. (2001) 'Defense Dept. confesses "bombing Red Cross on purpose,' November, www.awitness.org.

44   Conetta, C. (2004) 'Disappearing the dead,' p. 5.

45   Cordesman, A. (2001) 'The US bombing and Ramadan: the real problems we face because of our failure to understand asymmetric warfare and mistakes that turn "information dominance" into a self-inflicted wound,' *CSIS*, 9 November.

46   Di Matteo, E. (2001) 'CNN's secret memo: leaked e-mail orders staff to downplay civilian deaths,' *NOW*, 11 November, www.nowtoronto.com/issues/2001-11-08/news_feature.html.

47   Filkins, D. (2002) 'Flaws in US air war left hundreds of civilians dead,' *New*

York Times, 20 July.

48　Herman, E. S. (2002) '"Tragic errors" as an integral component of policy,' *ZMagazine*, September.

49　Soloman, N. (2001) 'Announcing the P.U.-litzer Prizes for 2001, ' *FAIR's Media Beat*, 14 December.

50　For his methodology see Herold, M. W. (2002) 'A dossier on civilian victims of United States' aerial bombing of Afghanistan: a comprehensive accounting [revised],' *Cursor*, March, www.cursor.org/stories/noncounters.htm.

51　Herold, M. W. (2001) 'An average day: 65 Afghan civilians killed by US bombs on December 20th,' *Cursor*, 29 December, www.cursor.org/stories/ ontarget.htm.

52　This is a partial display of Table 1 from Herold, M. W. (2002) 'Dead Afghan civilians: disrobing the non-counters,' *Cursor*, 20 August, p. 3, www.cursor.org/ stories/ontarget.htm.

53　Conetta, C. (2002) 'Operation enduring freedom,' *Project on Defense Alternatives*, 20 January, 'Red Cross warns Afghan children off cluster bombs, *Reuters*, 29 June 2002 and Herold, M. W. (2002) 'Above the law and below morality: data on 11 weeks of US cluster-bombing of Afghanistan,' *Cursor*, 1 February, www. cursor.org/stories/abovethe law.htm.

54　'Refugees and Humanitarian Aid,' *Council on Foreign Relations*, 2004, www.cfrterrorism.org.

55　Herold, M. W. (2002) 'Rubble rousers: US bombing and the Afghan refugee crisis,' *Cursor*, 16 March, www.cursor.org/stories/rubble.htm.

56　Steele, J. (2002) 'Forgotten victims,' *Guardian*, 20 May.

57　Filkins, D. (2002) 'Flaws in US air war,' *New York Times*, 20 July.

58　Conetta, C. (2002) 'Operation enduring freedom,' *Project on Defense Alternatives*, 20 January.

59　Rumsfeld, D. (2001) 'News transcript,' *United States Department of Defense*, 4 December.

60　'How many are dead: major networks aren't counting,' *Fair*, 12 December 2001.

61　Quoted in Corn, D. (2001) 'Pentagon denials and civilian deaths in Afghanistan,' *AlterNet*, 7 December.

62　Herold, M. W. (2002) 'Attempts to hide the number of civilians killed by US bombs are an affront to justice,' *Guardian* (London), 8 August.

63　Rumsfeld, D. (2001) 'Interview with Jim Lehrer,' *PBS News Hour*, 7 November.

64　'From victims of US bombs, forgiveness,' *Washington Post*, 9 February 2002.

65　Kristof, N. (2002) 'Merciful war,' *New York Times*, 1 February.

66　Conetta, C. (2004) 'Disappearing the dead.'

67　*Ibid.*

68　*Ibid.*

69　*Ibid.*

70　Kristof, N. (2002) 'Merciful war,' *New York Times*, 1 February and Arkin, W. (2002) ' Not good enough, Mr Rumsfeld,' *Washington Post*, 25 February.

71　Corn, D. (2001) 'Pentagon denials and civilian deaths in Afghanistan,' *AlterNet*, 7 December, p. 3.

72　Chernus, I., 'Are dying Afghans "collateral damage"?' http://spot.colorado.edu/ ~chernus/NewspaperColumns/WarAndPeaceIssues/CollateralDamage.htm.

73　Campbell, M. (2001) 'Bombing of farming village undermines US credibility,' *Toronto Globe and Mail*, 2 November.

74 Quoted in *ibid.*
75 Symonds, P. (2002) 'The makings of a protracted colonial war in Afghanistan,' *WSWS*, 22 March.
76 Quoted in Mosley, K. (2002) 'Fresh memories of war,' *Ithaca Journal*, 25 May.
77 See Hall, S. 'The West and the rest: discourse and power,' in Hall, S. and B. Gieben (eds.) (1992) *Formations of Modernity*, Cambridge: Polity Press.
78 Quoted in 'Message from a recon marine in Afghanistan,' 11 November 2001, usaattacked.com/MsgFromMarineInAfg.htm.
79 See 'Military strategy,' *OnlineNewsHour*, 29 October, www.pbs.org/newshour/bb/military/july-dec01/strategy_10-29.html and Hazen, D. (2001) '10 reasons to stop bombing Afghanistan,' *AlterNet*, 19 October.
80 Herold, M. W. (2002) 'Dead Afghan civilians: disrobing the non-counters,' *Cursor*, 20 August, www.cursor.org/stories/noncounters.htm.
81 Roy, A. (2001) 'Brutality smeared in peanut butter. why America must stop the war now,' *Guardian*, 23 October.

9 DODGING THE TERRORISM LABEL

1 Weber, M. (1965) *Politics as a Vocation*, Philadelphia: Fortress Press.
2 *Title 22 of the US Code, Section 2656f(d)*, www.cia.gov/terrorism/faqs.html.
3 United States Department of State, (2003) *Patterns of Global Terrorism*, Washington DC: United States Department of State.
4 Center for Arms Control and Non-Proliferation, 'Terrorism Definitions,' www.armscontrolcenter.org/ terrorism/101/definitions.html.
5 Constitutional Right Foundation, 'What is terrorism?' www.crf-usa.org/terror/What_Is_Terrorism_rev.htm.
6 For a discussion of the United States case see Grosscup, 2002: 1–9.
7 The informal surveys were conducted in the author's courses at CSU, Chico and numerous public lectures.
8 The reference is to characters popularized in Disney, W. (1937) *Snow White and the Seven Dwarfs*, Burbank: Walt Disney Productions, and Foster, H. (1937) *Prince Valiant*, Canada: Hal Foster.
9 Herold, M. W. (2002) 'US media discover (and still minimize) Afghan's casualties,' *Media Alliance*, 17 February, www.media-alliance.org/article.php?story=20031108153733172.
10 'Language, social representations and the media,' *Australian Psychological Society*, Australian Psychological Society.org.au/.
11 Herman, E. S. (2004) 'The war on terrorism,' Znet, 11 September.
12 Wilkinson, P. (1979) *Terrorism and the Liberal State*, New York: New York University Press, pp. 18–29.
13 Henzell-Thomas, J. (2002) 'The language of Islamophobia,' *New Humanist*, Summer, p 1.
14 Marcuse, H. (1998) *An Essay on Liberation*, Boston: Beacon Press.
15 To military officials and coaches, playing football is good training for war.
16 See Kellner, 1992.
17 *Chicago Tribune*, 12 April 2003.
18 Soloman, N. 'Media linguicide and class wars,' http://www.pairoducks.com Media.

19 For a list of military terms see 'Military aviation terms and definitions,' www.danshistory.com.

20 Kellner, 1992.

21 *Ibid.*

22 Cohn, C. (1987) 'Sex and death in the rational world of defense intellectuals,' *Signs*, 2, No. 4.

23 *Evening Chronicle*, 23 February 1991, cited in Kellner, 1992.

24 Reproduced in *In These Times*, 13 February 1991, p. 5.

25 Hart, L. (2003) 'Collateral damage,' 7 September. dada.com/artsints.html.

26 Kelsey, F. W. (1925) *Hugo Grotius: The law of war and peace*, Oxford: Clarendon Press.

27 Neumann, M. (2004) 'How we became barbarians,' *Counterpunch*, 16 December, pp. 3–4.

28 Shea, J. (1999) NATO press conference, 8 April, archiv2.medienhilfe.ch/topics/PBS/pbs-ser.pdf.

29 For a description of these weapons see 'Bomb types, varieties of cluster bombs,' *Americans Against World Empire*, www. againstbombing.org.

30 Rumsfeld, D. (2001) News briefing, Department of Defense, 25 October.

31 Myers, R. (2001) News briefing, Department of Defense, 1 November.

32 Conetta, C. (2002) 'Operation enduring freedom: why a higher rate of civilian bombing casualties,' *Project on Defense Alternatives*, 18 January, footnote 10.

33 Davis, M. (2003) 'Shock and awe,' in van Eekelen, B., J. González, B. Stoetzer and A. Tsing (eds.) (2004) *Shock and Awe: war on words*, Santa Cruz: New Pacific Press.

34 Grossman, Z. (2001) 'Killing civilians to show that killing civilians is wrong,' *Znet*, 21 October.

35 O'Hanlon, M. (2002) 'Counting casualties,' *SLATE*, 25 September and 'Pentagon report whitewashes civilian deaths in Yugoslavia,' *Human Rights Watch*, 8 February 2000.

36 Herman, E. S. (2002) '"Tragic errors" as an integral component of policy,' *ZMagazine*, September, p. 3.

37 Parenti, M. (1986) *Inventing Reality: politics and the mass media*, New York: St Martin's Press; Kellner, 1992; and MacArthur. J. R. (1993) *Second Front: censorship and propaganda in the Gulf War*, Berkeley: University of California Press.

38 Soloman, N. (2004) 'They shoot journalists don't they,' 24 March, www.antiwar.com and Lettice, J. (2003) 'Airstrike! the Pentagon simplifies media relations,' *The Register*, 20 March. In 2003–2004 nine journalists were killed in Iraq by US forces.

39 Coen, R. (2002) 'See no evil,' *EXTRA!*, January–February, Seth Ackerman, S. (2002) 'Afghan famine on and off the screen,' *EXTRA!*, May–June and Herold, M. W. (2002) 'The real "old" news America has now "discovered,"' *Cursor*, 13 February, www.cursor.org/stories/oldnews.htm.

40 Soloman, N. (2001) 'Killing civilians: behind the reassuring words,' *Media Beat*, 25 September.

41 Lieberman, J. quoted in Arnove, A. (2002) 'Cluster bombs: the civilian impact,' *ZMagazine*, March.

42 Quoted in Kiernan, B. (2003) '"Collateral damage" from Cambodia to Iraq,' *Antipode*, November, Vol. 35, Issue 5.

43 Rumsfeld, D. (2001) News transcript, Department of Defense, 4 December.
44 'US military vows to limit Iraqi civilian deaths,' *Houston Chronicle,* 9 March 2003.
45 *America's Debate,* 29 October, 2004, www. americasdebate.com.
46 Quoted in Kiernan, B. (2003) '"Collateral damage" from Cambodia to Iraq,' p. 854.
47 Meilinger, P. (2001) 'A matter of precision,' *Foreign Policy*, March.
48 Neumann, M. (2004) 'How we became barbarians,' p. 5.
49 Gowans, S. (2001) 'Our masters of propaganda,' *SWANS,* 12 November.
50 Herman, E. S. (2002) 'Body counts in imperial service,' *ZMagazine,* February.
51 Conetta, C. (2004) 'Disappearing the dead, Iraq, Afghanistan, and the idea of a "new warfare,"' *Project on Defense Alternatives,* 18 February.
52 Quoted in Wood, D. (2002) 'Status of women, children questioned after airstrike,' *New Orleans Times-Picayune*, 22 February.
53 For documentation of the various aspects of this policy, see McClintock, M. (1985) *The American Connection,* London: Zed Books; and Tayacan, (1985) *Psychological Operations in Guerrilla Warfare,* New York: Vintage Books.
54 Quoted in Gowans, S. (2001) 'Our masters of propaganda,' *SWANS,* 12 November.
55 Bush, G. W. (2005) White House press conference, 16 March.
56 Shawcross, 1972.
57 Herman, E. S. (2002) '"Tragic errors."'
58 Roberts, L., R. Lafta, R. Garfield, J. Khudhairi, G. Burnham (2004) 'Mortality before and after the 2003 invasion of Iraq; cluster sample survey,' *Lancet*, 29 October.
59 Quoted in Edwards, D. (2004) 'Znet commentary, 100,000 Iraqi civilian deaths – Part 1,' Znet, 23 November.
60 Rizer, K. (2001) 'Bombing dual use targets: legal, ethical and doctrinal perspectives,' *Air and Space Chronicles*, 1 May.
61 Mayer, J. (2005) 'Outsourcing torture,' *New Yorker Magazine*, 14 & 21 February.

10 TERROR FROM THE SKIES

1 Franti, M. and Spearhead, (2001) *'Bomb the World,'* www.inlyrics.com/lyrics/S/Spearhead/164622.html
2 Coser, L. 'Some social functions of violence,' in Barash, D. (2001) *Understanding Violence*, Boston: Allyn & Bacon.
3 *National Defense Strategy of the United States of America*, Part I. Section B, 18 March 2005, www.whitehouse.gov/nsc/nssall.html.
4 For this approach see Laqueur, 1987 and Hoffman, B. (1998) *Inside Terrorism*, New York: Columbia University Press.
5 Webel, C. P. (2004) *Terror, Terrorism, and the Human Condition*, New York: Palgrave Macmillan, p. 9.
6 For a discussion of why defining terrorism along the lines Webel does is more useful to understanding terrorism than those offered within the self-serving context of the terrorism industry see Grosscup, 2002: 1–19.
7 Jamail, D. (2005) 'Operation Matador: US claims over siege challenged,' *Inter Press Service*, 19 May and Shumway, C. (2005) 'Operation Matador, another offensive atrocity in Iraq,' *Educate Yourself*, 19 May, http://educate-

yourself.org/cn/operationmatadoratrocity19may05.shtml.

8   Kroth, J. (2002) 'The accidental terrorist: global diction of death and deed,' *Glimpse Magazine*, www.theglimpse.com/newsite/printarticle2.asp?articleid=10.

9   Buncombe, A. (2003) 'US admits it used napalm bombs in Iraq,' *Independent*, 10 August.

10 Herold, M. W. (2002) 'The bombing of Afghanistan as reflection of 9/11 and different valuations of life,' *Cursor*, 11 September, www.cursor.org/stories/heroldon911.htm.

11 Prashad, V. (2002) 'Aerial bombardment in the racist contemporary,' *ZMagazine*, 1 January.

12 Herman, E. (1982) *The Real Terror Network*, Boston: South End Press.

13 News report, *National Public Radio*, 17 July 2005.

14 Fineman, H. (2001) 'A president finds his true voice,' *Newsweek*, 24 September.

15 'Osama Bin Laden jokes, Taliban jokes, humor in a time of grief,' *America's Mad as Hell Humor Page*, www.almostaproverb.com/textjokes.html#weather.

16 *Sunday Times*, 16 March 2003.

17 *Ha'aretz*, 22 June 2005.

18 Herman, E. S. (1999) 'The US versus the rules of war: how Washington selectively invokes international law,' *ZMagazine*, 25 April.

19 Hersh, S. (2004) 'Interview with Amy Goodman,' *Democracy Now*, 26 January, www.democracynow.org.

20 Kroth, J. (2002) 'The accidental terrorist: global diction of death and deed,' *Glimpse Magazine*, www.theglimpse.com/newsite/printarticle2.asp?articleid=10.

21 Tonry, M. (2001) in Chien, A. J. (2001) 'The Civilian Toll,' *Los Angeles Times*, 11 October.

22 Marcuse, H. (1998) *Technology, War and Fascism*, London: Routledge.

23 Carr, C. (2002) *The Lessons of Terror*, New York: Random House, p. 64.

24 Mills, C. W. (1959) *The Sociological Imagination*, New York: Grove Press, p. 17.

25 Carr, 2002: 105–110.

26 Mills, 1959: 12.

27 Chomsky, N. (2001) 'An evening with Noam Chomsky, the new war against terror,' *The Technology & Culture Forum at MIT*, 18 October, http://web.mit.edu/tac/past/2001-2002/.

28 Dunnigan, J. (2004) 'The US Air Force x files,' 22 August, http://strategypage.com/dls/articles/20048220.

29 Carr, 2002.

Allen, H. R. (1972) *The Legacy of Lord Trenchard*, London: Cassell.

Arnold, H. H. (1944-45) *Report of the Commanding General of the Army Air Forces to the Secretary of War*, Washington: Headquarters, Army Air Forces.

Baddeley, J. F. (1908) *The Russian Conquest of the Caucasus,* London: Longmans, Green and Co.

Barash, D. (2001) *Understanding Violence*, Boston: Allyn & Bacon.

Baxandall, R., L. Gordon and S. Reverby (eds.) (1976), *America's Working Women*, New York: Random House.

Bederman, G. (1995) *Manliness and Civilization*, Chicago: University of Chicago Press.

Bendiner, E. (1975) *A Time for Angels*, New York: Knopf.

Berezin, M. (1997) *Making of the Fascist Self*, Ithaca: Cornell University Press.

Bidinian, L. (1976) *The Combined Allied Bombing Offensive Against the German Civilian 1942–1945,* Lawrence, KS: Coronado Press.

Boggs, C. (ed.) (2003) *Masters of War*, New York: Routledge.

Boyle, A. (1962) *Trenchard*, New York: Norton.

Buckley, H. (1940) *Life and Death of the Spanish Republic,* London: H. Hamilton.

Burlingame, R. (1952) *General Billy Mitchell: champion of air defense*, New York: McGraw-Hill.

Callwell, C. E. (1996) *Small Wars: their principles and practice,* Lincoln: University of Nebraska Press.

Carr, C. (2002) *The Lessons of Terror*, New York: Random House.

Charlton, L. E. O. (1936) *War Over England*, London: New York: Longmans, Green.

Chomsky, N. (1988) *The Culture of Terrorism*, London: Pluto Press.

Chomsky, N. (2000), *A New Generation Draws the Line: Kosovo, East Timor and the standards of the West*, London: Verso.

Chomsky, N. (2001) *9-11*, New York: Seven Stories Press.

Chomsky, N. (2003) *Hegemony or Survival*, New York: Metropolitan Books.

Chomsky, N. and E. S. Herman (1979) *The Washington Connection to Third World Fascism*, Boston: South End Press.

Churchill, W. (1931) *The World Crisis, 1916–18*, Part I, London: T. Butterworth.

Clausewitz, K. von (1873), *On War*, London: Trubner.

Clayton, A. (1986) The *British Empire as Super Power 1919–1939*, London: Macmillan.

Cline, R. S. and Y. Alexander (1984) *Terrorism: the Soviet connection*, London: Crane Russak.

Clodfelter, M. (1989) *The Limits of Airpower*, New York: The Free Press.

Condon, J. P. and J. M. Elliott (eds.) (2000) *Marine Corps Aviation*, Washington, DC: Deputy Chief of Naval Operations (Air Warfare) Naval Air Systems Command.

Cooke, J. (2002) *Billy Mitchell*, Boulder, CO: L. Rienner.

Cooke, M. (1996) W*omen and the War Story*, Berkeley: University of California Press.

Cooper, D. (ed.) (1969) *To Free A Generation*, New York: Collier Books.

Cottrell, R. C. (1992) *Izzy: a biography of I. F. Stone*, New Brunswick: Rutgers University Press.

Crane, C. (2000) *American Airpower Strategy in Korea: 1950–1953*, Lawrence, KS: University Press of Kansas.

Cumings, B. (1997) *Korea's Place in the Sun*, New York: W.W. Norton.

Danchev, A. (1998) *Alchemist of War: the life of Basil Liddell Hart*, London: Weidenfeld and Nicolson.

Davis, M. (2002) *Dead Cities*, New York: The New Press.

Davis, R. G. (2002) *On Target: organizing and executing the strategic air campaign against Iraq*, Washington, DC: Air Force History and Museums Program, United States Air Force.

Dodge, T. (2003) *Inventing Iraq: the failure of nation-building and a history denied*, New York: Columbia University Press.

Douhet, G. (1942) *The Command of the Air*, New York, Coward-McCann.

Douhet, G. (1998) *The Command of the Air*, Washington, DC: Office of the Air Force History and Museums Program.

Du Bois, W. E. B. (1995) *Black Reconstruction in America, 1860-1880*, New York: Touchstone.

Eekelen, B. van, J. González, B. Stoetzer and A. Tsing (eds.) (2004) *Shock and Awe: war on words*, Santa Cruz: New Pacific Press.

Ehrenfeld, R. (1990) *Narcoterrorism*, New York: Basic Books.

Eisenstein, Z. (1996) *Hatreds: racialized and sexualized conflicts in the 21st century*, New York: Routledge.

Ellsberg, D. (1972) *Papers on the War*, New York: Simon and Schuster.

Enloe, C. (2000) *Maneuvers*, Berkeley: University of California Press.

Fanon, F. (2004) *The Wretched of the Earth*, New York: Grove Press

Francis, S. (1991) *Soviet Strategy of Terror*, Washington DC: The Heritage Foundation.

Frankenburg, R. (1970) *Displacing Whiteness*, London: Duke University Press.

Frankland, N. (1970) *The Bomber Offensive: the devastation of Europe*, New York: Ballantine Books.

Fromm, E. (1973) *The Anatomy of Human Destructiveness*, New York: Holt, Rinehart and Winston.

Fuller, F. C. (1958) *The Generalship of Alexander the Great*, London: Eyre & Spottiswoode.

Futrell, R. F. (1961) *The United States Air Force in Korea 1950–1953*, New York: Duell, Sloan & Pearce.

Gauvreau, E. (1942) *Billy Mitchell: founder of our air force and prophet without honor,* New York: E. P. Dutton.

Geddes, P. and J. A. Thompson (1901) *The Evolution of Sex,* London: W. Scott.

George, A. (ed.) (1991) *Western State Terrorism,* New York: Routledge.

Gibson, J. W. (2000) *The Perfect War: technowar in Vietnam,* New York: Atlantic Monthly Press.

Gooch, J. (1981) *The Prospect of War,* London: Totowa, NJ: F. Cass.

Griffith, W. and J. Marciano, (1979) *Lessons of the Vietnam War,* Totowa NJ: Rowman and Allanheld.

Grogan, E. S. and A. H. Sharp (eds.) (1900) *From the Cape to the Congo,* London: Nelson Edition.

Grosscup, B. (2002) *The Newest Explosions of Terrorism,* Far Hills, NJ: New Horizon Press.

Gutman, H. (1925) *The Black Family in Slavery and Freedom, (1750–1925),* New York: Pantheon Books.

Hall, S. and B. Gieben (eds.) (1992) *Formations of Modernity,* Cambridge: Polity Press.

Hansell, H. S. Jr (1986) *The Strategic Air War Against Germany and Japan,* Washington DC: Office of Air Force History.

Herman, E. S. (1982) *The Real Terror Network,* Boston: South End Press.

Herman, E. S. and G. O'Sullivan (1989) *The Terrorism Industry,* New York: Pantheon Books.

Higham, R. (1966) *The Military Intellectuals in Britain, 1918–1939,* New Brunswick: Rutgers University Press.

Hirst, F. W., G. Murray and J. L. Hammond (eds.) (1998) *Liberalism and the Empire,* London: Routledge/Thoemmes Press.

Hobson, J. A. (1901) *The Psychology of Jingoism,* London: G. Richards.

Hoffman, B. (1998) *Inside Terrorism,* New York: Columbia University Press.

Horner, C. and H. Ullman (1996) *Shock and Awe: achieving rapid dominance,* Washington DC: NDU Press.

Houghton, N. D. (ed.) (1968) *Struggle against History,* New York: Simon and Schuster.

Hurley, A. (1964) *Billy Mitchell,* New York: Franklin Watts.

Jackson. R. (1974) *Storm from the Skies: the strategic bombing offensive, 1943–1945,* London: A. Barker.

Jamieson, P. D. (2001) *Lucrative Targets: the US Air Force in the Kuwaiti theater of operations,* Washington, DC: Air Force History and Museums Program, US Air Force.

Jones, N. (1973) *The Origins of Strategic Bombing,* London: William Kimber.

Jones, N. (1987) *The Beginnings of Strategic Air Power: a history of the British bomber force, 1923–1939,* London: F. Cass.

Kaku, M. and D. Axelrod (1987) *To Win a Nuclear War: the Pentagon's secret war plans,* Boston: South End Press.

Kellner, D. (1992) *The Persian Gulf TV War,* Boulder: Westview Press.

Kellner, D. (ed.) (1998) *Technology, War and Fascism,* London: Routledge.

Kelsey, F. W. (1925) *Hugo Grotius: The law of war and peace,* Oxford: Clarendon Press.

Kennett, L. (1982) *A History of Strategic Bombing,* New York: Scribner.

Kiernan, V. G. (1969) *The Lords of Human Kind,* Boston: Little, Brown and Co.

Kiernan, V. G. (1978) *America, The New Imperialism: from white settlement to world hegemony*, London: Zed Books.

Kiernan, V. G. (1982) *From Conquest to Collapse: European empires from 1815–1960*, New York: Pantheon Books.

Kohn, R. H. and J. P. Harahan (eds.) (1988) *Strategic Air Warfare*, Washington DC: Office of Air Force History, United States Air Force.

Kupperman, R. and D. Trent (1979) *Terrorism: threat, reality, response*, Stanford, CA: Hoover Institution Press.

Lambeth, B. S. (2001) *NATO's Air War for Kosovo*, Santa Monica, CA: Rand.

Landau, S. (1988) *Dangerous Doctrine: national security and US foreign policy*, Boulder: Westview Press.

Laqueur, W. (1987) *Age of Terrorism*, Boston: Little, Brown.

Liddell Hart, B. H. (1925) *Paris*, New York: Dutton.

Liddell Hart, B. H. (1927) *The Remaking of Modern Armies*, London: J. Murray.

Lindqvist, S. (2001) *A History of Bombing*, New York: The New Press.

Logan, R. (1965) *The Betrayal of the Negro: From Rutherford B. Hayes to Woodrow Wilson*, New York: McMillan.

Lyttelton, A. (ed.) (2002) *Liberal and Fascist Italy*, Oxford: Oxford University Press.

MacArthur. J. R. (1993) *Second Front: censorship and propaganda in the Gulf War*, Berkeley: University of California Press.

McClintock, M. (1985) *The American Connection*, London: Zed Books.

Macdonald, C. A. (1986) *Korea*, New York: The Free Press.

MacIsaac, D. (1976) *Strategic Bombing in World War Two: the story of the United States strategic bombing survey*, New York: Garland.

MacMullen, J. K. (2001) 'The United States Strategic Bombing Survey and Air Force Doctrine,' Thesis presented to the faculty of the School of Advanced Airpower Studies.

Marcuse, H. (1969) *Essays on Liberation*, Boston: Beacon Press.

McIlraith, F. and R. Connolly (1934) *Invasion from the Air*, London: Grayson & Grayson.

Mearsheimer, J. J. (1988) *Liddell Hart and the Weight of History*, Ithaca: Cornell University Press.

Meilinger P. S. (ed.) (1997) *Paths of Heaven*, Maxwell Air Force Base, Alabama: Air University Press.

Meilinger, P. S. (2001) *Airmen and Air Theory*, Maxwell Air Force Base, Alabama: Air University Press.

Mills, C. W. (1959) *The Sociological Imagination*, New York: Grove Press.

Mitchell, W. (1924) *Mitchell Papers*, Washington DC: Library of Congress.

Morrison, W. H. (1982) *Fortress without a Roof: the Allied bombing of the Third Reich*, New York: St Martin's.

Nardulli, B. R. (2002) *Disjointed War: military operations in Kosovo, 1999*, Santa Monica, CA: Rand.

Newsome, D. (1997) *The Victorian World Picture*, New Brunswick, Rutgers University Press.

Office of the Chairman (1986) *United States Strategic Bombing Survey: the strategic air-war against Germany and Japan*, Washington DC: Office of Air Force History.

Omissi, D. E. (1990) *Air Power and Colonial Control: the Royal Air Force*,

1919–1939, New York: Manchester University Press.

Osborn, S. (1860) *The Past and Future of British Relations in China*, London: W. Blackwood and Sons.

Overy, R. J. (1980) *The Air War, 1939–1945*, New York: Stein and Day.

Pape, R. A., (1996) *Bombing To Win: air power and coercion in war,* Ithaca: Cornell University Press.

Parenti, M. (1986) *Inventing Reality: politics and the mass media*, New York: St Martin's Press.

Parenti, M. (2004) *Superpatriotism*, San Francisco: City Lights Books.

Pearce, S. and V. Muller (eds.) (2002). *Manning the Next Millennium: studies in masculinities,* Evanston, IL: Black Swan Press.

Peret, P. (ed.) (1986) *Makers of Modern Strategy*, Princeton: Princeton University Press.

Putney, D. T. (2004) *Airpower Advantage: planning the Gulf War air campaign, 1989–1991*,Washington, DC: Air Force History and Museums Program, United States Air Force.

Reade, W. W. (1874) *The Martyrdom of Man*, New York: A. K. Butts & Co.

Rezun, M. (2001) *Europe's Nightmare: the struggle for Kosovo*, Westport, CT: Praeger.

Robertson, L. D. (2003) *The Dream of Civilized Warfare*, Minneapolis: University of Minnesota Press.

Robinson, D. H. (1962) *The Zeppelin in Combat*, London: G. T. Foulis.

Rodney, W. (1981) *How Europe Underdeveloped Africa*, Washington DC: Howard University Press.

Routledge, R. (1879) *Discoveries and Inventions of the Nineteenth Century*, London: Routledge.

Russell, B. (1938) *Power: a new social analysis*, New York: W. W. Norton & Company.

Said, E. W. (1981) *Covering Islam: how the media and the experts determine how we see the rest of the world*, New York: Pantheon Books.

Schaffer, R. (1985) *Wings of Judgement: American bombing in World War II*, New York: Oxford University Press.

Sederberg, P. (1989) *Terrorist Myths: illusion, rhetoric, and reality*, Englewood Cliffs, NJ: Prentice Hall.

Seversky, A.P. de (1943) *Victory through Air Power*, Garden City, NY: Garden City Publishing.

Shawcross, W. (1979) *Sideshow*, New York: Pocket Books.

Sherman, W. T. (1957) *Memoirs of General W. T. Sherman*, Bloomington: Indiana University Press.

Sherrod, R. (1987) *History of Marine Corps Aviation in WWII*, Baltimore, MD: Nautical & Aviation Publishing.

Sherry, M. (1987) *The Rise of American Airpower*, New Haven: Yale University Press.

Sherry, M. (1995), *Shadow of War*, New Haven: Yale University Press.

Sigaud, L. A. (1941) *Douhet and Aerial Warfare*, New York: G. P. Putnam's Sons.

Smith, D. M. (1976) *Mussolini's Roman Empire*, New York: Viking Press.

Smith-Rosenberg, C. (1985) *Disorderly Conduct*, New York: Alfred A. Knopf.

Spencer, H. (1865) *Education: intellectual, moral, and physical*, New York: D. Appleton and Co.

Stannard, D. E. (1992) *American Holocaust: Columbus and the conquest of the New World*, New York: Oxford University Press.

Sterling, C. (1981) *The Terror Network*, New York: Reader's Digest Press.

Stoler, A. L. (2002) *Carnal Knowledge and Imperial Power*, Berkeley: University of California Press.

Stone, I. F. (1952) *Hidden History of the Korean War*, New York: Monthly Review Press.

Tayacan, (1985) *Psychological Operations in Guerrilla Warfare*, New York: Vintage Books.

Taylor, F. (2004) *Dresden: Tuesday, February 13, 1945*, New York: HarperCollins.

Terriane, J. (1965) *The Right of the Line: The Royal Air Force in the European War, 1939–1945*, London: Hodder and Stoughton.

Tohmatsu, H. and H. P. Willmott (2004) *A Gathering Darkness: the coming of war to the Far East and the Pacific, 1921-1942*, Lanham, MD: SR Books.

Travers, T. and C. Archer (eds.) (1982) *Men at War: politics, technology, and innovation in the twentieth century*, Chicago: Precedent.

United States Department of State (1987) *Patterns of Global Terrorism*, Washington, DC: Department of State.

United States Department of State, (2003) *Patterns of Global Terrorism*, Washington, DC: Department of State.

Veale, F. J. P. (1968) *Advance to Barbarism: how the reverse to barbarism in warfare and war-trials menaces our future*, London: Mitre Press.

Vicinus, M. (ed.) (1972) *Suffer and Be Still: women in the Victorian Age*, Bloomington, IN: Indiana University Press.

Virilio, P. (2000) *Strategy of Deception*, London: Verso.

Warden III, J. A. (1988) *The Air Campaign: planning for combat*, Washington, DC: National Defense University Press.

Wavell, Lord (1960) *New Cambridge Modern History, vol. 12*, Cambridge: Cambridge University Press.

Waxman, M. C. (2000) *International Law and the Politics of Air Operations*, Santa Monica, CA: Rand.

Webel, C. P. (2004) *Terror, Terrorism, and the Human Condition*, New York: Palgrave Macmillan.

Weber, M. (1965) *Politics as a Vocation*, Philadelphia: Fortress Press.

Wilkinson, P. (1979) *Terrorism and the Liberal State*, New York: New York University Press.

Williams, W. A. (1976) *America Confronts a Revolutionary World, 1776–1976*, New York: Morrow.

Wintringham, T. (1943*) The Story of Weapons and Tactics: from Troy to Stalingrad*, Freeport: Books for Libraries Press.

Wrigley, C. (ed.) (1986) *Warfare, Diplomacy and Politics: Essays in Honour of A. J. P. Taylor*, London: H. Hamilton.

Wyman, D. S. (1984) *The Abandonment of the Jews: America and the holocaust, 1941–1945*, New York: Pantheon Books.

Zinn, H. (1995) *A People's History of the United States*, New York: Harper-Perennial.

Zinn, H. (2002) *Terrorism and War*, New York: Seven Stories Press.